The Memories, Letters, and Documents

of

Moltke the Younger

*Colonel General Helmuth von Moltke
Koblenz, August 1914*

The Memories, Letters, and Documents

of

Moltke the Younger

Edited and with a Foreword by

Eliza von Moltke

Legacy Books Press
Military Classics

Published by Legacy Books Press
RPO Princess, Box 21031
445 Princess Street
Kingston, Ontario, K7L 5P5
Canada

www.legacybookspress.com

The scanning, uploading, and/or distribution of this book via the Internet or any other means without the permission of the publisher is illegal and punishable by law.

This translation and edition first published in 2021 by Legacy Books Press

1

This translation and edition © 2021 Legacy Books Press, all rights reserved.

ISBN: 978-1-927537-57-2

First published as *Erinnerungen Briefe Dokumente 1877-1916: Ein Bild vom Kriegsausbruch, erster Kriegsführung und Persönlichkeit des ersten militärischen Führers des Krieges,* by Der Kommende Tag A.-G. Verlag, Stuttgart in 1922.

Printed and bound in the United States of America and Canada.

This book is typeset in a Times New Roman 11-point font.

Table of Contents

Publisher's Note 3

Foreword. 4

Part I – A Memorandum, Moltke's Reflections and Reminiscences
. . . . 11
    A Memorandum by Moltke 13
    Reflections and Memories 17

Part II – Moltke's Thoughts and Deeds in Excerpts from Letters to
    his Bride, 1877-1878 31

Part III – Moltke's Thoughts and Deeds in Excerpts from Letters
    to his Wife, 1879-1914. 53

Part IV – Moltke After the Battle of the Marne 309
    Moltke to Reich Chancellor v. Bethmann Hollweg 311
    Moltke to Reich Chancellor v. Bethmann Hollweg 315
    Moltke to His Majesty the Emperor. 320
    Moltke to General —— 323
    Moltke to Field Marshal General v. Hindenburg. 326
    Moltke to His Majesty the Emperor. 327
    Moltke to His Majesty the Emperor. 330
    Moltke to Field Marshal General v. Hindenburg. 334
    Moltke's Speech on the Birthday of His Majesty the Emperor,
        27 January 1915. 336
    Moltke to General Ludendorff. 338
    Chief of the General Staff of Field Army No. 227. 340
    Moltke to General —— 341
    Telegrams from the Emperor to Moltke. 344
    Moltke on the Retreat on the Marne. 346

Part V – Moltke's Final Years 355
    Moltke and the Founding of the "German Society 1914"
    357

Excerpt from a Letter by Moltke 361
Excerpt from a Letter by Moltke 363
Moltke's Speech at the Funeral Service for Field Marshal
    General Freiherr von der Goltz 366
Telegram from His Majesty the Emperor............ 370
Letter from Crown Prince Wilhelm 371

About the Author 373

Publisher's Note

This translation was created with the assistance of DeepL Pro translation software. While all possible efforts have been taken to avoid translation errors, some errors may still be present in the text.

To improve general readability, some modifications have been made to the formatting of paragraphs throughout the text. All efforts have been made to preserve the author's voice and meaning while making these changes.

All references to "the editor" refer to Eliza von Moltke.

Foreword

In the spring of 1919, I decided to publish the notes of my husband, Colonel General von Moltke, on the outbreak of the war, so that the truth would be known in good time before the conclusion of the peace negotiations in Versailles. For in these records I had proof that Germany was not guilty of the world war in the sense that its opponents claimed, in order to be able to bring about a violent peace in their favor. While these records reveal the full extent of the incompetence and helplessness of Germany's political leadership during the decisive period, they also provide incontrovertible proof, through the presentation of hitherto unknown, most important facts and events, that the German government did not want the war. Even in the days of the outbreak of war, this government believed in the will of England to prevent the expansion of the war, so that the Emperor and the Reich Chancellor, who were caught in this error, intervened in an obstructive manner in the course of mobilization.

The attempt to present this proof of Germany's will for peace at Versailles, and thus to make the violent peace based on

Germany's guilt* impossible, failed. The records were to appear at that time in order to put before the people and nations the bare facts and thereby to create a counter-effect against the concealment of the truth. This attempt to appeal to the public also failed, because the appearance of the records was prevented by the intervention of certain persons. Since this took place in 1919, many things have happened. The Peace of Versailles, whose articles of debt German negotiators signed, has brought the greatest calamity upon Germany and the world. In the meantime, a whole literature has arisen in Germany dealing with the reasons for the loss of the war. Again and again, reference is made to the Battle of Marne and the failure of the first Supreme Army Command, especially to the alleged incompetence of Moltke. In the book "Erinnerungen" (Memories) of the former Crown Prince Wilhelm, edited by Karl Rosner, it is said that Moltke "in a misunderstood sense of duty, against his will and in recognition of his inadequacy" had taken on a task that was beyond his strength. That had become his undoing. His and ours.

Sentences of this kind are what make it my duty to publish the present book. In Moltke's own words, a picture of his work and his views is to be given through the publication of letters from his early days up to the records during the war. Only through this can the outrageous accusations be refuted. These letters and documents will show where the "inadequacy" lay and how Moltke's

---

* Article 231, p. 122, of the official edition of the Versailles Peace Treaty reads:
The Allied and Associated Governments declare, and Germany acknowledges, that Germany and her allies are responsible as authors for all loss and damage suffered by the Allied and Associated Governments and their nationals as a result of the war imposed upon them by the aggression of Germany and her allies.

The correct translation is: The Allied and Associated Governments declare, and Germany acknowledges, that Germany and her Allies are responsible for all loss and damage caused by them to the Allied and Associated Governments and their nationals, arising as consequences of the war imposed upon them by the aggression of Germany and her Allies.

I say the above, in spite of this somewhat ambiguous version of the article, not out of a mistaken interpretation of it, which the Germans are otherwise accused of, but because what is said is its actual effect and [Germany's] treatment on the part of the victors is in reality so (The Editor.).

personality combined the greatest sense of responsibility with a comprehensive overview of the circumstances and the will to act, setting aside all personal concerns. When, on January 7, 1905, the Kaiser and Moltke met to discuss his acceptance of the post of Chief of the General Staff, for which the Kaiser had selected him on the advice of Count Schlieffen, Moltke made his acceptance conditional on the Kaiser's not interfering personally in the military leadership. For eight years of peace, the Emperor conquered his nature. He did it because he knew that he had no more loyal advisor than Moltke. When it came to the real war, not only to maneuvers, on August 1, 1914, for the first time he did not listen to the proven long-time collaborator, he intervened in military necessities and gave an order over Moltke's head, which had to endanger the entire deployment.

It is not true the recurring claim that Moltke had been seriously ill long before the war. His last visit to Karlsbad shortly before the outbreak of the war was also for family reasons and had nothing to do with his long healed illness. Moltke went in full health fresh and energetic on 1 August to the castle. Only what he had to experience there in the afternoon hours of the 1 August hit him hardest. It was up to the Chief of Staff to take military measures in such a way that the Fatherland would not be shattered in the midst of a wall of enemies; politics built on sand failed, and therefore the military order was the only possible one. On Moltke, who for years had recognized the political, economic and military situation of Germany with a clear eye, who had always pointed out the dangers that threatened Germany, the responsibility rested entirely on his shoulders in these hours in which he had to fight for the execution of the mobilization plan. After those hours, when all his objections were overheard, Moltke was a different man. His confidence was shaken. The relationship of trust between him and the Emperor was destroyed. His conviction from then on was: Where such conditions are possible in a country, misfortune must result. Although Helmuth von Moltke had for a long time taken a serious view of the relevant circumstances, he had always believed that the emergency would trigger the necessary forces in the leading personalities, which unfortunately did not happen. "I can well wage war against the external enemy, but not against my own

Emperor," were his words after the preceding experiences. The only man who was able to fight on 1 August, after the complete failure of German policy, had to make the militarily necessary decisions, who in these moments had to fight against lack of understanding and short-sightedness in military and political terms, this man, when he was finally given back the possibility of action late in the evening of August 1, 1914, was struck to the core by what he had experienced that afternoon. That is the terrible truth. The impression of these experiences, which could not be erased from his consciousness, continued to afflict Moltke for the next few years, and the effects of these hours became apparent when the first major setback in the war occurred.

Whoever knew Moltke's sense of responsibility and consciousness will understand that these experiences of August 1 must have had a profound effect on him. The fact that our contemporaries lost the understanding for such "imponderables" and that their thinking and judging became so coarse, is the reason for the wrong assessment of Moltke's personality, as well as, in my opinion, a main cause for the bleak conditions of our present time.

Moltke's intention to launch new operations after the retreat on the Marne had restored freedom of movement to the armies was not carried out under the direction of General von Falkenhayn. Instead, the war of position began, which Moltke wanted to avoid at all costs, since he saw in it the greatest danger for the German army. The decision was not made on the Marne, but a few weeks later in the east. That was when the struggle for leadership of the war between East and West began. General von Falkenhayn, as Chief of the General Staff, refused Field Marshal von Hindenburg the troops he had requested in November 1914; the victory over the Russians that was surely hoped for was thus thwarted. Perhaps history will one day judge this dark chapter more harshly than we are now willing to do, and then recognize the causes of much that followed.

Moltke had been back in Berlin since the beginning of December 1914. He now began to familiarize himself with the economic situation; he saw the dangers and evils in the country, he raised his warning voice. This aroused the displeasure of those men who now had power in their hands and who tried to prevent his activity. At the same time, several personalities decided to approach the Emperor, saying that General von Falkenhayn was a misfortune for the country, that the army had no confidence in him. Field Marshal von Hindenburg demanded his departure if General von Falkenhayn continued in command. Moltke wrote to the Emperor, and the crown prince also interceded in the matter. But everything was in vain at that time. The clear-sighted did not prevail. Twenty months later, in September 1916, three months after Moltke's death, what he had advised to be done at the right time was carried out. At that time he was the only one who proposed in detail the strategic plan for the demand of the leading figures in the East in an authoritative position; later, when others fell for the same, it was unfortunately too late for many things. For the dangers for Germany, which Moltke had seen coming if everything remained as it was then, had occurred and had created a desperately serious situation in the face of the superior strength of the enemy. What could have been achieved if Moltke's advice had been followed in 1915, what would the war situation have been like if the necessary troops had been sent to the East in November 1914 or later in August 1915? Moltke said countless times in 1915 that with the mass of troops made available by the Grand Headquarters for the East, fine tactical successes could be achieved, but not a thoroughgoing strategic main blow such as would be necessary in the East.

It is certainly convenient and relieving for many who today pass over these drastic questions to lay all the blame on Moltke. Since he is dead today and cannot defend himself, which he would otherwise certainly do very vigorously, it is my heavy obligation to stand up for him. It is the obligation to defend him against those who keep talking and writing about the "weak-minded," "incapable" Moltke, who was not up to his task. Moltke took the most difficult decision of his life to initiate a new effective war action in the West after the difficulties that had arisen by gathering the main part of the armies further back in a new front formation. That his conviction to continue the war effectively in this way could not be carried out is due to the fact that the leadership was taken away from him before the execution. Throughout his life, Moltke proved that he was not afraid to act and to use his person ruthlessly where the good of the country was at stake. His conviction of the inadequacy of others paralyzed him at the beginning of the war and prevented him from fully developing his powers at the decisive time.

Thus, what Moltke thought, felt, worked, and suffered may testify for him, and all those to whom it will be inconvenient may consider that they have caused the publication by their own conduct; for truly the decision to make these publications was not taken lightly of heart, but out of the realization that duty demands that we stand up for a man who is being slandered in the most outrageous manner.

Moltke was the most faithful servant of his king and fatherland, who died of a broken heart out of concern for his people and country, because he foresaw and experienced in advance exactly how everything had to come and become in view of the conditions that prevailed in Germany. These publications are intended to contribute to the recognition of the truth, so that the way can be found to defeat untruthfulness, which as a destructive force wants to destroy all true life, which will turn Germany more and more into a heap of ruins, as Moltke already felt and wrote down in the spring of 1904.

Would that the Germans would finally stop tearing themselves apart, denigrating their best men. Only in this way can Helmuth von Moltke's firm belief be fulfilled: the rebirth of the true German nation, built on truth and knowledge. Then his sufferings for his fatherland will not have been in vain, then his "tragedy" will be transformed into a "heroism" that will bring blessings to Germanness and whose fruits later generations will reap. "You will know the truth, and the truth will make you free."

This is the leitmotif of my publications.

Because a clear picture of Moltke's work and personality is to be given, the following arrangement of the contents of this book has been made.

Preceded by the documents that give the present a proper and true picture of the events of late July and early August 1914 in Berlin, the focus of this first part is Moltke's own transcription of his recollections of the decisive events and their political and military significance. Through the memoirs, as one can be convinced, an account of the outbreak of war is given which, despite its brevity, contains more and more important than anything that has hitherto appeared about it. The picture of future historiography, as one can be further convinced, will be much more similar to this account than to the others.

Then follow all those documents which show Moltke's development in a vivid way, up to the point in his life when he consciously had to make such a difficult decision as no other personality of the present or past known to him.

The conclusion is formed by expressions of his life's earnestness after his dismissal from the position of the Chief of the General Staff, which are in every line a proof of the fact that he wanted to sacrifice his best forces as the most faithful servant of his people until his death.

Berlin, October 1922.

Eliza von Moltke
née Countess Moltke-Huitfeldt.

Part I – A Memorandum, Moltke's Reflections and Reminiscences

A Memorandum by Moltke

Berlin, July 28, 1914.

Assessing the political situation

There is no question that no European state would face the conflict between Austria and Serbia with anything other than human interest if it did not involve the danger of a general political entanglement which today already threatens to unleash a world war. For more than five years, Serbia has been the cause of a European tension that has been weighing on the political and economic life of the peoples with an almost unbearable pressure. Until now, Austria has endured the constant provocations and the political agitation aimed at destroying the state's existence with a long-suffering weakness that has led it from regicide in its own country to the murder of princes in neighboring countries. Only after the last atrocious crime did it resort to the extreme means of burning out with red-hot iron an ulcer that threatened to poison the body of Europe continually. One would think that all Europe should have known to thank him. All Europe would have breathed a sigh of relief if its troublemaker had been duly chastised and thus peace and order established in the Balkans, but Russia sided with the criminal country. Only with this did the Austro-Serbian affair become the weather cloud that can be unloaded over Europe at any moment.

Austria has explained to the European cabinets that it does not seek territorial acquisitions at the expense of Serbia, nor does it want to touch the existence of this state, it only wants to force the restless neighbor to accept the conditions which it considers necessary for continued coexistence and which, as experience has shown, Serbia would never keep uncoerced, despite solemn promises.

The Austro-Serbian affair is a purely private dispute, in which, as I said, no one in Europe would have a deeper interest, which would in no way threaten European peace, but on the contrary would consolidate it, if Russia had not interfered. It was this that gave the matter its threatening character.

Austria mobilized only part of its forces, 8 army corps, against Serbia. Just enough to be able to carry out its punitive expedition. Russia, on the other hand, is making all preparations to mobilize the army corps of the military districts of Kiev, Odessa and Moscow, 12 army corps in all, in the shortest possible time[*] and has similar preparatory measures in the north, opposite the German border, and on the Baltic Sea. It declares its intention to mobilize if Austria moves into Serbia, since it cannot admit the destruction of Serbia by Austria, although Austria has declared that it has no intention of doing so.

What will and must be the further consequence?

When Austria moves into Serbia, it will face not only the Serbian army but also a strong Russian superiority, so it will not be able to carry out the war against Serbia without securing itself against Russian intervention. That is, it will be forced to mobilize the other half of its army as well, for it cannot possibly hand itself over to a Russia ready for war at its mercy or at its disfavor. But the moment Austria mobilizes its entire army, the clash between it and Russia will become inevitable. But this is the *casus foederis*

---

[*] Side note (Moltke's): Has been done in the meantime.

for Germany. If Germany does not want to break her word and let her ally be destroyed by the Russian superiority, she will have to mobilize on her part. This will also result in the mobilization of Russia's other military districts. Then, however, Russia will be able to say, I am being attacked by Germany, and thus it will secure the support of France, which is bound by treaty to participate in the war if its confederate Russia is attacked. The French-Russian agreement, so often praised as a purely defensive alliance, which is supposed to have been created only in order to be able to counter Germany's plans of attack, has thus become effective and the mutual fracturing of the European cultural states will begin.

One cannot deny that the matter is skillfully staged by Russia. Under continual assurances that it is not yet "mobilizing" but only making preparations "just in case," that it has "so far" not called up any reservists, it is making itself ready for war to such an extent that, if it really does declare mobilization, it can be ready to advance in a few days. In this way it puts Austria in a desperate position and shifts the responsibility to it by forcing Austria to secure itself against a Russian surprise. It will say, "You, Austria, are mobilizing against us, so you want war with us."

Against Germany, Russia assures that it does not want to do anything, but it knows very well that Germany cannot stand idly by and watch a warlike clash between its confederate and Russia. Germany, too, will be forced to mobilize, and again Russia will be able to say to the world: "I did not want the war, but Germany brought it about." – This is how things will and must develop, unless, one would almost say, a miracle occurs to prevent at the last hour a war which will destroy the culture of almost the whole of Europe for decades to come.

Germany does not want to bring about this terrible war. But the German Government knows that it would fatally injure the deep-rooted feelings of loyalty to the Confederation, one of the most beautiful traits of German emotional life, and would put itself in contradiction with all the sentiments of its people if it did not want to come to the aid of its confederates at a moment which must decide their existence.

According to the available news, France also seems to be

taking preparatory measures for a possible later mobilization. It is evident that Russia and France are going hand in hand in their measures. Thus, when the clash between Austria and Russia is inevitable, Germany will mobilize and be ready to take up the fight on two fronts. For the military measures we intend to take, if they occur, it is of the greatest importance to obtain clarity as soon as possible as to whether Russia and France are willing to go to war with Germany. The further our neighbors' preparations progress, the more quickly they will be able to complete their mobilization. As a result, the military situation is becoming more unfavorable for us by the day and, if our probable adversaries continue to prepare themselves calmly, may lead to disastrous consequences for us.

Reflections and Memories

Homburg, November 1914.

The European war of 1914 was not unexpected to those who looked at the world without diplomatic bias. For years it had been looming like a weather cloud in the political sky, the tense European situation was urging to be unleashed, and there could be no doubt that the conflict between two major European states would unleash war on almost the whole of Europe. This had to be the consequence of the treaties and agreements concluded between the members of the two groups of powers, which bound state to state in the event of war. It was certain that Germany would take an active part in a war which seriously threatened the existence of the Austro-Hungarian monarchy, and it was equally certain that France would stand by Russia. For years the Entente had been hostile to the Triple Alliance. That the latter would fail in the test of seriousness, that Italy would not fulfill its binding obligations, was, however, not to be expected. The previous agreements between Italy and Germany had been revised and renewed the year before the war, and in the spring of 1914 they had been renewed in binding form. Italy had undertaken to place 2 cavalry divisions and

3 army corps at Germany's disposal in the event of war between Germany and France; General Zuccari, who had been designated as the leader of these auxiliary troops, had visited me in Berlin; the transport of the troops had been worked out with the cooperation of the Austrian General Staff. Everything had been discussed in detail. Likewise, a naval agreement between Germany, Italy, and Austria had been formally concluded and signed, according to which a joint action of the Austrian and Italian fleets was to take place with the addition of the German ships present in the Mediterranean at the outbreak of the war. All these agreements were so clear and so binding that there could hardly be any doubt as to Italy's loyalty to the League. The documents produced on this subject, the declarations made by the Italian side on behalf of the government, which had received the King's approval, are in our archives. Nevertheless, Italy broke its word. It declared its neutrality and indifferently disregarded all treaties. A more ignominious breach of word is perhaps not to be found in history. Germany and Austria stood alone when war broke out.

English diplomacy had known how to keep clear of binding treaties, to preserve the policy of a free hand. There were, however, agreements between England, France and Belgium for the eventuality of cooperation, but England could justifiably claim that she had not entered into any binding treaties. If, therefore, the attitude of England at the outbreak of the war remained doubtful, all the probability was that she would be found on the side of Germany's adversaries if war broke out between Germany and France. The opportunity to eliminate the inconvenient competitor on the world market, to intervene where there was a prospect of crushing Germany with superior force in union with Russia and France; the long years of stirring work initiated by King Edward VII. The long years of agitation initiated by King Edward VII for the encirclement of Germany, the hope of destroying the dreaded German fleet and thus gaining unrestricted rule of the seas, world domination, made it probable from the outset that England would be found in the ranks of our enemies.

The hope of our diplomacy to initiate a good relationship with England, which for years was the magnetic needle according to which our policy was set up, had to prove to be mistaken as soon as the brutal English interests could find an opportunity to assert themselves. England has always known how to put a moral cloak around her selfish actions. So here, too, the violation of Belgian neutrality by Germany had to serve as a pretext for declaring war on the latter. It may be left open whether England would immediately have actively entered the war against us if this violation of neutrality had not occurred. In any case, she would have intervened as soon as the danger appeared that France would be overpowered by us. None of the continental powers, least of all Germany, should, according to the old practice of English policy, have become so strong that there was danger of hegemony. Perhaps it would have been more convenient for England to wait with her intervention until the continental states had exhausted themselves in the war. But that England would always, sooner or later, have acted against Germany had to be reckoned with by every impartial observer under all circumstances. All the courtship of our diplomacy was lost from the outset in the face of a state which, like England, pursues only a selfish policy of interests. It might not have been so difficult to realize this even before the outbreak of the war. I think it would have been easier to reach an agreement with France or an understanding with Russia than a reliable neutrality on the part of England. Our eyes, however, were fixed on England as if hypnotized, and when she declared herself against us at the very beginning of the war, we were confronted with Austria, without any other ally, and even without any preparation for gaining one, by the overwhelming power of our enemies.

The outbreak of the European war has been postponed for years by the fear of the people. It was this fear that prompted all the cabinets to repeat over and over again that all their efforts were directed toward the preservation of peace.

It would have been better for us if, in recent years, we had looked the coming events, the war that was unmistakably at the door, firmly in the eye and had also prepared ourselves diplomatically for it. The highest art of diplomacy, in my opinion, consists not in maintaining peace under all circumstances, but in constantly shaping the political situation of the state in such a way that it is in a position to be able to enter into war under favorable conditions. This was the immortal merit of Bismarck before the wars of 1866 and 1871. His constant concern was a coalition of France and Russia, which has now occurred and forces us to war on two fronts. That the German people had a clear feeling that hard times were ahead for the fatherland is proved by the acceptance of the defense bill of 1912 demanded by the General Staff and the War Ministry.

The war on two fronts had been expected by the General Staff for years. That it would become necessary at the moment when the rivalry of Russia and Austria in the Balkans would lead to open conflict was clear enough. We all knew that France, on the side of the Tsarist Empire, to which it had given its billions to better prepare for the war, would absolutely take part in it.

One might ask whether Germany would not have done more wisely to leave Austria to her fate, instead of taking upon herself, faithful to the Confederation, the immense gravity of the expected war. The view has been expressed several times that the disintegration of the Austro-Hungarian monarchy could not be stopped after all, and that there was really no reason for Germany to plunge into the adventure of a war for Austria's sake, the gravity of which was clear to everyone. The possibility must be admitted that Germany, if it had surrendered the allied monarchy, could have been saved from war at first. But apart from the fact that the German people would have had no sympathy for such a felony, in my opinion the abandonment of Austria would have been a political mistake which would have been severely avenged within a short time. The Anglo-French policy of encirclement was directed primarily against Germany. It would have remained in force if Germany had separated from Austria, and in a few years we would have stood before the war with the same coalition that is now attacking us, but then without, or perhaps even with, a hostile Austria. Then we would have stood all alone. This war that we are waging now was a necessity that is rooted in the development of the world. Nations and individuals are subject to its law. If this world development, which is usually called world history, did not exist, if it was not guided by the world development plan according to higher laws, the theory of development, which is recognized with regard to the living beings of the earth, would not be applicable to the highest living being, man, in his summary as a people. Then world history would be nothing but the confused result of coincidences, and one would have to deny it any planned development. But that such a development takes place, history itself teaches in my opinion. It shows how the cultural epochs take turns in progressive succession, how each people has to fulfill its specific task in the development of the world and how this development takes place in an ascending line.

Germany, too, has its cultural task to fulfill. The fulfillment of such tasks, however, does not take place without friction, since resistance must always be overcome; they can only come to fruition through war. If one were to assume that Germany would be destroyed in this war, then the German spiritual life, which is necessary for the spiritual further development of mankind, and the German culture would be eliminated; mankind would be set back in its overall development in the most disastrous way.

The Romance peoples have already passed the climax of their development; they cannot bring any new fertilizing elements into the overall development. The Slavic peoples, first and foremost Russia, are still too far behind in culture to be able to take over the leadership of mankind. Under the rule of the ruffians, Europe would be returned to the state of spiritual barbarism. England pursues only material goals.

A spiritual further development of mankind is only possible through Germany. That is why Germany will not be defeated in this war; it is the only nation that can take the lead of mankind to higher goals at this time.

It is a tremendous time in which we live.

This war will result in a new development of history, and its outcome will dictate to the entire world the trajectory on which it will have to proceed in the coming centuries.

Germany did not bring about the war, it did not enter it out of a desire for conquest or out of aggressive intentions against its neighbors.

The war has been forced upon him by his opponents, and we are fighting for our national existence, for the continued existence of our people, our national life. Thus, we fight for ideal goods, while our opponents openly state that their goal is the destruction of Germany.

Never has a more just war been waged by a state, and never has it affected a people more moved by ideal feelings. As if in one fell swoop, all divisions, all party differences, all material interests receded; the people stood together with one accord, and everyone was ready to sacrifice goods and blood for the fatherland. The high idealism of the German people, which even the materialistic current of the long years of prosperity could not destroy, broke through victoriously. The people recognized that there are higher and more valuable goals than material welfare; they turned to them with all the fervor of Germanicism.

Such a people are invincible.

The external cause of the war was the assassination of the Archduke-Throne. As soon as it became apparent that Austria was making far-reaching retaliatory claims against Serbia, Russia took the side of the murderers. It feared that its prestige in the Balkans and its position as protector of all Slavs would be lost if it handed Serbia over to Austria without support. Therefore, Russia was determined to go to war from the outset and immediately began preparations for mobilization, which were at first kept very secret. In my opinion, it only wanted to gain time when it declared shortly afterwards that the mobilization now openly ordered in the southern military districts was directed only against Austria, that there should be no mobilization against Germany. While mobilization was already in full swing, the Minister of War gave his word of honor to the German military attaché that no mobilization would take place. It is known that then, while our Emperor was still trying to mediate between Russia and Austria in an honest way, the mobilization of the northern military districts was pronounced in Russia as well. Although the Tsar declared that this mobilization was not directed against Germany, that Russia did not want war against Germany, he nevertheless demanded that we see ourselves at the mercy of a fully armed Russia without any war preparations of our own.

This was, of course, impossible for Germany. The moment Russia mobilized its entire army, we were also forced to mobilize. If we had not done so, Russia would have been able to invade our unprotected country at any time and make a later mobilization impossible for us.

There can be no doubt in the mind of any unbiased person that it was Russia that ignited this war. It knew very well that Germany would not allow its ally Austria to be destroyed, but it had gained time by its deceitful behavior and was already far advanced in its mobilization as Germany began hers.

As already mentioned, the war against two fronts had been worked on in the General Staff for years. Already under my predecessor, Count Schlieffen, the advance through Belgium had been worked out.

This operation was justified by the fact that it seemed almost impossible to force the French army to a decision in the open field without violating Belgian neutrality. All the news seemed to make it certain that the French would wage a defensive war behind their strong eastern front, and one had to be prepared to face a long-lasting war of position and fortification if one proceeded frontally against this strong front. Count Schlieffen even wanted to march through southern Holland with the right wing of the German army. I modified this so as not to force the Netherlands on the side of our enemies as well, preferring to take upon myself the great technical difficulties caused by the fact that the right wing of our army had to squeeze through the narrow space between Aachen and the southern border of the province of Limburg. In order to be able to carry out this maneuver at all, we had to take possession of Liege as quickly as possible. From this arose the plan to seize this fortress by a *coup de main*.

The question of whether we would not be better off waging a defensive war has also been repeatedly considered by the General Staff. It was always answered in the negative, since with it the possibility of carrying the war into enemy territory as soon as possible became obsolete. The possibility that Belgium would protest against a march through, but would not oppose the same by force of arms, was reckoned with. The communiqué I drafted to the Belgian government, which guaranteed the King the existence of the monarchy, was written in this spirit. The passage contained in it, in which Belgium was promised territorial enlargement in the case of friendly behavior, was deleted by the Foreign Office when the communiqué was handed over.

There is certainly much to be said against action by Belgium, but the course of the first weeks of the war has shown that, as intended, it forced the French to confront us in the open field and that they could be defeated. That the defeat of France failed at the first attempt was due to the rapid assistance of England.

The *coup de main* on Liege was a daring enterprise. If it failed, the moral blow would be severe. What prompted me to order it in the first place was the hope that it would bring the Aachen-Liege railroad into our possession undestroyed. This succeeded, and the fact that we later had the railroad to Brussels and beyond to St. Quentin at our disposal has been of incalculable benefit.

The day before mobilization, a dispatch had arrived from London saying that England had made a commitment to France to protect the French north coast against German attacks from the sea. The Emperor demanded my view, and I declared that we could unhesitatingly undertake not to attack the French north coast if England would remain neutral on that condition. In my opinion, the struggle against France would be decided on land, and an attack from the sea could be omitted if England's neutrality depended on it. This dispatch was obviously England's first attempt to dupe us, at least to delay our mobilization.

In response to the news arriving on July 28 or 29(?),[*] that general mobilization had been ordered in Russia, the Emperor had issued the declaration: imminent danger of war. On 1 August, at 5 o'clock in the afternoon, His Majesty the Emperor ordered mobilization for Germany. August 2 was the first day of mobilization.

I was on my way back from the castle to the General Staff when I received the order to return to the castle immediately, that an important message had arrived. I turned around immediately. In addition to His Majesty, I found the Imperial Chancellor, the Minister of War and several other gentlemen in the castle.

The Imperial Chancellor, who, as already indicated, saw the most important goal of his policy in establishing a good relationship with England, and who, strangely enough, still

---

[*] July 30. (The editor.)

believed until this day that general war, or at least England's participation in it, could be avoided, was obviously excited by the contents of a dispatch that had just arrived from the German ambassador in London, Prince Lichnowsky. So was His Majesty the Emperor. The dispatch stated that Secretary of State Grey had informed the Ambassador that England wished to undertake that France would not enter into war against us if Germany for her part undertook not to take any hostile action against France. I must point out that mobilization had already been ordered in France on the same day as in Germany, and that we were aware of this. As I said, there was a joyful mood.

Now we only need to wage war against Russia! The Emperor said to me: "So we just march with the whole army in the East!" – I replied to His Majesty that this was impossible. The deployment of an army of millions could not be improvised; it was the result of a full, laborious year's work and, once determined, could not be changed. If His Majesty insisted on leading the entire army to the East, they would not have an army ready for battle, but a desolate heap of disorderly armed men without rations. The Emperor insisted on his demand and became very indignant, telling me among other things: "Your uncle would have given me a different answer!" which pained me greatly. I never claimed to be equal to the Field Marshal. The fact that it would have been a catastrophe for us if we had marched into Russia with our entire army, with a mobile France behind us, no one seemed to think of. How could England ever have prevented – even assuming good will – France from stabbing us in the back! – Even my objection that France was already mobilizing and that it was impossible for a mobile Germany and a mobile France to agree peacefully not to harm each other was to no avail. The mood became more and more agitated, and I stood there all alone.

Finally I succeeded in convincing His Majesty that our deployment, which was intended with strong forces against France and with weak defensive forces against Russia, would have to proceed according to plan if the most disastrous confusion was not to arise. I told the Emperor that after the deployment was completed it would be possible to transfer any number of strong parts of the army to the East, but that nothing could be changed in the deployment itself, otherwise I could not assume any responsibility.

The reply dispatch to London was then drafted to the effect that Germany would be very happy to accept the English offer, but that the deployment once planned, even on the French border, would have to be carried out first for technical reasons. We would not do anything to France, however, if she would also keep quiet under England's control. That was all I could achieve. The nonsensical nature of this whole English proposal was clear to me from the outset. Already in earlier years I had been told by the Foreign Office that France might possibly remain neutral in a war of Germany against Russia. I believed so little in this possibility that even then I had declared that if Russia declares war on us, we must, if France's attitude is doubtful, declare war on her at once. Now, as a guarantee that France would not be defeated, I demanded the temporary surrender of the fortresses of Verdun and Toul to us. This proposal was rejected as a vote of no confidence in England.

In the course of this scene, I had come into an almost desperate mood; I saw from these diplomatic actions, which threatened to interfere with the course of our mobilization, the greatest disaster for the war ahead of us. I must interject here that our mobilization plan provided for the occupation of Luxembourg by the 16th Division on the first day of mobilization. We absolutely had to secure the Luxembourg railroads against a French *coup de main*, since we needed them for our deployment. It hit me all the harder when the Reich Chancellor now declared that the occupation of Luxembourg must not take place under any circumstances, that it would be a direct threat to France and would make the offered English guarantee illusory. While I was standing by, the Emperor, without asking me, turned to the wing adjutant on duty and ordered him to immediately telegraph to Trier the order to the 16th Division not to invade Luxembourg. I felt as if my heart should break. Once again there was a danger that our deployment would be thrown into confusion. What this means can only be fully appreciated by those who are familiar with the complicated work of a march, which is regulated down to the smallest detail. Where every move is regulated to the minute, every change must have a disastrous effect. I tried in vain to convince Her Majesty that we needed the Luxembourg railroads and had to secure them; I was dismissed with the remark that I would like to use other railroads instead of them. The order remained.

With that, I was discharged. It is impossible to describe the mood in which I arrived home. I was broken and shed tears of despair. As the dispatch to the 16th Division was presented to me, repeating the order given by telephone, I thrust the pen on the table and declared that I would not sign it. I cannot put my signature, the first after the announcement of mobilization, under an order that revokes something that is prepared according to plan and that will immediately be perceived by the troops as a sign of uncertainty. "Do what you want with the dispatch," I told Lieutenant Colonel Tappen. "I won't sign it."

So I sat idly in my room in a dull mood until at 11 o'clock in the evening I was ordered back to the castle to see His Majesty. The Emperor received me in his bedroom; he had already been to bed, but had got up again and thrown on a skirt. He gave me a dispatch from the King of England, in which he declared that he knew nothing of a guarantee by England to prevent France from participating in the war. Prince Lichnowsky's dispatch must be based on a mistake or he must have misunderstood something. The Emperor was very agitated and told me, "Now you can do whatever you want." – I immediately went home and telegraphed to the 16th Division that the invasion of Luxembourg should be carried out. To motivate this new order at least a little, I added: "Since it has just become known that mobilization has been ordered in France."

That was my first experience in this war. I have the conviction that the Emperor would not have signed the mobilization order at all if the dispatch of Prince Lichnowsky had arrived half an hour earlier. I have not been able to overcome the impressions of this experience, something was destroyed in me that could not be rebuilt, confidence and trust were shaken.

The *coup de main* against Liege was scheduled for August 5. In the evening of that day a message arrived from there, according to which it could be assumed that the enterprise had not succeeded. In any case, our troops had not penetrated the city. I had to report it to the Emperor. He told me: "I thought so right away. This action against Belgium has brought war with England down my throat." – The next day, when the news came that the city had been taken from us, I was bowled over.

After the first rapid and victorious advance of our armies through Belgium into France, the setback came from the attack of strong French and English forces from Paris against our right wing. The 2nd Army had to withdraw its right wing, the 1st Army also had to be withdrawn. The situation was critical. I had gone out to the army high commands. As I was at A.O.K. 4, a radio message came from the 2nd Army that strong French forces were turning eastward against the 3rd Army. I was eager to leave the 3rd Army standing, as well as the 4th and 5th.

As I got to A.O.K. 3, General v. Hausen told me that he could not hold the line assigned to him, that his troops were no longer efficient. I was therefore forced to assign to the 3rd Army a shorter and farther back line, but at the same time I had to withdraw the 4th and 5th Armies as well, in order to re-establish a closed army front. I had to issue the corresponding order immediately on the spot, on my own responsibility. It was a difficult decision that I had to take without being able to obtain His Majesty's permission beforehand. It was the most difficult decision of my life and it cost me my lifeblood. But I foresaw a catastrophe if I had not taken back the army. At 3 o'clock that night I arrived back in Luxembourg at the Grand Headquarters.

On September 13, I reported to the Emperor what I had ordered and motivated – the Emperor was not ungracious, but I had the impression that he was not entirely convinced of the necessity of the withdrawal. I must admit that my nerves were very down because of everything I had experienced and that I must have given the impression of a sick man.

On September 14, in the afternoon, General v. Lyncker appeared at my office and told me that the Emperor had told me that he had the impression that I was too ill to be able to continue the operations. His Majesty had ordered me to report sick and return to Berlin. General v. Falkenhayn was to take over the operations.

At the same time, my former chief quartermaster, General v.

Stein, was relieved and given command of a reserve army corps. All this came over me without any preparation.

I immediately went to General v. Falkenhayn and informed him of His Majesty's order. He was completely surprised. We went together to the Emperor, who told me that he had the impression that I had been weakened by my two cures in Karlsbad and needed to recover. I told the Emperor that I did not think it would make a good impression in the army and abroad if I were sent away immediately after the army's withdrawal.

General v. Falkenhayn concurred with this view. The Emperor then said that Falkenhayn should act as Quartermaster General and that I should remain *"pro forma."* Falkenhayn explained that he could only take over operations if he had a completely free hand. I could only acknowledge this.

So I stayed at headquarters while everything was taken out of my hands and I stood there as a spectator without any influence. Perhaps no one will understand this. I took this martyrdom upon myself and covered the further operations with my name, for the sake of the country and to spare the Emperor from being told that he had sent away his chief of staff as soon as the first setback occurred. I knew what disastrous consequences that would have. Later I asked His Majesty to send me to Brussels to assist in the capture of Antwerp. I could no longer bear to be present at the Grand Headquarters without activity and completely sidelined. The Emperor approved my request, and I went to Brussels and from there to the headquarters of General v. Beseler at Fildonk. I was there three times, in between again at the Grand Headquarters, to which the restlessness because of the further operations drove me back again and again. I was able to provide General v. Beseler with some auxiliary materials, bridge trains, and a Landwehr brigade. At the surrender of Antwerp I was present at Fildonk. The Emperor had given me authority to conclude the eventual surrender, which I meanwhile ceded to Beseler, to whom alone the honor was due.

After the surrender, I returned to the Grand Headquarters. I now had nothing more to do, was exhausted and almost in despair about my attitude. I went to the Emperor and told him that I could no longer bear this state of affairs. He was astonished as I explained to him that I was completely excluded, and said that he still regarded me as the real head of operations. After I had explained the facts to him, he said that this was not his intention, that he would remedy the situation, that he would think it over and change it. The next day I fell ill with an inflammation of the gall bladder and liver and had to go to bed. The mental excitement of the last weeks, my desperate mood and situation had had a pathogenic effect on the physical organism. After I had been lying down for eight days, the Emperor visited me and sat by my bedside for an hour. He was very kind and gracious, but did not return to my official functions. Two days later I received his second visit. He provided me with an apartment in Homburg Castle and advised me to go there for some time to recuperate. He also admonished my second adjutant, Captain Köhler, to take good care of me, and was again very gracious. I went to Homburg a day or two later, it was on 1 November.

On November 3, the order was signed appointing General v. Falkenhayn as my successor. I was in the air without any official function.

I have made these cursory notes without having notes or any material at hand. There may therefore be some errors in dates etc. in them. Also, I was still ill when I wrote them. They are intended only for my wife and must never be known to the public.* The martyrdom I bore was great. I believed I owed it to the Emperor and the country. If I have done wrong, may God forgive me.

I am firmly convinced that the Emperor never realized what he had done to me. He kept his gracious attitude toward me even after I left.

---

* I consider the publication of Moltke's records necessary today, so that the truth about important events may become known. (The editor.)

Part II – Moltke's Thoughts and Deeds in Excerpts from Letters to his Bride

1877–1878

Creisau, * *1 September 1877.*

Today is the 1st of September. Seven years ago today I stood on the battlefield and listened with a trembling heart to the rolling of the firefight in front of us around the heights surrounding Sedan. At the same hour as I write now, the iron dice were still rolling here and there and no one knew who would succeed in the throw. Now, after seven years, the church bells are ringing throughout the German Empire and thousands of hearts are bowing before the One who guides the destinies of the nations with a strong hand, and from thousands of German hearts a prayer of thanksgiving is rising up for the fact that the dream which the German people have dreamed for centuries has become reality, has become truth, and that we have seen the sun of unity rise full and bright, even if from a bloody dark night, the sun for which our fathers and forefathers bled and of which they saw only the first redness of the morning sky.

---

* Second Lieutenant in the 1st Guards Regiment on foot, assigned to the War Academy.

General Staff Berlin, 4 October 1877.

I am pleased that you liked "Faust." I am always drawn back with irresistible force to this book, which I have already read so countless times that I know it almost completely by heart. It is a work that unites all the sounds of poetry, from the praises of the archangels to the mocking laughter of hell – from the thoughts of strength of a titanic struggling man's spirit to the naive chatter of an innocent girl's heart. The greatest thing our German literature has ever created.

General Staff Berlin, 13 October 1877.

It may be enough for today with the work, my thoughts, which I have tied long enough on books and paper, now also want to have their will and push with force away from here and move towards the north, far into the distance. If I could wander with them! It is already late at night. I have been so absorbed in my work that I have not noticed how the hours have passed and the hand of the clock has gradually moved further and further. All around me reigned the silence of the night. Sleep has descended upon the city; with a soft beat of wings it has come and blotted out the sound of the day. He, the friend of the poor and miserable, is now already beautifying many a face, which a few hours ago still feared hardship and worry, with a quiet, peaceful smile, and brings sweet dreams to the afflicted, in which he can forget the troubles of the day. Nothing stirs in the quiet rooms that abut mine, only my clock ticks its busy monotony and my lamp casts its quiet yellow glow on this sheet of paper on which I paint the black letters. It is the time I love to work. When the cars no longer rattle through the streets and no loud noise draws one's attention away, then one's mental powers awaken, then one can grasp and understand everything so easily and quickly that it is a true pleasure, then I really feel what it means to work with pleasure and to fight against the books as

---

* First Lieutenant.

against an enemy that must be defeated so that one can feel the joy of the consciousness of victory. And I am not alone in these hours dedicated to work. Spiritually and figuratively you are with me, my faithful comrade, you work with me and endure with me until I push back the books and say stop for today. Day by day I feel more and more that I have the strength to accomplish something, and the thought of You is for me the ever bubbling spring from which I draw strength to go forward, forward, forward, as I owe it to You and to my name.

General Staff Berlin, 1 November 1877.

I have often thought that the thoughts of the human spirit are a model for him, how he will become later. This is how I think of the soul after death. The body is then stripped off and becomes dust and ashes, as is its destiny, it returns to the earth from which it is formed and to which it belongs, but the consciousness remains alive, and as we can now move in thought from one place to another in an instant, so we can then really wander through the infinite spaces of creations; Just as we can now in thought take ourselves ahead of time or go back in it to the days of our earliest childhood, even to the misty distances of the oldest known history, so we can then in reality take ourselves back and forth, time has then ceased to carry us along with it without our will, we then stand above time, that is, it no longer exists and that is eternity.

I find beautiful the idea of thus being able to wander from world to world through the infinite pillars of heaven, to see what we can now only guess at, and to enjoy bliss in it as it is promised: in beholding the glory of God revealed as we can comprehend it, namely in the all-powerful works of the Almighty Creator. I like this thought better than the rigid rest of death, of which it is said that man sleeps until the trumpet of the Last Judgment wakes him from his slumber. We already sleep so much here on earth, shall we then begin even more after death! - Do not believe, however, that I am of the opinion of the spiritists. According to my opinion we have finished with the death with this earth and do not come back there. I think, you will understand me and will not think me for a mystic enthusiast.

General Staff Berlin, 7 November 1877.

You don't have to believe in these stupid war rumors. France still has too much to heal from its wounds to feel like getting new ones. But if we have to march, you too will grit your teeth and let me go to do my duty like everyone else. My blood and body belong to the king and the fatherland, but my heart is my property.

General Staff Berlin, 7 November 1877, evening.

Are you afraid that it will be war again? If that is the case, I say to you, believe nothing of what the others speak, because I can assure you that it will not be war. A war does not fall from the sky so easily, but announces itself beforehand like a thunderstorm gathering on the political horizon, and even if one believes that it must break out now, it often remains with a harmless weather lightning. Here with us, no one knows anything about war; everything is as peaceful as it has ever been.

Academy Berlin, 11 November 1877.

Do you know where you are getting this letter from? You certainly can't guess. Just listen to how oblivious I am today. Here I am sitting in the academy at my green-painted wooden table, all around me sit the officers and listen with the most attentive faces to the lecture of Major von A., who tells us how old Frederick, the great king, fought his battles in the Seven Years' War. How he moved his small army here and there, defeating the Austrians here and the French there, and how he made poor little Prussia great and powerful through all dangers, in spite of the myriad of enemies surrounding it, without any other means of support than those which his ingenious spirit always created anew out of itself. Now I should actually direct my eyes to the maps spread out before me and follow in my mind the multitudes of the great king over Dresden into the Bohemian regions! – In confidence I will tell you that I will sit down at home tonight and work through everything, so that nothing will be lost to me.

General Staff Berlin, 13 November 1877.

And now I want to tell you one more thing: No human being is good in and of itself, because otherwise we would not be human beings. Everybody has his mistakes and weaknesses. It depends only on the fact that one recognizes his mistakes and tries to improve them. This striving must be present in every human being if he does not want to sink deeper and deeper into himself. With good will, however, much can be done. We both want to see that we make each other better and that one helps the other in this.

Do you remember how we once talked about the hieroglyphs in the Egyptian tombs? I have to think of them when I sit in front of your drawings and first try to make clear to myself whether it is a human being or a landscape that I have in front of me! – How often I dwell in thoughts on the beautiful hours when we sat together, rejoiced together and made nonsense like children, and then again how you listened to me so attentively when I read you the treatise on the chorus in Greek tragedy. It was so nice to find interests in you that responded to everything.

General Staff Berlin, 27 November 1877.

As I happen to look up and my gaze falls on the books lying on the table in front of me, there's someone sitting on top of a thick book, saying nothing at all, and holding out a sheet of paper to me with the words "Christmas" written on it. I nod at him and say: "Schongut! I've known you for a long time, too, and I know that you live in my books, so that when I open them, you come out of them and hang around on my desk day and night. It's all right, my little friend, we must wait, the time will come. But then, when it comes, you shall go with me to Sweden and visit your comrade.

How happy you will both be!"

General Staff Berlin, 28 November 1877.

You ask me in your last letter if I don't find the entertainment of the big world terrible. I can't say that I do. You can't talk to everyone about everything, and before you find someone who is interested in something other than what directly affects him, you have to search for a long time. You are quite right when you think that there are so few really clever people. But it is a true luck that one has invented then this conversation which you find so terrible. What should one do in a society and with a person who only knows how to say yes or no to something he doesn't hear every day, and even that not always, if one didn't have this conversation, which one can put on like a pair of worn slippers and in which all the world knows how to slurp along. What should one talk about with such a person?

If I'm extremely indifferent to a person, I'm also happy to choose an extremely indifferent subject for conversation; like goes with like. So we talk for half an hour, and afterwards everyone thinks that they have had a good time. Everything is happy and satisfied and everyone thinks of himself: "You are much more important than the other!" – And because everyone thinks this, everyone is also amiable, for man is never more amiable than when he is pleased with himself. That one would have something of it, of this kind of entertainment, I do not want to claim now, but it is just the big way, on which all find themselves together and find their way, and which is so broadly trodden that nobody can miss it. This entertainment is conventionally established like all rules of decency and good manners, which are really foolish and wonderful enough at times, and yet, if one did not want to follow them, we would in time get back to eating acorns like our ancestors and beating ourselves to death with knickknacks.

General Staff Berlin, 8 December 1877.

As I got up this morning, the white frost was on the trees and the lawns in front of the house. The first light troops, which winter sends ahead to reconnoiter whether it can follow with the main force or whether here and there a careless flower, left behind by the departing autumn, is still nosily lingering above the earth. These last late bloomers are driven away by the frost; whatever green plant life was still there is destroyed and the way is cleared for King Winter. He can come with snow and fog, and then with frost and clear sunshine, but without warmth, as it were a mirror image of the hot summer sun; the same sun, the same rays, but without awakening life, without warming the rigid earth, without making the moist steam of budding spring rise from all furrows. And this difference is only because the sun's rays fall on the earth a little more obliquely than in summer, although the earth is closer to the sun in winter than in summer!

But I don't want to lecture you on physics, I just want to tell you how weak these first winter attacks are, because today at noon it is already dripping again from all the roofs and the wet and humid haze, in which we have been wrapped for a month, lies again on the city like a widow's veil. I feel the same as you, I don't like this weather either and love nothing more than a good, real frost, where all senses sharpen in the cold. Now everything here looks dull and sleepy, people have boring faces and an unhealthy appearance!

General Staff Berlin, 9 January 1878.

Put a person on a desert island after his birth and let him grow up there without coming into contact with other people. What do you think that he would become? A reasonable animal, nothing more, a creature that knows no other interests than its belly, eating and sleeping. What do you think this unfortunate man would say if he suddenly came into the world and began to understand that there are other interests besides the things that occupied him until now? He would understand nothing and feel terribly stupid. Now it is not at all impossible that this person has the best talents in the world, and if he has them, they will develop as soon as the opportunity presents itself, and in a short time he will be just as clever as the others. But the better he is, the more he will feel the oppressiveness of his ignorance, for if he did not feel it, he would not feel the need to educate himself and would remain stupid and simple-minded all his life.

General Staff Berlin, 12 January 1878.

To recover from yesterday, I went today after the Academy to the Picture Gallery, where some new, very beautiful paintings are displayed. I wandered around there for a long time, trying to trace the spirit with which one or the other artist has created his figures. One can think so much about some paintings, so little about others, but all of them look at you mutely and meaningfully, as if they wanted to say: If you want to understand me, think about me. Forget yourself and the time and world in which you live, and put yourself in my world and in my time. Then the figures come to life and the stories of the past they represent come to life and rise from the old gray time with its joys and pains, its good and evil deeds.

General Staff Berlin, 24 January 1878.

If a person confronts you with petty thoughts, a person who crawls in the dust and who feels comfortable in the dirt, then let all the pride of your soul roar like a hurricane, turn away full of contempt from everything that is small and mean, and hold fast to the ideal, to the true and beautiful, then be proud, proud in your faith in truth and right, proud against petty people, proud against lies and slander. Always turn your gaze upward, never downward, open your heart wide where truth and beauty meet it, but close it firmly against all that is unjust.

General Staff Berlin, 28 January 1878.

How fortunate it is that, at the time of the Tower of Babel, music saved itself from the confusion of languages and remained the common property of all nations! Think if every nation had its own music as well as its own language, which the foreigner could not understand or could only learn with difficulty; fortunately, music is above the nations, so that all can unite in its common enjoyment and understand it and enjoy it.

General Staff Berlin, 10 February 1878.

Today I was in church, it is a very good pulpit speaker, only he has the fault that he can not help bringing politics into his speech. In my opinion, the sermon must remain free of everything that is not directly related to our faith. An *ecclesia militans*, that is, a church armed for battle, is not to my liking. Our religion is that of love and forbearance, of humanity and forgiveness, therein lies, in my opinion, the high beauty of the same. The God of my heart is not a God of vengeance, but a God who welcomes the sinner, who turns to him with a penitent heart, the God who looks at the heart and not at the confession, a God who is equally close to all people and who lets himself be found by everyone who seeks him.

But we are living in a time where things are fermenting from the bottom up and are stirring in all corners of the world. Here in Berlin, in the big city, where much need and misery has come together with many people, the spirits begin to heat up more and more. It even penetrates the pulpits and resounds from the mouths of preachers, it penetrates religion and wants to suffocate it. The enlightening teachings of science exert all their dangerous influence on the masses, who hear these teachings without being able to digest them, and who write individual extracted sentences of them on the banners of their socialist aspirations. Bad times are coming, if not yet soon, they will come; you and I will still be in the midst of the storm.

My poor fatherland, you beautiful, proud empire, whose mighty eagle spreads its wings over all seas, what will they make of you! As long as the army holds out, all is well, there is a good and healthy tribe in it, and military honor is strong in it, but the army is formed from the people, and when the beams become rotten, the house collapses.

These nonsensical people, they do not know what they are doing, they put the torch to the powder keg without thinking that they are blowing themselves up with it; they think they can direct the movement and do not consider that the raging torrent of the unleashed mob will wash them away like straws when the dam they are slowly undermining is broken. They call themselves the people's benefactors and do not heed the nameless misery they will bring upon the same people they want to gratify; if only they would take an example from the Girondists of the French Revolution, noble men with the best intentions, who found the fruits of their people – gratification on the scaffold of the guillotine.

Now I have come too far and you are shaking your head over this political letter. Do you like to read it after all, why should you not have a part in what concerns us all so closely. By the way, don't worry, everything is still only in the beginning, but I see it coming, how it will become. If you were here, we could talk better with each other and you would have your political opinion just as well as I do, because you should stand by my side with equal understanding in that, too. Farewell, my comrade. We stand firm at our post.

General Staff Berlin, 10 February 1878.

A knot and a piece of national color, that's what I have from your work. Shall I send you one of mine, too? What will it be? Some thoughts about tactics and fortification or a piece of war history, from which one can see that people have fought each other as long as the world has stood, that they have shed their blood for phantoms that burst in their hands like soap bubbles. I could also send you black and white war history, so everyone has his two-color work!

1878

General Staff Berlin, 16 February 1878.

We are just beginning to look at politics somewhat attentively. What may still develop there, if only the big pot of the conference boils, provided that it comes at all so far and not before still the Englishmen under the unbelievable leadership of their Israelite prime minister get themselves a lesson for the too humane fingers. I begrudge them from the bottom of my heart, this nation with its haughty presumption toward the outside world, the dismissed phrases of humanity on its tongue, and in its heart nothing but a desire for profit, cotton and trade policy.

General Staff Berlin, 22 February 1878.

The flowers also have a language, even if not in words, they speak to the heart, it only depends that the heart understands them, that it is receptive to the language of the fine leaves that sit so gracefully on the style, that delight the eye with their light colors, that carry their fragrance from Sweden and bring greetings!

General Staff Berlin, 28 February 1878.

It is quiet around me, one could almost believe that one could hear the breaths of the passing month. He goes away into the endless past to the infinite number of his brothers, a passed second beat at the big clock of the time and, nevertheless, how infinitely much has crowded together in him. What will his successor bring? The waves of the political current are running high. What will become of it?

General Staff Berlin, March 22, 1878.

On His Majesty the Emperor's Birthday!
    May the good God preserve him for us for a long time to come, may he hear a thousand and one thousand wishes for the salvation

of our beloved Emperor, which on this day rise up to him from all regions of the German Empire, this Empire which he has made great and powerful, this Empire whose dream, which it has dreamed for hundreds of years, he has brought to fulfillment, the childhood dream of the young Germany, which it held on to until its manhood, which its poets sang in countless songs and which it carried in its heart, although it was torn and disintegrated, like its most precious treasure, this ideal of the German people, which was its guiding star in the night of bondage and oppression; the red of the nation that shone for us in the wars of liberation, now the sun has risen and shines far and wide over all German land, as far as the German tongue sounds, German unity has been won and our Kaiser has won it for us. Through blood and struggle with unheard-of sacrifices it has been won, the best of the country's children have remained and their corpses rest like memorial stones in foreign soil, but their death is not lost, from the bloody seed the golden harvest has sprouted.

"Do not forget the faithful dead!" – they died a beautiful death, but we shout from the bottom of our hearts: "Long live our Emperor!" – On the Königsplatz under the Victory Column a battery has been raised and now shot after shot follows in rapid succession!

How I know them, these voices that speak so powerfully to the heart, these heavy hammer blows in the music of battle, how often did their sound surround me while we stood there on the bloody field, while death held its harvest and when the humanly weak heart wanted to tremble, when it became hot and the number of comrades in arms became smaller and smaller, then the fresh sound rolled over and called with a mighty voice: Still the Prussian eagle flies high, stand firm, comrades, victory is ours!

Your heart will also feel German with the man to whom you are so dear, your strong courageous heart understands what it means: to love one's fatherland and one's king, and since you have given it to me, this heart, it will also rejoice with me and thank God that he has given us these sanctuaries in a time when materialism and disrespect are spreading. How they disperse, the many people who stood around the guns, in the streets the crowd is breaking up, men and women and children, yes go ahead, even if there are some among you who would like to rebel against the warrior state that lies so ironclad on the people, you are all Germans after all, and when the fatherland and the Emperor call, you are all there and hold the shield of German honor high and pure in a strong German hand, so that all enemies who stretch out their hands for the sacred German goods must shatter against its iron strength, because you all love it so much, your German fatherland.

General Staff Berlin, 1 April 1878.

So today is the day I have waited for so long – now may his successors also hurry on their journey to the regions of the past from which nothing returns, the only thing that has power to visit these dead is memory. Memory and hope, these two gifts of God that we human beings have received to embellish our life on earth, one belonging to the past, the other to the future. Thus, they always touch each other with beginning and end, without ever being able to change territories.

The space of hope becomes narrower and narrower with the coming years, with them the area of memory wider and wider, and in the middle of both, just there, where one begins, the other ends, man stands with his beating heart, which lives and trembles under the influence of both. Always it hopes, and yet how seldom does memory keep what hope had promised, and yet this remains eternally young and eternally new, until with the last breath hope ceases and memory completes its long list.

That is, after all, how I feel. I have much of both. Memory shows me such beautiful hours, hope paints me even more beautiful ones, and the closer the hour approaches when it is to be fulfilled, the faster the heart beats towards it: Come soon, how long is it until then – and then again: Do not hurry so quickly past, you fleeting time, can you be nowhere to be grasped, nowhere to be held? – But reason also wants to join in, how would it look in the world if everyone could set the time like his pocket watch according to his desires and discretion, how could a calm world history unfold with such a *charivari*, which the people could record, which the children could learn in the schools. It is already better in such a way as it is, and nevertheless how gladly everyone would make the watchmaker at the infinite time gear, if he were only not such a powerless weak human being. An atom in the long chain of the living, a sun dust which is blown away, and one does not see his trace any more, a nothing whose insignificance one recognizes only from the fact that his disappearance leaves no gap.

And yet, what a world of feelings stands still when a human heart stops beating. What an abundance of thoughts goes out at the moment when the living blood no longer flows through the veins, thoughts that spanned the world far and wide, that penetrated into everything that has moved the human race for millennia, that hurried ahead of time in the flight of the giants and pondered into the distance what will come of good and evil. How it has trembled in sorrow and pain, how it has rejoiced to the shining sky of happiness when its hand touched it, how it has hoped and waited, how it has endured and bled, and how it has loved – this little human heart, this nothingness that disappears without way or trace, what a world it has sheltered within itself! The days come and go, in the string of pearls of eternity hour follows hour and we move with the unknown, like the skipper on the sea, who follows the winds that drive him and has only the compass that shows him his direction. My compass points to the north, so it is well able, at the helm of my ship of life sits hope, the wind is favorable and the sails swell. Happy sailing! – I know that I am not shouting it alone. I am not alone in this barren world.

General Staff Berlin, 3 April 1878.

Now I have had enough of everything that is called society, drawn a line under it and drawn a conclusion. What comes out of it? Not much profit that I would have had. The same people as always, the same interests, the same circles of thought, which I already got to know last winter and which have now confronted me again. How petty they are, these people who have nothing in their heads but their dear person, for whom their ego is the god to whom everything is sacrificed.

I don't know whether I am judging more sharply this year than in the past or whether my observation is perhaps more unbiased than last year, but I have never noticed the inanity of society people as I have this winter, and if I am to be honest, I myself have never felt so foolish as I have in the past months, when I played the amiable person in societies without my heart being in it. I want nothing from this society, I find nothing in it worth stooping to when one sees it at one's feet, it offers nothing to rise to, it is only a copy of the everyday man with all his faults, all his petty interests, all his egoism, his narrow-mindedness, his frivolity.

Now all this has perished, all these pleasures and vanities have lost their value, I have found the true value of life. You once wrote to me: "The life of the great world has no lasting value." Truly, you were right, I believe that you are very often right, only you must always tell me so.

General Staff Berlin, 13 May 1878.

You must have read about the assassination attempt on the Emperor. The enthusiasm of the countless crowds gathered in front of the palace was indescribable. I went there immediately after the news had come. Head to head the crowds stood, singing "Hail to thee in the victor's wreath," "I am a Prussian," etc., Most moving of all was how the whole mass of many thousands sang the old beautiful Lutheran hymn, "Now give thanks to God." – The Emperor stepped out on the balcony and the air trembled with endless cheering acclamations. The rage at that swine of a fellow was colossal; I think the people would have torn him apart if the police had not protected him. All night long the people stood in front of the palace and, when on the next day the Emperor drove out again as usual: When the Emperor drove out again the next day as usual, the streets were full of cheering people, the carriage had to drive at a walk, little was missing, they would have unharnessed the horses to pull the beloved Emperor himself, whom everyone wanted to see, to whom everyone wanted to shout.

General Staff Berlin, 25 May 1878.

If people in Paris have their fortunes told about the war, I think you can only feel sorry for them. Then you can be quite sure that no one will come. Besides, I trust the political situation more than the gossip that comes from the mouth of an old woman and with which I don't want to pollute my ears. How can one be so...like that!

General Staff Berlin, 31 May 1878.

I think you have been to Versailles in the present days and have looked at the wonderful paintings of Horace Vernet in the castle. How many times I have wandered through these halls and enjoyed the beautiful pictures. One in particular has remained in my memory, a raid of a Moorish camp by French *chasseurs a cheval*, furthermore the storming of the Malakoff, where the little drummer runs past so quickly in front of the gap in the wall to regain the protective rampart.

This collection is beautiful, and it is to be regretted that Germany has not also produced a battle painter, who from the rich and glorious development of its war history in a similar way as Vernet has fixed the most important episodes for posterity. The pictures of battles painted by our painters are mostly cold and without life, without action and unnatural, I know of only a few exceptions for the better. It is strange that we know how to fight battles but not how to transfer the spirit of battle to canvas!

In any case, you must not leave Paris without having seen Versailles, especially Trianon, all these places of such great historical interest, these quietly hidden lawns where the unfortunate Marie Antoinette held her shepherd's games, while the black clouds of the Revolution were already gathering so threateningly over her head, this head that still laughed and joked so harmlessly and yet was later to become a bloody monument to the unleashed powers of a long oppressed people.

General Staff Berlin, 3 June 1878.

You can imagine the feelings with which I am writing to you today. I can still hardly come to my senses, I cannot believe and understand how it is possible that such an outrage could happen. How we stand there before the peoples of the whole world. The murderous hand of this nefarious knave has burdened our people with a disgrace that will cling to them as long as history will exist. Our old Kaiser, the man who made Germany what it is, the man, the only one in the world, who today united in himself the hopes of peace of all, it is too base, too mean.

How we stood there after the happily completed war, a newly united people, strong and powerful, proud of our strength, proud of our Kaiser, the people's favorite, how high beat the heart when one said to oneself: You are a German and you can be proud of it, – now shame and disgrace lie upon us, our Crown Prince in England mocked by German workers, our ships wrecking each other, our Kaiser in his own capital wounded by murderers' hands, twice in so short a time. Our Reichstag weak and inactive, miserable cowardly fellows who dare not stand up against what they call the people's rights, thus unleashing the bloody passions of the rabble, our ministers flirting with liberalism, our industry lying idle, its products pushed aside abroad, all over and done with, and now this insult.

I was so happy in the thought of being able to bring you to our German country, what must you think of us now! How can I get back to Sweden, where people will point fingers at me and say: "This is one of those who shot their Emperor."

This has come like a hailstorm that destroys the young seed, crumples it and pushes it to the ground, to the ground deep in the dirt. What does it help us if thousands also want to cover our Emperor with their bodies with joy, if we are ready to shed our heart's blood for him at any moment, what does it help us! The cowardly murderer's hand seeks the ambush and the shame of the deed lies on all of us.

General Staff Berlin, 4 June 1878.

Here I sit again with the pain and shame in my heart. I cannot shake off the feeling that an indelible shame lies on our nation. The blood cries out to heaven and accuses the people for whom it has cared and worked throughout a life of 81 years. These boys abroad who pillory the name of the German people so that everyone must cry fie on us, who sully with their foul hands the hospitality which a foreign nation bestows on our Crown Prince, who drag in the mud that which is sacred to every man of honor, who disgrace their people, disgrace and disgrace forever. It is hard to bear this if one has only some sense of decency and good name. Yes, it is worse than when misfortune and poverty befall you. Misery and sorrow can hurt and consume and wear a person out, but honor at least is immaculate, so what does all misery say?

We have lost our German honor, at least that is how I feel, and have lost it through the fault of these beasts who do not deserve to be born of a German woman, who even the animals would expel if they had reason, for they stand far below the animals and roll in the dirt with their disgusting bodies. And we have to stand by and watch how the German name is desecrated, and can do nothing, – we cannot catch them, after all, these scoundrels who skulk in the dark, who only grin out from time to time under the shield of our humane liberal legislation, where they are safe, quite safe, and can laugh with their ugly satanic grimaces. No revolution, no revolt, afraid are the dogs to step out freely and fight for their principles. Everything is done quietly and secretly, solved stone by stone, where there is no danger. If I had only one of these fellows under my fingers, if I had twenty or a hundred against me, I would thank my God on my knees and go to battle against this cast of humanity with joy such as I have never known. But I would put on gloves, because one might be tempted to touch this filth.

What else are we to do in this country when our Emperor dies, they will shoot the Crown Prince too, and our Reichstag will wrap itself in the mourning mantle of its humane laws, to which they sacrificed the life of the noblest Hohenzollern who ever lived, will shrug its shoulders and say: "We had to uphold the liberal laws." They will sit, these humane sleepers, until the state building collapses over them too and buries them under its ruins, until the howls of bloody red socialism ring through the streets, until the torches of the people's army lay the young German Reich in ashes and our enemies set their foot on the neck of our torn people. There is no nation that has so little patriotism as the Germans.

I immediately telegraphed to Uncle Helmuth.* Yesterday he came. He also received a threatening letter, the writer tells him: "You have spent your whole life working with the sweat of the workers," etc. A too mean piece of work, but nevertheless painful for a man who has spent his whole life only doing his duty and has contributed so much to raising this Germany to the height on which it stood. Truly, one could feel disgust at the cowardice and indecision of the sentiments that seem to prevail. If I were a free man, I would tie up my bundle and turn my back on the whole pack of rascals, go to America or to Africa to the Hottentots.

---

* The Chief of the General Staff Field Marshal Count Helmuth Moltke.

Part III – Moltke's Thoughts and Deeds in Excerpts from Letters to his Wife

1879–1914

Lauban, 19 July 1879.

Yesterday we moved in here. A friendly little town, unfortunately our last quarters, the day after tomorrow our general staff tour will be over. I could have gone on riding like this all summer. I feel so healthy that I always feel like singing and jumping. I think I can also be satisfied with my work. Our major even said of an expose I had worked out: I don't know how it could be done better. You can imagine how proud I am.

Potsdam, 29 July 1879.

So: Potsdam! There I sit again in my old garrison, from which I had flown out for three years, a fledged bird that fate has led back to its old nest. I feel quite at home. The old familiar sounds of the chimes on the garrison church ring so familiar in my heart and ears, the handsome guys in their tight posture, the command, the tight discipline, the bumpy stone paving, the empty streets, all good and dear old acquaintances who greet me as if not a hair's breadth had changed in them during the three years of my absence. Three years! What a long time! Ten times the same period of time and a human life is gone. Withered like the flowers of the field and blown away by the wind.

On Sunday we arrived here and reported back to the regiment. I am commanded to lead the infantry company while the captain is on leave. This is very pleasant. I can put myself on duty and gradually get used to the little finesses of the practical soldier again. Right on Monday we had a big exercise in the battalion. We marched off in the morning at 4:30. First we had a big battle and then we moved into bivouac. We had beautiful weather. Our bivouac site was under shady oaks, through whose dark green leaves the sun cast green-gold reflections that played tremulously across the soldiers' bare helmets. Soon the bivouac fires were burning, and tightly packed the soldiers stood around their cooking cauldrons in which meat and potatoes were simmering for the midday meal. We officers sat on our field chairs at our small field tables, and while we waited for our meal, cooked by the orderlies, to be ready, we smoked our cigars and listened to the regimental music, which played its merry tunes in front of the bivouac. Or we would lie lengthwise on our backs in the grass and watch the little blue clouds of our cigar float light and airy through the green leaves until they were lost in the blue of the high sky that stretched above us like a crystal bell.

In 1½ hours the meal was ready and we dined in the green with an appetite known only to the soldier who has been on his feet from sunrise. After the meal, the soldiers began to perform their dramatic dances. Always two and two, polonaise, quadrille, always around the music. One has a big stick in his hand and commands the dance. He is a Lorraine man from the Metz area who, when he joined the regiment, understood only French. Wonderfully the French words sound in the German *bivouac, en avant, changez les dames*! etc., but all understand them and flawlessly execute the prescribed tours. At another point, a recruit is "bounced." A long line of soldiers stand vis-a-vis each other with their hands firmly grasped. On this chain bridge of arms the bounced man is laid and in a tactful throw he is flung high into the air, caught falling down again and thrown up again until he has reached the end of the row and – not always in the gentlest way – finally reaches the ground again after his flight. Loud cheers and laughter resound through the air. When the music is silent, the soldiers, camped on the ground, start their choral singing. The old songs, how well I remembered them and how easy it became to join in. Thus it gradually becomes dark and as evening falls, we set out to do another night exercise. Outposts are set up, slogans and field cries are issued, and soon darkness and silence lie over the company that was so loud and merry earlier. Night has fallen. On the horizon stands a dark bank of clouds, through whose veil the moon peeps out from time to time, as if it wanted to cast an astonished glance at the nightly military exercise. Deep silence all around.

The night wind whispers softly in the tops of the poplars. The air is warm and soft, refreshing in the forest. Now and then the faint call of a post sounds through the darkness, summoning a returning patrol. Slogans and field cries are exchanged, then the patrol moves on, quietly, shadowily disappearing into the darkness. Now everything is silent again. Suddenly, far ahead, a brief light flashes. Immediately after, the crack of a gunshot comes through the night to our ears. Two to three other shots rattle behind, then everything is silent again. Now shots are fired again, five or six in quick succession. First you see the flash, then comes the bang. The field guards hurry to their rifles, in two minutes the whole company is lined up like a dark wall, not a sound is heard, no one speaks a word, everything goes on the quiet shouting of the officers, who stand like a dark dot in front of their platoons. Now comes a report from the advanced patrols. The enemy has made a reconnaissance on the causeway against our position, but has moved off again as he came upon our patrols. The guns are reassembled, in a few minutes there is the same silence as before. At 11 o'clock we get the order to march off. At 12:45 hours we are in our quarters. That was the first day I was here.

Wüstemark, 11 September 1879.

We are very well situated in a mill in the middle of the forest. All alone, me with my oldest officer and the ensign. Two miles from

Wittenberg. I am all alone with my company. Very pleasant. Last night we bivouacked in pouring rain. That was less pleasant. But what a man can't stand. The clothes dried on our bodies the next morning. But the night was bad. The water ran down your collar and out of your pants. I was on outpost with my company and was lucky, as you will see in a moment. My major told me, "If you are attacked, your defense is naturally in the hollow." But I saw at once, with my innate military acumen, that my defense was not in the hollow of the forest in which I was bivouacked, but on a present ridge. I let the Major be and dug trenches on the heights and set up a defensive position there for my company. When we were indeed attacked the next morning, the colonel came and expressed his appreciation of the expedient arrangement, and the major, who had heard the praise, came to me and told me that "I would now also like to occupy with my company" the position that I had "so skillfully" set up. Truly, the enemy attack was repulsed, and I was so proud that an ordinary strategist like Uncle Helmuth seemed very small to me! – I feel as well as possible. Healthy and strong and full of zest for life and joy in my activities.

Wittenberg, 14 September 1879.

Here I sit in the old Luther city on the Elbe. Today is again a day of rest. We are on a village Dabrun near the city and drove in today to see the sights of the same. Very interesting indeed. For a long time I stood in front of the door of the old massive castle church, on which Dr. Martin Luther once nailed his ninety-five theses and thus threw the spark into the turbulent spirits that in a few years fanned the giant torch of the Thirty Years' War, which scorched Germany's flourishing fields and set back its culture by centuries. At the same time, however, in this European conflagration, the old, matted religion was cleansed and purified to new, purer views.

Now a door of ore is embedded there, in which the sentences of Luther are engraved in the metal. In old, ponderous Latin. At that time the German language was not to be found in the mouths of the church fighters. The *ecclesia militans* fought with the Roman sword. Today it is different, and we owe our unified language, perhaps the only some thing we have, in the best part to that Wittenberg monk who fearlessly took up the fight against Pope and Emperor and fought through it victoriously.

Then we went to Luther's apartment in the old university. His living room is still unchanged. The benches on the walls, the big table, the stove. Portraits of Luther painted by Cranach. At that window with the dull lead-framed panes sat Mrs. Katharina Bora, his wife, and looked out for the Herr Doktor when he returned home from the college. In the auditorium of the university building still stands the old, high-built chair from which he lectured and on which, almost a boy, he delivered his doctoral dissertation and obtained his doctoral hat. All this is interesting to see. It is like the old spirit of the Reformation when you walk through these rooms. Old-fashioned, strong, homely and coarse. But healthy and lasting. It was a great, mighty time, and Luther was a whole man.

Potsdam, 22 September 1879.

If the nonsensical and unfounded agitations of the Russian press against Germany had led to a conflict between the two states, which is happily avoided by the journey of our Emperor, then, of course, according to the impartial and absolutely correct opinion of the foreign countries, Bismarck would have been the troublemaker again! Don't you want to grant us poor Germans even the right, which otherwise goes through the civil legislation of all states, the right of self-defense?!

Wildberg,* May 30, 1880.

As you can see, I have now arrived at the first place of my destiny. Yesterday I finished my preliminary practice and this morning I left here. I had a so-called ladder wagon on which sat my large suitcase and all my instruments, Max and myself. The former on

---

* Assigned to the Kgl. Land Survey.

top of the suitcase like an Arab on the back of his camel. Pluto behind, so we went down the causeway with ups and downs. Finally, we had to load up the good Pluto as well, because he was getting tired and could no longer come along. It was a wonderful ride, you should have seen us. Half a mile before Wildberg, the wagon suddenly tilted to one side, one of the front wheels had run off. There we sat. Fortunately, we had not been knocked over, so that the instruments had suffered no damage. I left Max with the driver to sort things out and went ahead on foot. They soon followed.

Here I found a serviceable waggoner's inn, in which I have lodged. A room where the wallpaper hangs down from the wall in large rags. The bed promised a painful night. My dinner consisted of roast pork and potatoes, all swimming in grease. This establishment proudly goes by the name "Hotel to the Old Times"! After I had dined, I made a reconnaissance around the village, which wrongly bears its name, for it is neither wild nor mountainous; on the contrary, the whole area flat as a plate, I will have trouble seeing the level lines running. On one side there are vast meadows, quite marshy, in the middle of them a peculiar ruin from ancient times. It cannot be called a mansion, because it is only an earthwork, circular, with ramparts of house height and a ditch with water all around. On one side you can still see the pillars of an old bridge. The colossal structure was obviously built by man. Many thousands of feet of earth must have been necessary to build it in the boggy ground. But it must have been a fixed position. An old robber baron must have had his nest here, unassailable in the marshy meadows, which were only connected to the solid land by an embankment, on which the road now runs. The thing makes a peculiar impression. One can see the mighty ramparts in the flat meadows from far away. All around at their foot there are trees. The whole thing is circular. I went inside. Inside was a large empty space, no trace of masonry, but I soon realized that there was. A part of the inner wall had been cut off, the owner had used the earth to fill in the marshy meadows. During this cutting a piece of an old foundation was exposed, but not bricks, but granite and joined without mortar. These are called cyclopean walls, and they are always evidence of very great age.

Furthermore, I found a continuous layer of charcoal in the same tapping, from which I concluded that the buildings that had stood here must have burned down once. Then the fort had apparently stood uninhabited for a long time, because a layer of earth about three meters thick followed over the coals again. Later it was rebuilt and then burned down again, as a second layer of coals proved to me, over which there was again two meters of earth. In this second layer I found also already stones, to which mortar stuck, thus a later time. That the lower layer, thus the whole building, must be already very old, I found confirmed by shards of pots, which I scratched out. These were made of unfired clay. I took a handle and the rim of a pot as souvenirs. Both show the crude craftsmanship of antiquity. Hand made decorations, impressions and grooves. Where might the hands be now that worked these shards, lying here before me on the table, looking at me so gray and ancient? I asked a worker who was planting turnips on top of one embankment if coins had never been found, to which he replied in the negative. So it must have been a powerful society that lived here.

I also found a piece of iron, but it was so eaten through with rust that I couldn't tell what it had been, it crumbled in my hand. The worker showed me the blade of a hatchet he had dug up, also very rusty, but obviously of recent origin, so I had no desire for it and left it. The old potsherds I scraped out of the lowest layer are much more interesting to me, they are many hundreds of years old, as far as my imperfect judgment goes, still from pagan – probably Wendish times. Tomorrow I will drive over the terrain that I am to survey, two and a half square miles. The day after tomorrow the work begins.

Wildberg, 6 June 1880.

Today is Sunday, and it rained all day, from morning to evening, without a break. This is really terrible. I sat and drew all day long until my eyes hurt, then I walked around the room whistling and singing and declaiming, it all didn't help, I'm terribly bored! – Pluto lies in the middle of the room on his back and stretches all four legs in the air, he is very comfortable, he would like that the topographizing would never come to an end. I do have a good entertainment, namely Treitschke's *German History of the Nineteenth Century*. You may have heard talk of this book, which the whole world is reading now; my captain lent it to me as a consolation, and I must confess that I do not remember ever having been so captivated by a work of history. The whole book is dramatic. One feels and lives with the characters, one thinks, hopes and fears with them, one is so vividly transported back into the time it describes that one is amazed to find oneself in reality when one closes the book. And at the same time, a spirit of patriotism and German patriotism blows through the whole thing, without ever doing violence to the historical truth; it is wonderful.

Vichel, June 19, 1880.

I received word yesterday from my captain that he would come today to work with me. He ordered me to a certain place where he wanted to survey, in order, as he wrote, to help me a little forward. When he arrived, however, I had already recorded all the surrounding terrain fixed and ready, so that he said he saw that I needed no help, was very much astonished at how much I had already finished, and said that after my previous achievements he had no doubt that I would be one of the first to finish. He was very pleased in general and left after half an hour without having helped me. I can already stand on my own feet!

Vichel, 21 July 1880.[*]

I have my "Faust" as a constant companion again. You should see me when I stand bent over my measuring table and declaim monologues from "Faust" aloud in the middle of the blowing bush

---

[*] Publisher's note: Due to a typographical error in the original German edition, this date is uncertain.

grass, while I measure the distances with the compass. Occasionally I have to laugh at myself, which then sounds again quite peculiar and lost through the still air. A person who laughs at himself is always something wonderful in solitude, just as well that it is not the cutting laughter of scorn or despair, but the comfortable inner laughter of a fantasist who, in the midst of the most practical and prosaic work, cannot refrain from quenching his soul's thirst for beauty with a sip from the crystal fountain of Goethean poetry. Thus the hours fly by like minutes, and again and again I discover new beauties, which until now have been carelessly hurried past. Such a working day of twelve to thirteen hours always satisfies me. When I go home in the evening, I have a certain joyful feeling of satisfaction.

Nackel, 21 July 1880.

See how beautiful the world is ! What would man be if he could not hope. A stunted existence, burrowing in dark, unclear pain and tormenting himself with secret horror. Grieving and weeping for the past, for what was lost, for what was not achieved, anguishing with self-reproach in nameless agony. No, hope, this true daughter of heaven, according to the beautiful old legend, was given to mankind when all suffering had flown over them from Pandora's box; it alone outweighed all suffering. The eyes of the people are directed forward, one should also look forward, towards the light that brings us the morning. He who looks back and looks back becomes a pillar of salt like Lot's wife. Open eyes and open hearts, you see, that is my view and opinion.

Segeletz, 4 September 1880.

I did celebrate a certain small triumph today, as my captain told me that I was the first to finish. Even the old topographers, who are already surveying in their eighth to tenth year, are still behind me. He went over everything very carefully with me, I think, in fact, he thought I had worked cursorily in the great achievement of nearly thirty minutes last month, but he found nothing and, touched, squeezed my hand as he drove away and said: "A really extraordinarily industrious work, which I can hold up as a model to many an old topographer."

Wildberg, 6 September 1880.

So now I'm back where I started, back at the starting point after three months of work in the great circle. This time I am here with a much lighter heart. If then it meant: to begin, my being here now means: to stop, and I will do that with a thousand joys as soon as the last stroke of the work is done. It seems so strange to me that my laborious work is now really almost finished that I can't even get into the thought that it always seemed as if it could never be finished. The summer, of course, has passed me by without me actually having a feeling that it is over. I still think that the larks should be singing and the strawberries should be there, and yet the first yellow leaves are already falling from the trees, and the swallows are preparing to leave. The storks are already gone, migrated over the sea, towards the sun.

Our earthly sun, which shines on all, has meant it quite well with us in the last days. It has heaped such a glow on the top of our heads that animals and people lay there motionless and panting, waiting only for the moment when the glowing fireball would sink below the horizon and the shadows of the evening would bring a cooling, albeit slight. Only the topographer moved through the glow of the path, without skirt and vest, with open shirt, yet almost languishing.

Berlin, 18 June 1881.

You should see that when we have our apartment here in Berlin again and have settled in a little, you will soon like it here. Only now you are faced with uncertainty and only see the past in the beautifying light that it always assumes, thanks to the benevolent order of the world, when it has beautiful hours to offer. We forget the bad so quickly, the pleasant settles in the memory, and that is good. But we should also look to the future with firm courage and hold on to hope, this good fairy of the human race, who stands by man's side from the cradle to the grave and casts bright highlights into the darkness of the future with her golden shining torch. And after these streaks of light man hunts all his life like the child after butterflies. He who loses hope has lost everything, for he then has a broken courage and a dead heart, and is as good as if he had already died. Therefore, let us let the past have its right and rejoice in the sunny memories, but above what lies behind us, let us not forget what lies ahead. When we rejoice in the past, let us hope for the future and not become unfair to what will sooner or later become the past.

General Staff Berlin, 21 June 1881.

I have just come down from upstairs, where I have been sitting and working from 10 to 7 o'clock. The day after tomorrow I am to give a lecture on the genius of the Austrian army, and I have to gather the material for it from all sorts of instructions, reports, ordinance sheets, and so on. A laborious task.

General Staff Berlin, 23 June 1881.

Today I gave my presentation. It went well and my superiors were satisfied. From July I have been assigned to lead the exercises in surveying. Where? I do not know yet.

Charlottenburg, 10 July 1881.

If only I could be with you to rejoice with you in the magnificent gigantic nature, whose entire undreamt-of magic must already hold you captive. What sensations will assail you when your gaze falls for the first time on these rigid snow-capped peaks, which tower up into the blue sky with eternal, unchanging silence, the clouds weaving like a wreath around their foreheads, looking down from an icy calm on the restless hustle and bustle of the people below with their quarrels and quarrels, their tears and joys, their hatred and love. Does one not feel, as it were, that one has come closer to nature when one penetrates in this way into the mighty forms it has created? Don't you think you can still feel the breath of the almighty Creator blowing around these mountain peaks, don't you feel infinitely small when you look up at the rock faces that have already stood long before the first man began to learn his unhelpful earthly life? How wonderful it is to look at the rich nature. Admittedly not lovely and delicately curved. Roughly and jaggedly it confronts us here, but full of strength and marrow, full of mysterious showers of an all-powerful world spirit and mighty creator. This strengthens and steels heart and senses. You will see how the nerves become firm in the contemplation of the great and how the chest becomes wide and the blood pulsates more quickly when breathing in the spicy mountain air.

You must have gone over Lake Constance and then up the Rhine valley? You are now close to the source of this ancient German river, around whose vine-covered banks so much German and Frankish blood has flowed. Later, you will see this prince of the river in its lower course and become intoxicated by its enchanting beauty. The poet sings, "To the Rhine, to the Rhine, don't go to the Rhine," for once you have seen it, once its charms have spun around your heart, you will be sick with an eternal longing for its green banks! – How great is the piece of world history that is attached to this stream, whose weak trickling source you will have seen. You are enthroned now so many thousand feet above us other mortals who continue to spin our existence in deep sandy plain.

Berlin, 15 July 1881.

You write so beautifully and so interestingly that I savor everything you have seen together with you once again. From your letter I can see so clearly how much your inner life has awakened more and more and is pushing towards the light, towards the knowledge of itself and of the outer world surrounding you. Continue to let everything you see have an effect on you, open your inner being to the magnificence and beauty of the world, and you will feel for yourself how you will daily have purer enjoyment of these pleasures and daily learn better to enjoy with an unclouded inner being and to rejoice in the beautiful life. Then, when you yourself feel happy inside, you will also make others happy and from the consciousness of being in harmony with your fellow men, you will again draw an ever new moment of happiness. That is why I attach so much importance to this journey, because I know that nothing is more suitable to draw a mind away from itself and towards the outside world than a journey with its daily new images, its compulsion to pay attention to everything, its interest in things never seen before and its inner wanderlust, which is inherent in every human being and is awakened as soon as the post horn blows and the wheels rattle on the stone pavement. This forces the mind out of itself, and as new impressions approach it every day, it has no time to sink into musings, no time to speculate and brood, for the beautiful world beckons outside in all too golden a way, the brooks leap from the rocks, the larks rejoice loudly with delight – who would not like to sing with them with fresh sense from a free breast!

Berlin, 20 July 1881.

I received a letter from Uncle Helmuth today asking if I could have ten days leave, he would like to take me on a trip to the Tatra Mountains. But I don't think I will get leave, because from the 22nd on I am the only officer in my department, since all the others are on leave.

Creisau, 30 July 1881.

Let me tell you how everything happened! I already wrote you from Kandrzin that I had to leave without all my things, because the suitcase was not at the station. I had prepared everything so beautifully, writing paper, pen and ink with me, now I had to travel without being able to take a piece of it with me. Fortunately, L. lent me a few shirts and stockings, which were packed into Uncle Helmuth's small carry-on suitcase, that was all our luggage! We drove the first day to Ratibor, where we stayed in a small hotel, Uncle Helmuth and I both in one room. By the way, he was of course recognized everywhere, although, as he said, he wanted to travel completely incognito! We arrived in the evening at 7 o'clock, went to the hotel, I always with my suitcase, travel blanket, etc. in my hand – and then immediately left again to see the city.

On the way back, the mayor, dressed in tails and a white bandage, met us, greeted Uncle Helmuth and asked him for the honor of being allowed to accompany him to his hotel. Uncle Helmuth was rather short-tempered, did not understand what the man said, and so we went through the city, the mayor always in the gutter alongside with the convulsive effort to make conversation, which he completely failed! – The next morning there was a large gathering at the train station to see Uncle Helmuth depart. The railroad administration had had a saloon car put on the train, which was very pleasant for us, since it had windows all around and so one had an unobstructed view of the really charming area of the Krkonoše and the Sudeten Mountains. Uncle Helmuth's arrival was always announced in advance by the railroad administration by telegraph, so that all conductors and railroad officials were already averted.

In Oderberg, the railroad crosses into Austrian territory. Here, too, everything was very polite and very curious. The Austrian railroad administration allowed the saloon car to continue on its way, and so we drove into Austria, admired and marveled at! Now came a truly magnificent ride through the increasingly mountainous country towards the Carpathian Mountains. The railroad crosses the Tablenkau Pass at an altitude of a thousand meters above sea level and then descends into the Váh Valley, where it rises again, always following the course of the Váh River upstream. The area becomes more and more magnificent the further we go. Following the course of the river in many twists and turns, through tunnels and in sharp curves around rocky outcrops, the railroad climbs uphill. On the other side of the Tablenkau Pass, the watershed between the Danube and the Vistula, everything becomes characteristically Hungarian. The people working in the fields show the picturesque costume of the Hungarians, the wide white pants and shirts, with the felt hat with a wide brim, the women all in high boots with white shirt and coverlet or the legs wrapped up to the knees with felt rags. All the grain is cut with the sickle and put on in peculiar almonds. Small melancholy horses, which nevertheless perform and endure a lot, poor huts covered with decaying thatched roofs, but everywhere an abundant vegetation, which shows its original rich creation in mighty, waving cornfields.

From Rattek we leave the Pest Railway and take the Rashov branch line to our destination Poprard. Now the highest peaks of the Tatras, covered with eternal snow, are already visible on the left, while the less steep Tatra Mountains rise on the right. The ride on this last stretch is enchantingly beautiful. The closer one gets to the Tatras, which rise as a quite separate mighty group almost abruptly from the flatter plain, the more beautiful becomes the sight that this imposing mountain range offers. The peaks are very steep. Rugged rock faces of gray granite, rising steeply vertically, up to the third part of the height dense coniferous wood creeps up in the ravines, then come pines and stone pines, above them bare rock with long snow-filled valleys and the very pointed peaks that stare rough and torn into the blue sky.

The lighting of the whole parts is wonderful. Blue deep shadows alternate with brightly illuminated walls, sometimes one of the drifting clouds hangs like a wafting veil around one of the mountain tops, cannot detach itself from it, branches out in the cracks and gorges as if it wanted to suck itself in, It surges up and to the side, but still does not release the peak, which has completely disappeared into it with its pointed rock spires, then creeps down and tears apart, and above it the rock spires suddenly stare again, torn gray and unmoving, into the blue sky. This ever-changing spectacle is wonderfully beautiful, and I can well say that I had already fallen in love with the mountains before we had even set foot in them.

Finally, at 8 o'clock in the evening, we arrived at Poprard and got out. Uncle Helmuth had told the conductor that he wanted to stay the night in Poprard, but as a row of country wagons, harnessed to small, skinny Hungarian horses, stopped next to the station, and several coachmen in the most ragged costumes imaginable offered to drive us, Since the evening was beautiful and the air refreshingly cool after the hot ride in the coach, Uncle Helmuth suggested that we drive that same evening to Schmeks, the spa where we were to stay for a few days and which was a good hour away. "And," he added, "we will have the advantage of arriving incognito!" We did have that advantage, and how we got it, I will tell you tomorrow, because tonight, it is 2 o'clock, my eyes are closing. More tomorrow with fresh strength.

Creisau, 31 July 1881.

Now you shall have the continuation of my letter broken off yesterday evening. So, we drove in the evening at 7:30 from Poprard on a small greasy wagon without springs, harnessed with small, greasy horses, to Schmeks – up the mountain trail. Since we had only a small carry-on suitcase with us, there was no difficulty in getting away. The path climbs continuously from Poprard on. Schmeks lies at the foot of the Tatras, hidden in the middle of a dark green fir forest, with the stony, rocky ridge rising immediately behind it. It was a wonderful evening, a balmy air that was sucked in with all one's chest and invigoratingly filled the lungs.

At 9:30 we arrived in Schmeks. We asked the porter for a room and were immediately told that there would probably be no more rooms available. The director was called and, of course, we were first presented with the usual question of whether we wanted to stay longer or just a few days. After we said that the latter was our intention, we had decidedly gambled. We were really completely incognito, as Uncle Helmuth had wished, and had to bear the consequences! After we had been led into two false houses, we finally found in a third one, lying high on a lean-to, a meager accommodation in a very small room with a moderate bed, a small window to the courtyard and a right cellar air. Uncle Helmuth was very indignant. "This is supposed to be the first bath in Hungary!

It's like a hut in the Krkonoše Mountains. A terribly uncivilized nation," etc. But he had to make a virtue out of necessity, and I was glad to have a place to sleep prepared for me on the rock–hard sofa.

After our luggage had been deposited, we went down to a lower-lying house, on the outside of which was written in large letters "Dining House." We entered a large hall that sat crowded with people, male and female. With difficulty we found a shelter at the corner of a table just in front of the open door, in the most beautiful train! – In the middle of the room, at a table, sat the spa doctor and the clergyman, who had a lot of small prizes in front of them, a bag with numbers, and from time to time shouted something in Hungarian in a loud voice through the room, of which we of course did not understand a syllable. Almost all the guests had small lottery cards in front of them, which they looked at attentively, and at last it became clear to us that the whole company was engrossed in a raffle game, which was just in full swing when we entered. How general the interest in this game was, we were soon to learn to our sorrow by the fact that all the waiters also held a lottery card in their hands and divided their attention between this and the guests very much to the disadvantage of the latter. After a long effort, I managed to persuade one such jack, engrossed in his card, by shouting loudly, to bring us a fried chicken during a pause made by the crier, which we ate down to the stiffest bones. We had to give up the attempt and retire to our cellar-like room, where Uncle Helmuth crawled into his much too short bed with many groans and sighs, while I settled in on the sofa. We were thoroughly incognito!

The next morning found us up early. It was glorious weather, the sun cast its glare on the steep rock faces at our heads, deep blue, almost purple, the shadow-filled gorges stood out from the walls, here and there a narrow strip of snow blown into the cracks of the rock. A magnificently beautiful sight. The air thereby so clear and beautiful, one sipped it neatly like the most delicious wine. It was as if breathing was happening all by itself, as if someone else was breathing for us and we were just enjoying it. We took a wagon and drove up to the Kohlbach valley on a steep and uncomfortable path, which only these Hungarian cats can overcome. Here we found a refuge, a kind of log cabin, where there was excellent Hungarian wine and good trout, and we sat on a terrace with a beautiful view over the valley, where the Kohlbach comes roaring down, and a wide view over the grain-flowing plains at the foot of the mountains. While Uncle Helmuth remained seated, I set off and climbed up the valley for another hour on a rather difficult path to the so-called giant waterfall of the Kohlbach. It is very beautiful, but it does not deserve its name because of the insignificant amount of water.

As I turned around again, the high mountain peaks were still just as high above me as if I had stayed at the bottom of the plain. That is the beauty here in the mountains, that everything is still as nature created it. Here are no artificially dammed waterfalls, no costumed alpine dairymaids, no musically educated shawm players dressed in picturesque peasant costumes, no carefully hewn distant views, no ruins, no ruins that cling to the steep rock, weathered from time immemorial, and yet were bricked up and artificially aged only last year for the sake of the view, no cast-iron bridges and comfortable footpaths, no railings with ornate knobs in front of every ten-foot precipice – pure and unadulterated nature confronts us, rough and jagged, just as it was created.

The firs that have fallen over the gorge here with their roots torn out have surely been tossed by the wind, the water has been roaring over the same boulders for thousands of years, no human hand has regulated its course here, no sluice dams it up to let it run free for a minute in exchange for 50 pennies. Here and there a barely trodden footpath stretches rough and reckless over roots and rocks on the slopes, it is only the foot of man that has trodden it, not the hand that has made it for convenience. Where you step on a precipice, no railing restrains your step, one more and you lie shattered between the rocks. A few makeshift footbridges are artlessly cut across the stream. A few barely hewn fir trunks, a resinous railing on one side is enough to get across and to be able to climb on the other side.

All this is wonderfully beautiful, movingly powerful, when one is suddenly transported from our merciless civilization, as if by magic, into the midst of primeval nature. The vegetation springs up powerfully everywhere, the lichen moss hangs long-bearded on the firs, blueberries and fairies grow high and luxuriantly around the damp dark trunks, and above them the jagged craggy granite, rising to the sky, sharply lifted from the ether and intermingled with its deep blue shadow. No human voice as far as the ear can hear, barely the sound of a bird scurrying by. One could believe to be the only human being in these lonelinesses, the first human being perhaps and the last, and the far stretched picture of the fruit-yellow plain with the villages huddled in the valleys is just only a picture, is no reality, only a symbol of human earth life, up here in the God-created loneliness the strong breath of the creating power blows around us, ancient, but eternally young, mild and sweet as well as rigid, strong and unbending. I longed to go up to where the clouds were striving in vain to reach the mountain peaks, but, down below, Uncle Helmuth was sitting and waiting, so back and back in the wagon with him down to our basement!

Below, the gypsies were playing in front of the so-called Promenade Square. Violin, cymbal and clarinet without notes, one plays in front, the others wildly behind, even if many an adventurous leap runs under, but all keep the general direction like a herd of wild horses, which roar in a furious gallop behind the lead stallion over the Puszta. We had become hungry, and yet it was impossible for us to get something to eat. In the dining house, the kitchen was "closed" at 7:30 in the evening, they don't serve food again until night, now you can't get anything!

Then Uncle Helmuth, resentful and hungry, retreated to his room to pass the time with an English novel; but I strove out the criss-cross, followed the roaring streams down the valley, climbed up again, swarmed around under the firs, and was heartily glad not to meet anyone who could have spoiled my enjoyment. It is a heavenly nature, and from what I have seen of the Alps, i.e., the tour over the St. Bernard from Lake Lucerne to Lake Lugano, the Tatras are in no way inferior to them in wild romantic beauty.

As I returned tired and drifted off, Uncle Helmuth was still sitting by his book, gloomy and in a very bad mood. He had made another attempt to get a better room, but in vain. The director had tapped him on the shoulder and said, "Yes, look, you can be glad that you were accommodated at all and didn't have to lie on straw." – So we were still incognito in the highest degree.

"Tomorrow we leave," said Uncle Helmuth, "but then I will collect fiery coals on their heads. They don't consider us full – (of course, I thought), but when we leave, I'll sign up: Count Moltke, Field Marshal General, Knight etc. with all titles and dignities!!!" – I was sorry to have to leave again, I wanted to see more of the mountains and accordingly used a stratagem.

As we went down to dinner again, I stayed behind and then asked a waiter if he had not seen whether Count Moltke had already gone in? – Now you should have seen! – Who? The Count Moltke? The field marshal? The famous – oh! and from mouth to mouth went the news! All of a sudden all the waiters were supple and attentive, all of a sudden the host rushed over and ordered us to be seated, all of a sudden it was said: what do your Excellency order? I will have something cooked especially for Your Grace, please Your Excellency to take a seat here, here is a padded chair, there is no draught here, this wine is recommended, no, not that one, Your Excellency, it is only a country wine.

Suddenly there was a waiter standing behind each chair to adjust it, suddenly someone was jumping for toothpicks, someone was jumping for water, someone was jumping for wine, suddenly the tablecloth wasn't quite fresh, the bread was torn off the table because it was yesterday's bread, and fresh bread was put on the table, and then the innkeeper started to shout with a thunderous voice at a waiter who was walking too slowly: what kind of waitress that was, whether he hadn't heard that Your Excellency wanted to eat quickly, so he ran into the kitchen himself and came back breathless with the venison fillet that he had had roasted especially for Your Excellency! Please, Your Grace, is Your Excellency satisfied? Is it soft? Shall I make another one? Here you are, Your Grace!

And Uncle Helmuth, calmly and comfortably allowing himself to be fixed, winks at me across the table and whispers, "Someone must have recognized me."

But that he was not dissatisfied with the broken incognito, I saw by the quiet smirk of the corners of his mouth! – Now also the movement among the guests. All heads turn to look at us. Everyone who comes in has already found out and casts a long curious glance at Uncle Helmuth. After a quarter of an hour, the director also arrives, but not to pat Uncle Helmuth on the back again, but to say that a very nice room has been arranged for him: the minister's room, Excellency! The best room we have. Lord God, he turns around, I might have pulled my hair out, as I heard that I put Count Moltke in that room up there! Your Grace, Excellency, the things are to be brought down immediately. And three stout house servants will be sent to fetch the things! Two of them can then turn back, because the first one is already coming towards them triumphantly, swinging our suitcase in his hand, he has already brought down Excellency's "things" by himself!

The revelation of Uncle Helmuth's true nature thus brought us the double advantage of being well served and receiving a better room. We were still having our supper when, from the crowd of guests filling the hall, an elderly gentleman rose, walked up to Uncle Helmuth and said in a dignified tone: "Excellency, I greet you in the name of the guests!"

This elderly gentleman turned out to be a Catholic provost from Szegedin, the city that was almost completely destroyed by the flood of the Theis River last year. He was the president of the entertainment committee of the guests and his name was Oltvarrgi Päl-prepost, päpai Kamares, Ferencz József Rend Lovag Keresztese. From this long message of his visiting card I can only understand: Provost, papal chamberlain. This brave provost talked a lot, of which Uncle Helmuth understood only the tenth part, and finally informed us that tonight in the dance hall of the bath the great Anna Ball would be celebrated, which would take place on St. Anna's Day in all spas of Hungary in the same way. Your Excellency would certainly be interested in watching a real Hungarian Szardas. Your Excellency would not be in any way inconvenienced, could watch from a corner, etc. To my astonishment, Uncle Helmuth really agreed, and so we went to the Anna Ball in the evening!

This ball was not opened until 10:30 and began with a Szardas, like all balls in Hungary, as the clergyman, who knew a lot about entertainment, assured me. In one corner of the large dance hall the gypsies had positioned themselves and directly in front of them seven to eight couples who had lined up for the Szardas. I must say that I had imagined this famous dance quite differently. The gentlemen in tailcoats and white collars, patent leather boots, the ladies in large ball gowns. Very pretty appearances, especially striking because of the wonderfully pretty little feet and the excellently fitting footwear. Gentleman and lady stood vis-a-vis. The gentleman with both hands clasped his lady around the waist, the lady placing her hands on the gentleman's shoulders. The gypsies played wild dances with a lot of fire, and the couples jumped up and down in front of each other, crowded together, without moving from the spot. Sometimes they lifted themselves up on their toes, sometimes they made whirls with their feet, but no gentleman let go of his lady in order to perform the dance in changing pas, bends and twists, as it lives in our imagination. Thus the whole made the impression of a society of fools, who jumped tirelessly up and down, until the sweat ran in large drops from their foreheads and master and lady gasped for breath. It looked wonderful, the large hall completely empty, only the ladies not dancing around the walls, and then in one corner, often dancing so close to the gypsies that they had to raise their violins so as not to bump into the heads of the dancers, this confused tangle of figures jumping up and down in the most elegant ballroom! – Had such a scene occurred in a German ballroom, one would have immediately sent for the mad doctor; here the whole society sat and stood in mute amazement watching the few couples who, in the great heat, were indulging in such an enormously strenuous activity!

Uncle Helmuth, who had been watching the spectacle through the door for ten minutes, pushed his way home shaking his head, while I stayed on, as I was interested in observing how long a person would be able to endure this jumping around! – The whole dance lasted over half an hour. Every now and then a couple would fall off, always the ladies first, who would retreat while violently balking at their master, only to sink onto a chair, completely exhausted. When they had recovered somewhat, they re-entered. Others, apparently endowed with stamina calves and lungs, held out longer.

After a quarter of an hour, all the gentlemen were sweating as if they were in a Roman bath. They let go of one hand to run a handkerchief over their dripping foreheads, but without pausing in their bouncing. The ladies, likewise always bouncing, strongly needed the fans. Then, as if ashamed of their weakness, the gentlemen jumped twice as high as before, shook the hand with the handkerchief at the gypsies right under their noses, called out to them, and these brown guys then played at it with renewed fire.

Gradually fewer and fewer couples remained, the completely finished ones lay and hung around on chairs, at last only one couple danced, but even here the lady was completely finished, after she had made vain attempts to tear herself away, then to bring her dancer to a halt, however with the same success, with which an inexperienced person unfamiliar with arresting would try to stop the pounding piston of a steam engine, she had resigned herself to her fate, standing motionless still and letting her master bounce up and down on her like a young filly tied to a stake. I am convinced that this gentleman would still be bouncing like a rubber ball today if the strength of the gypsies, whose trembling hands were no longer able to guide the bow, had not gradually worn out. Suddenly the music stopped, and the gentleman, who had beaten all the others and even danced the music to death, made one last hop and led his wavering lady to her place, which she would not have been able to leave again within twenty-four hours, measured by North German standards. Thus ended this wild witches' sabbath, in which neither grace nor agility, neither beautiful figures nor intricate ways of dancing were to be noticed, but in which it was merely a matter of jumping up and down in as small a corner as possible, pressed as closely as possible between the gypsies, for as long as possible, and in which a lot of sweat was shed, which still made the damp floor steamy after the dance had stopped, while gypsies, gentlemen and ladies, sweating for breath with loud gasps, took a compulsory break! – I felt sorry for the poor ladies. Some of them were charming, graceful apparitions, who retained a certain dignity even in the dance, while at times a flash of movement appeared among the gentlemen, which was unpleasantly reminiscent of the lurching contortions of the Parisian cancan par excellence.

I did as Uncle Helmuth had done, shook my head, told my provost, who had watched the dance with shining eyes, that I had found it very beautiful, in any case very original, and sought my bed to be awake the next morning at 5 o'clock, where I had ordered a guide to climb the so-called Polish ridge, which, forming the divide between Galicia and Hungary, stands out sharply and jaggedly against the sky. For, lo and behold, Uncle Helmuth had graciously decided to stay another day in Schmeks, and I wanted to take advantage of the opportunity.

Heavy clouds, rolling fog, a heavy sultry air, that certainly gives a rainy day, as I stepped outside the door at 5 o'clock in the morning. But, the day must be taken as it is, surely it will not come again, so up and whether all the floodgates of heaven would like to open over me!

In front of me stood the ordered guide, a boy of fifteen to sixteen years, with a good-natured German face, a genuine descendant of those expelled Saxon Protestants, who settled everywhere in Spiš County and still unmistakably preserved their Germanic ancestry, as well as the language is almost everywhere German. He had in a sack on his back provisions for both of us; laced shoes, a mountain stick with hammer on top and looked very quaint and nice.

Another lad, scarcely three cheeses high, dressed in a jacket which had evidently been discarded by his father, and through the sleeve of which he was vainly endeavoring to get his hands free, came dragging a little horse, which, with bowed head and drooping ears, patiently met the awful fate of dragging my weight of two hundred pounds the first half of the way up. I really got on this little animal, as my guide assured me it had carried much heavier loads. But since I bumped into pieces of rock and roots with my feet almost touching the ground at every step, I put an end to the torture after ten minutes, sent the horse back together with the boy and explained to my guide that I wanted to make the tour entirely on foot. He looked at me in amazement, for the tour is quite strenuous and takes about eight hours.

So we set out on foot, he in front of me, I following him step by step. Now I want to remind you that I only had a suit with me and only one pair of shoes, so that rain was something I had to fear very much, and yet I was not to be spared it. For the time being, however, it was only cloudy, and sometimes a breeze even drove the fog aside and a golden ray of sunlight fell over the mountains, giving me good courage to continue my journey. Always ascending on a footpath, which is washed out by the water, full of stones and boulders, we reached the border of the coniferous forest after one and a half hours of climbing. Unfortunately, it had become so dull again that nothing could be seen of all the beautiful vistas we passed according to the guide.

After two hours, leaving the rocky valley in which we had climbed so far, we arrived at a rough log cabin built by the Carpathian Association for the benefit of tourists, where we rested and had breakfast. The "good path", as my guide said, stopped here, and from now on we came to the difficult path. After half an hour we continued. Now soon came the first bad path. A steep rock wall, over which the water sprays down in eternal rain. Under these heavy drops the climb goes up, now it became already precariously steep, and if one looked back, the fall precariously deep. After overcoming this first difficulty, we came to a valley called "The Flower Garden." And indeed it deserves this name and the great reputation it enjoys for its beauty in the whole area.

I already had the feeling that we must be at about the highest point, and now think of my amazement when a lucky gust of wind suddenly broke the fog that enveloped us, and I had the following sight.

We were standing on a moderately large meadow, on which the most luxuriant grass was growing, in the middle of which the Felka River was flowing gently over flat stones, murmuring with crystal-clear water, and all around us thousands of the most colorful flowers were blooming and smelling. There stood the deep blue gentian, forget-me-nots as deep dark as the sea, yellow filled meadow roses, who can name them all, the manifold flowers and herbs, which unfolded their glowing calyxes up here in the mountain-high solitude and stood nodding at the bank of the glass-clear water. And, all around this blooming splendor, enclosing like the iron box of the miser guarding his treasures, towered sky-high, iron-gray, bare, jagged and torn the vertically steep rock faces – how was my feeling when I looked up there, bending back my neck, I who had already believed to be on the heights and who now saw that I stood deep below the peaks in a closely enclosed valley! This moment was wonderfully beautiful and moving, the most beautiful thing I had seen and experienced, when the fog suddenly flew away, as if a magic hand had swept it away, as if the curtain rose in the theater and revealed magnificent decorations. Only to one side, the one from which we had come, was the valley open; here the Felka roared down in a precipitous fall more than a hundred feet deep, and over the edge of this precipice, up the walls of which we had climbed, the delighted gaze sank for miles beyond, down over the plain below, until, at the very back of the horizon, blue mountain shadows, as if painted with fairy hands, delicately and fragrantly closed the picture, over which the sun spread its warm rays, pure and golden. All this gazing and marveling lasted only a minute, then the wet gray mist crept in again, heavy and uncouth, extinguishing all magic, obscuring all distance vision, enveloping all beauty. Perhaps this wonderful picture has impressed itself on me so deeply because I was only granted a brief moment to enjoy it. But now it stands before me as if surrounded by all the charms of an indescribable beauty, a wild, rough magnificence, combined with the loveliest grace and fragrant floral splendor, rock and stone, damp walls, steep cliffs and jagged ridges, a flowering meadow, a murmuring silver stream and then a view into the distance, as if one could fly over the world with one's eyes – where will one find such a union again, and when – yes, when will I see such a thing again!

In the end, I was lucky that the fog came again, otherwise I could have been like the knight Toggenburg, and instead of sitting here in Creisau today and writing faint impressions of beautiful experiences on paper, I might still be sitting up there, wondering and looking, until the winter cold would have come over my warm blood, until my eyes would have frozen and frozen, until after year and day I would have been shown to the travelers as an oddity, as a misshapen stone, as a rock spike or who knows what! – So then it came crawling as with a thousand feet, winding around the rocky corners, wrapping us up, blowing cold into our faces, and startling me out of silent wonder.

We continued to climb toward the heights in dense fog. Now every path and footbridge ceased, a quarter of an hour after we left the flower garden, our foot already stepped on the first snow field. We continued over huge boulders, over which we climbed and jumped and under which invisible, but in the depth loudly roaring water flowed. Fortunately I didn't fall down, otherwise I would have broken my leg for sure, but when the travel guide says: "The word 'path' here is to be understood only very euphemistically, because it takes a gem hunter's skill to climb these granite boulders and translate gaps" – and further: "The panorama is indeed very rewarding, but whoever is not free from giddiness, with strong nerves and with capable hamstrings, should refrain from this last part of the part" – so, thank God, all the preconditions applied to me, and I made the whole way without feeling actual fatigue. The very last part was the worst, here it went up so steeply on smooth granite walls, over scree that was wet and slippery from the fog, then again only a crevice to put the foot in, only a loose tuft of grass to hold on to, that I really thought for a moment: Yes, up it goes, but how should one ever get down again!

Finally we were on top of the actual ridge. A narrow ridge, barely two meters wide, sinking steeply on both sides into the infinite depth. How deep it was, one could not see, because the fog enveloped everything. Now a sharp, wet and cold wind whistled over the heights, I had become very warm from climbing and pressed myself shuddering into a crevice to seek some shelter and catch my breath. In large beads, the mist settled on my clothes and covered me and my companion with a damp, glittering veil. The air was thin and rough. There was nothing to be seen of the famous view of Galicia on one side and Hungary on the other; only at our feet, blinking blearily through the fog, was the so-called "frozen lake," which, covered with ice throughout summer and winter, bears witness to the altitude at which we found ourselves. So I had to be content with the awareness of being on top, of having reached the goal I wanted to reach, but unfortunately I had to do without the fruits of my labor.

We waited for a quarter of an hour to see if the fog would not lift for a moment, but it remained immovable, impenetrable. So I had to give up the view and we started the descent. This was even more difficult than the ascent. At first my guide had to adjust my foot here and there, while I slid down on my hands and with permission – piece by piece. Later it went better and I came forward alone, but often still came places where I had the consciousness that a wrong step would plunge me without salvation into the depth. After half an hour I had become so confident that I could easily follow my skilful guide, who told me that I had a lot of climbing ability and strongly advised me to climb the Gerlsdorf peak, the most difficult and breakneck section in the whole Tatra. Gradually we came back to the field covered with granite boulders in ever thicker fog. On the way we startled a pack of chamois, which were running wildly over the sharp ridges. We did not see them, only heard the sharp beat of their hooves on the rock, small stones and boulders loosened under their fleeting feet and rolled, jumped and bounced in a hundred thuds and rumbles into the depths. Only after a while did the sound come up to us of them clattering below or plummeting into the water. After ten seconds everything was dead silent again, only the fog around us, no sound of a living being in the sublime silence of the mountain giants. Then my guide uttered a long-drawn-out whoop, we stood and listened, ponderously, as if smothered in fog, the echoing reverberation came back twenty-fold.

As we passed the flower garden for the second time, we plucked a mighty bouquet; blue, yellow, pink, purple, a hundred-colored we gathered the flowers together, a splendid glowing bouquet, such as could probably not be tied in any garden tended by human hands! A strong smell permeated the flowers, spicy, herbaceous, true children of the mountains.

After four hours, since we left it, we arrived back at the blockhouse and sat down to breakfast with a primeval appetite. Here everything was consumed that the satchel contained and what the bottles could offer, and then, while we were still sitting and resting, the rain began to pour down. First in small pauses, as if to test its strength, then incessantly, tirelessly, straight and steady, a real continuous downpour. And we sat and waited. My guide lit a fire and, impaled on a piece of wood, fried the last piece of bacon. The rain continued to pour down calmly and steadily. Then I made the great decision to brave everything and with my skirt collar turned up, my neck pulled into my shoulders, I went into the flowing wet, down on the two-hour way home. The bouquet had well of it, fresh as if it had just broken, we brought it down, but I –! From my shoes, from my sleeves and pants the water flowed, as I stepped into our room, and now – not a piece to change! I undressed, wrestled the water out of my clothes, stuffed my shoes with stockings and handkerchiefs, hung everything over chairs to dry and – went to bed! – I had to do it like Kato did when his only toga was given to be washed, which, by the way, should not have happened too often!

Uncle Helmuth was downstairs in the coffee house, it was 3 o'clock. I had just warmed up, he came back, and now my suffering began! – It continued to rain quietly and he sat down with a book to read. After a while he got bored with me lying in bed and started to intrigue me to get up. Fortunately I had shirts and underwear with me from L., so so far it went quite well, but then I could not get into my wet shoes. The kitchen was "closed" as usual, so there was no fire for drying. With unspeakable effort I finally wedged my feet, which were somewhat swollen from the unaccustomed climbing, into the wet leather, but could not take a step in them for the first five minutes. Then I had to put on a pair of Uncle Helmuth's pants, which reached halfway below my knees and which I could not close over my stomach. Uncle Helmuth claimed that they fit like a glove, I want to believe that, only that the cast was a good bit too short and too tight! For this I put on L.'s summer topcoat, which made up in width and length for what the leggings wore out, and so I was to go down with Uncle Helmuth to have dinner! Energetically, however, I refused. Wet as they were, I put my own clothes back on and consoled myself with the thought that they would dry best on my body. In the meantime, Uncle Helmuth had decided to have tea in his room, and I went downstairs alone, wet and chilled to the core.

The next morning the sun shone bright and clear in the sky, sparkling in the rain-heavy fir branches over the millions of drops that sat entangled in them. There was a brilliance and sparkle, a flashing and melting together of light and shadow such as I had never seen before, and at the same time an air so balmy and pure, so invigorating and invigorating, that one could not get enough of the blissful pleasure of breathing it in, indescribably refreshing. But we prepared for departure. My heart was heavy as I saw merry societies, glad of the beautiful day, climbing into the mountains, as everyone hurried to make up in the open air for what yesterday's rainy day had cost him in room seats, – we packed our little suitcases, climbed onto a springless wagon, and off we went, down the stony mountain path to the railroad station!

Goodbye, you beautiful piece of God's world, you magnificent mountain nature with your crystal water, your blue-grey rock faces, your diamond flashing fir darkness, how I would have liked to stay there, how in two days, like a child who smiles and cries, you captured my whole heart with sunshine and rain. But this I vowed to myself, that if God lets us live, then you and I will travel here again for a few weeks and enjoy the beautiful nature together, breathe the pure air of the mountains together and listen to the strange sounds of the cymbal and violin together, from which the brown gypsies elicit their wild tunes.

We drove all day. At 8 o'clock the train left Poprard, in the evening at 10:30 we were in Neisse, the next morning at 6 o'clock we went on, at 12 o'clock we were in Creisau – where I found my suitcase! – Thus ended our short journey, which nevertheless brought me a wealth of the most wonderful memories. Uncle Helmuth sends you the flowers which I have pinned up here. He himself climbed down a steep mountain to pick them, took them himself, dried them and gave them to me here with the words: "When you write to Eliza, greet her from me and send her this bouquet from the Tatra." – I was so touched by the old gentleman.

Creisau, 2 August 1881.

Today Uncle Helmuth and I took a long trip, he armed with the pruning shears, I with a saw, and raged terribly among the young saplings!

General Staff Berlin, 29 August 1881.

A general staff officer who cannot ride in terrain is useless, and since I have not been able to ride so far, I must learn now. I know that I am risking my neck, but I would rather break my neck than stand at a post that cannot be filled with consciousness. I have to be able to ride, and I will learn, and if I fall a hundred times, it won't help.

The air of maneuvers is already beginning to blow and seems strange to me. One longs to get out of the confines of one's four walls, out into the open, fresh field life among living soldiers, with sweat and physical toil instead of these paper armies that present the same boring numerical face to one every day. How I look forward to the few days when I am to attend the maneuvers in Holstein, it will be too wonderful.

General Staff Berlin, 8 September 1881.

The maneuvers at the X. Corps are now finished, and for the meantime, until they begin at IX Corps, Uncle Helmuth has gone to Kiel. The Emperor is going to Danzig, where the meeting with the Emperor of Russia is to take place, of which all the newspapers are now full. Bismarck is also going there. The Emperor is said to have been unwell during the last few days of maneuvers. He attended one day of them in the car, which he has never done before.

Itzehoe, 12 September 1881.

The parade was very nice. At 9:30 we drove out to the Lockstadt artillery range, a large plain where the whole IX. Corps was deployed. At 11 o'clock the Kaiser, the Crown Prince, Crown Princess, Prince Wilhelm, etc. arrived. The march past was very good, although not as impeccable as I saw from the Guards Corps in Berlin. I liked the Mecklenburg regiments best, beautiful tall people. A huge crowd gathered here. Wherever the Emperor is seen, he is greeted with endless cheers. The weather held during the whole parade. But no sooner had the Emperor climbed into his carriage and departed than a veritable downpour fell. How strange, as if it had only been waiting until the Emperor was in the dry carriage!

Itzehoe, 13 September 1881.

I can't tell you how immensely comfortable I feel in this fresh, lively maneuver life. In the midst of the troops, in the open air, in the battle, seeing everything, observing, and not in the limited field of vision of the front officer. On horseback, where the main moments of the battle take place, criticizing, examining and judging, it is too beautiful. Only the quarters would have to be a little worse, a straw sack or bivouac, no feather bed and then a little more danger. In a word, a real battle, a real campaign, and then I would like to lead the battle myself according to my own ideas! And if not, just a moment when once again the whistling of bullets would be heard and success would have to be wrested from the enemy with blood and iron! As the Arabian horse inhales the hot breath of the desert, so I inhale the smell of powder in long, deep breaths. Here is my element, here is my life, feeling and thinking. I would welcome a campaign with a thousand joys and throw myself into the tumult of war with true lust. What could be more beautiful than the soldier's life. The man standing on his own feet, facing the enemy, and now the fight to the death begins. But you don't have to take it so seriously. I still have a nose full of gun smoke, and that always intoxicates me like young wine. But twice as much you feel your inner life pulsating. All nerves tense, all senses sharpened, you beautiful, glorious war life! I believe I was born to be a field soldier, and I thank God that he has brought me into a career in which one feels one's heart beating in overflowing professional joy.

Itzehoe, 14 September 1881.

The maneuver yesterday was very nice. The whole army corps maneuvered against a marked enemy. It started with a big horse battle, where four regiments burst against each other. Since there was not the slightest dust, the whole field of attack could be beautifully overlooked. Then the infantry developed, went forward to the attack, supported by an artillery position of 12 batteries, 48 guns. The Emperor looked very fresh. It granted a beautiful sight when he, followed by the shining entourage, galloped across the field, about two hundred officers of the most diverse armies of the world behind him. Uncle Helmuth also appeared from time to time. Prince Wilhelm rode with me for a long time yesterday. I think he is glad to find an old acquaintance among the masses of strangers. The Crown Princess is also always out on horseback. The Crown Prince handsome and imposing as always.

General Staff Berlin, 25 September 1881.

Yesterday evening we all went together, in civilian clothes of course, to a people's meeting in which Pastor Stöcker was to speak. He is the founder of the so-called Christian Social Workers' Party and has often spoken against the overgrowing Jewry. A huge hall, Tivoli, was filled with at least two thousand people who received him with bravos and hand clapping. I had heard much of the pastor's ravishing eloquence and was very curious about him. He spoke very nicely and in places even with flaming enthusiasm. When he said that social reform must start from the family, that the righteous, faithful old German marriage, the firm union between man and woman, must be restored, an endless cheer, a minute-long clapping of hands and bravo broke out. One got the impression that all these men, workers and merchants, were striving with all their hearts to rebuild a national Germany. Towards the end of the two-hour speech Stöcker became a little too unctuous and at the end fell completely into the pulpit tone. That is a pity, the first half was in places truly beautiful and often ravishing.

General Staff Berlin, 26 September 1881.

I now have a job that interests me very much, namely to prepare a report on this year's major Austrian maneuvers. One has to gather the material from newspaper news and military sheets, which is rather tedious. I have been told privately that I should take over the Scandinavian section as section chief in the winter, but this seems unlikely to me, since our captains are not yet section chiefs, and I am still the eternal premier lieutenant.

Uncle Helmuth rode from Schleswig to Eckernförde with his officers in one go, quite a feat! How I would have loved to have been on that trip! But one must not ask too much.

Ragaz, [*] *26 April 1882.*

As you can see, we have now arrived here, but only to leave again tomorrow or the day after tomorrow. The baths here have not yet been opened, but since it is not possible to bathe, Uncle Helmuth does not want to stay here and is already talking about going to Berlin or Creisau. I suspect that he will go back to Berlin first, and since you can always count on him to last a day or two shorter than he said before, you needn't be surprised if we arrive back in Berlin in three or four days!

Now I must tell you how and where we have been wandering around these days. You can believe that we made an exhausting tour, and to call this kind of traveling a pleasure, you have to have Uncle Helmuth's views on comfort! – So, from Zurich, Uncle Helmuth and I left for Lucerne at 9 o'clock in the morning. It was intended that we should stay the day in Lucerne and continue the next day via Lake Lucerne. But since the weather was so nice, we only ate some breakfast, – I ran there in a hurry and looked at the Lion and the Glacier Garden, and then we took the ship across the lake at noon. Splendid weather, a delightful ride. Towards evening we arrived in Fluelen, where we spent the night. The next morning we had taken two seats on the post, banquet, climbed with a ladder our airy seat and drove in sorry weather into the mountains, towards the Gotthardt. Although the railroad is already completely finished and is used by worker trains on the whole distance from Lucerne to Milan, it will be handed over to the traffic only next month. Until now, one has to travel by mail to Göschenen, where the large main tunnel that passes under the Gotthardt begins. Until

---

* Personal adjutant of Field Marshal Count Helmuth von Moltke and Captain in the Grand General Staff.

then, we had the opportunity to admire the colossal constructions that have been built to make this railroad line possible. On sky-high viaducts, the railroad crosses deep abysses to disappear and reappear in tunnel after tunnel. Twice it makes a complete loop, i.e. goes over itself, so that the two tunnel openings are exactly on top of each other. It is really a gigantic construction that has been carried out here, and one does not know what to admire more, the enormous forms that nature has created here, or the audacity of the tiny people who pierced all these rock walls, bridged these chasms and cut a thin iron path right through the heart of the mighty mountain giants.

In Göschenen we boarded the train and immediately after the start we immersed ourselves in the night of the Gotthardt tunnel. The lamps were plugged in and so it was exactly the same as if we were driving at night. Only when we opened the window, the hazy suffocatingly warm air flowed in and reminded us that the workers had to suffer from a heat of up to twenty degrees when drilling the tunnel!

The journey lasted almost three quarters of an hour. In the middle of the tunnel we stopped for a moment and it looked peculiar how, under torchlight, the railroad workers moved while their flickering shadows scurried in grotesque distortions along the dark arch. At Airolo, we suddenly emerged again into the sunshine of the open landscape. The eyes first had to get used to the light. Now we went back to the post office, actually we wanted to spend the night in Biasca, but since we were on the road once, we got back on the train in Biasca and arrived in Bellinzona at 9 o'clock in the evening, where we stayed for the night. We had just been on the road for twelve hours, and I had not been able to get Uncle Helmuth to take anything to eat. I was only able to get him a cup of coffee, and from time to time a small sip of the port wine I had brought from Berlin. In Bellinzona we ate little and poorly and then went to bed. The next morning we were up at 5 a.m., and at 6 a.m. we took the train to Como. Now it was already raining gently, but persistently, nevertheless we went for a walk, from which we came home soaked and then I managed to pack Uncle Helmuth, who was quite tired and starved, to bed. He then slept until 12 o'clock, where we had a hot breakfast. Actually, we were supposed to stay in Como for a day and from there visit some beautiful points on Lake Corner, but since the weather was bad, Uncle Helmuth decided he would rather go on right away. So we went on board at 2 o'clock and sailed up the Corner Lake to Colico. Although it was really horrible weather, this lake delighted me to the highest degree. In sunshine it must be heavenly there. Cypresses everywhere, with flowering creepers winding up them, roses covered with blossoms on all the houses, it is really indescribably beautiful. We passed the beautifully situated Villa Carlotta, which belongs to our Crown Prince.

In the evening at 8 o'clock we arrived in Colico, where we wanted to spend the night, but since we just saw the post office ready to leave, Uncle Helmuth decided to drive that same evening to Chiavenna, where we arrived at 12 o'clock at night. So we were on the road for eighteen hours. Since the mail from Chiavenna continues over the Splügen at 2 a.m., we stayed there for the night, and extra mail was ordered for the next morning at 6 a.m. to Splügen. Now I had secretly smuggled a bottle of wine and some cold food into the car and had made the firm decision to force Uncle Helmuth to eat on the lonely country road if necessary!

We drove uphill in glorious sunshine. This road is one of the most beautiful I have seen. In unbelievably steep serpentines it climbs up and opens always new views into the valley and on the white mountain heads, which lay before us. During the night it had snowed above and the snow lay deep down into the valleys on the green leaves of the walnut trees, which were just beginning to sprout down here. Everything was shining in the sunshine, but the high peak of Splügen was shrouded in a small gray cloud and our coachman shook his head apprehensively and said that it would not be clean up there!

At 12 noon we were at the snow line and now had to leave the carriage to be pressed into a small sled. Here we also had breakfast from the supplies we had taken with us. Good that I had something with me! – Our one horse was harnessed in front of the sled, the other ran behind it like a dog. So we went over the pass for almost two hours in the snow. The higher we got, the more uncomfortable it became. A fierce wind whistled against us, it snowed quite heavily, in places it was bitterly cold. Then again we came to a sheltered place, where suddenly the sun shone, so brightly that one could not open an eye, and so hot that one felt its rays burning properly.

Then in the next moment again all gray haze and icy snow straight in the face. Downhill we went in a great hurry. In the deep snow that filled all the cracks and crevices, we went straight downhill, skipping the switchbacks of the road. Our poor horse slid on all fours and was always close to rolling over. It looked funny how the single horse dutifully slid behind us on all fours with an astonished face as well.

At 2 o'clock we had the snow behind us and got back into the wagon. We then passed the romantic and beautiful Viamala and came to Thusis. You can imagine that I thought of you especially vividly here. You have been here, too. Then we arrived in Chur at 7 o'clock in the evening, where we had a proper lunch. It was the first time since our departure from Zurich, but Uncle Helmuth was now so far gone that he said: "If I don't get something to eat soon, I'll turn over."

At 8 o'clock we then took the train to Ragaz, where we arrived at 9 o'clock after an uninterrupted tour of fourteen hours. Here I immediately put Uncle Helmuth to bed with a hot water bottle and this morning he was quite lively again. Only in the face we both look crab-red. The rapid change of sun heat and snow flurries makes us both like snakes in the skin of our faces. This morning we already took a long walk and I looked at the beautiful Tamina Gorge. Then we ate and just now Uncle Helmuth had a little lie down, but is up again now. Now we will not stand it here much longer and as I suspect will arrive in Berlin again in the near future!

What do you say to our "small pleasure trip to the upper Italian lakes with some time stay at some beautiful point", as uncle Helmuth called it before? Should one believe that he counts eighty-two years? "But" – he says – "if one can travel with all comforts as we do, there can be nothing more comfortable!"

Wildbad Gastein, 2 August 1882.

Now we are happy here. We have seen a lot of beautiful things, and I have also had my share of trouble, as you can imagine, without which a trip with Uncle Helmuth cannot be completed! – You will have received my card from Vienna. The next day we drove to Ischl, a magnificent tour along the shore of the lovely Traunsee, unfortunately under constant rain. We arrived there in the afternoon, lodged in the Hotel Elisabeth, the same one in which a scene from Ouida's "Moths" is set, and the balcony on which Correz sat and let his voice be heard was also right there, with the roaring Traun below. Everything was right! – After we ate, we took a long walk in the beautiful surroundings of this charmingly situated place. At the table, sitting next to us, was Wegner from the Wallner Theater, the "youngest lieutenant," whose comedy, even in a civilian relationship, was a source of great amusement to Uncle Helmuth and me. She obviously studied Uncle Helmuth, I'm afraid she'll bring him on stage next!

The next morning we drove to Aussee, where we again walked the surroundings in the pouring rain, then ate and after dinner drove on to Lend. This tour also offered much of beauty. The mountains of the Salzkammergut are magnificently beautiful. They stand more isolated in single massive stacks, which makes the gigantic masses of them more impressive than the Alps. In Lend we stayed the night from Monday to Tuesday in the hotel "to the Post" with miserable beds, uncle Helmuth and I in a small room together. Both almost without sleeping, although we had calmed down by six to seven solitaires! Actually, Uncle Helmuth wanted to come here that same evening with the mail, where we would have arrived at 12 o'clock, but since it was already gone because of a train delay, we had to stay and now drove here this morning with extra mail, where we arrived at 11 o'clock in the morning. Immediately after arrival, Uncle Helmuth took his first bath, then he went to sleep, and I went out, met the Emperor, who looked youthfully fresh and inquired about Uncle Helmuth. Then I was invited by return for tonight to a *soiree dansant* at Count Lehndorff's, where we are to dance for the Emperor.

Wildbad Gastein, 3 August 1882.

I had quite a good time last night. The Emperor sat in a corner all evening and watched. He obviously enjoyed himself very much. He looks splendid, fresh and healthy. This morning we went a few hours without rain. Uncle Helmuth and I went to the promenade, where we found the Kaiser sitting on a bench, who greeted Uncle Helmuth very warmly. Uncle Helmuth is there today for dinner. Since 12 o'clock it rains again, it is really to despair. I still made a tour into the mountains. The fall of the Ach is really wonderfully beautiful. It comes roaring down six hundred feet high in a very narrow gorge, all white spray and foam. Just outside our window it plunges into its basin with a thunder-like roar. Above the basin stands a cloud of water dust as high as a house, in which the steam of the hot water flowing down mixes. The snow-covered summits of the mountains stood out splendidly against the deep blue sky, as it cleared up for a moment, unfortunately only for such a short time. Uncle Helmuth asks you to write quite a bit about Creisau, weather and harvest. He wants to take eighteen baths.

Wildbad Gastein, 4 August 1882.

Uncle Helmuth was very pleased about the messages concerning weather and harvest. We continue to live quietly here. At 7 o'clock in the morning, Uncle Helmuth takes his bath and then lies in bed for another two hours. Then we drink coffee and read the newspaper, after which we go to the promenade at about 10:30 hours, meet the Kaiser, who is sitting on some bench and always greets Uncle Helmuth very kindly. At 2 o'clock we have lunch, then drink coffee somewhere and walk again until 8 o'clock, where we have tea in Uncle Helmuth's room and then play solitaire until 10 o'clock.

This afternoon we took a small single carriage and drove to a place called Bockstein, which is half an hour higher up in the mountains. From there we walked back. On the way, Uncle Helmuth explained that the main thing in the cure was to remain calm and not to exert oneself. We had already climbed up and down for two hours in the morning and were now walking back for an hour. He was completely exhausted, and I scolded him properly and will not tolerate any more such extravagances from now on. For the rest, he is in good spirits and quite mobile. I think the baths will do him good, as long as he behaves sensibly.

The surrounding area and the country itself are indeed of a delightful beauty. Wherever you go, there are always new beauties. In every valley a roaring waterfall, but the king of all, the Achenfall, in the middle of the lodging houses. Uncle Helmuth knows every step here and always knows where to find a view or other beautiful spot.

Wildbad Gastein, 6 August 1882.

Yesterday Uncle Helmuth and I went to the Kaiser's for dinner. Today there is a solemn service in the small Protestant church. I have just accompanied Uncle Helmuth there. The whole court is there, and the very small church was full to suffocation. I cannot know when we will return, but I believe that Uncle Helmuth will declare his cure over on the 20th and then hurry home in forced rapid marches; he has given me a very special greeting for you.

Wildbad Gastein, 8 August 1882.

The rain falls quite soft and straight down with an equanimity that can make you despair. All the paths are groundless, the whole area shrouded in a monotonous gray. The little grain that is built up here stands rotting and full-grown in the fields, it is too dreary. If you can't get out here, it's just growing out. Sitting in the parlor all day with Uncle Helmuth, who is just starting to get in a bad mood, is not one of the greatest comforts! Yesterday we had dinner with the Emperor. Today he left with his whole entourage. The moment when he left accompanied by the entire bath with cheers, the sun was shining, ten minutes later it started raining again!

Wildbad Gastein, August 14, 1882.

Uncle Helmuth does not want to stay here longer than until the 19th. Then, if the weather is good, he wants to make a tour of a few days to Berchtesgaden, the Königsee, Reichenhall, Salzburg and intends to arrive in Creisau around September 1. But I already know these pleasure tours, which are projected to eight days and then raced through in one or at most two days! – Yesterday I bought a chess set and played a game of chess with Uncle Helmuth. Since I checkmated him after a hot struggle, he declared that the game was upsetting him too much, and we returned to solitaire to calm down! This night he had slept badly, as he said, still as a result of the excitement from the chess game! Otherwise he is doing very well. The cure agrees with him very well, he goes every morning two to three hours without complaints and looks excellent.

Dresden, Palais, 17 September 1882.

I have already had to interrupt this letter three times. In the meantime, we have been with the Emperor, the King and all the hustle and bustle at Professor Schilling's, where we saw the plaster design for the national monument on the Niederwald, then barracks inspection in the Albrechtstadt and a big breakfast with the Emperor's regiment, just returned, and in half an hour we are to leave again, for a big garden party. After that, dinner at 5 o'clock, theater tonight and then *soiree* at the Minister of War – and that's what you call a free Sunday!

Merseburg, 15 September 1883.

The parade yesterday was very pretty, a little very dusty, but otherwise well done. The Emperor looks very well, Prince Wilhelm in his hussar uniform is developing more and more to his advantage. Uncle Helmuth's mare walked excellently, yesterday as today. Tomorrow we will all go together, accompanied by the

Emperor, to Halle, where a tour of the city and inspection of the sights there will be undertaken. The day after tomorrow, there will be a large celebration in the evening, which the estates will give to the Emperor, in connection with a theater performance, to which the Grand Ducal troupe from Weimar will come. On the 18th, there will be another such celebration. On the 20th, we go to Homburg.

Merseburg, 18 September 1883.

Yesterday was too exhausting for the Emperor, so that he had to give up his intended trip to Halle. Consequently, we did not drive, but instead visited the very beautiful old cathedral, which has been quite skillfully renovated recently, and the quite pretty castle garden and courtyard. The historic Raven is enjoying the best of health. Many years ago, one of the old bishops of Merseburg had one of his pages executed because he suspected him of having stolen a valuable ring from him; this was a Krosigk. After a few years, the missing ring was accidentally found in a raven's nest on one of the towers during a reconstruction. As compensation, the bishop gave the brother of the beheaded man a considerable estate, on which, however, there was an obligation to maintain a raven in the castle in memory of the innocently executed man. At the same time the Krosigks got a raven with a ring in its beak in their coat of arms. This raven is still kept in a large cage. When it dies, it must be replaced immediately, since the possession of the estate still in the family depends on its maintenance.

In the cathedral is a magnificent organ that takes up the entire height of one of the nave's wings, some beautiful old oak carvings, and the unsightly bronze tomb of Emperor Rudolph, who was mistaken for a saint by the formerly Catholic population and kissed quite bare in some places. Otherwise, there is absolutely nothing to see in the city itself. Thank God today's rest day will soon be over, and tomorrow the maneuvers will start again.

Merseburg, September 18, 1883.

We have just returned from the maneuver field, tired and dusty. Maneuver life has always been my greatest pleasure. On the days when Goßler goes to dinner with Uncle Helmuth, I eat with the comrades and sit with them in the evening in the pub, drinking beer and listening to anecdotes, which I really enjoy, after I have not seen a soldier for so long and have not been able to converse with any comrade in a harmless and informal manner. Uncle Helmuth is always very amiable and cheerful, a completely different person than usual. He also enjoys the maneuvers, and he has thawed out in a way that one would not think possible with him.

Merseburg, 19 September 1883.

This evening we had a great pleasure. At 6:30 Prince Albrecht had ordered the organist to the cathedral to play for him on the wonderful organ. Uncle Helmuth and I were also there and listened with delight to an Adagio by Mendelssohn and several preludes by Bach. If you closed your eyes, you literally had the feeling as if the mighty waves of sound could pick you up and carry you away with them. It was wonderful. Today's last day of maneuvers went very nicely.

Homburg, 23 September 1883.

On the 20th in the evening we arrived here at 7 o'clock, at 7:30 we had to be back at the castle for dinner, it all went head over heels. The next day parade, at 5 o'clock dinner, at 7 o'clock theater, yesterday corps maneuvers. The weather was cloudy, and around 12 o'clock it started to rain, so that we came home soaked at 3 o'clock. Dinner at 5 o'clock and theater in the evening. Today is Sunday, and so I have a free morning. At 2 o'clock is officers' race, to which we want to go out. On the 28th we are at the National Monument near Rüdesheim, from there we go to Wiesbaden in the evening.

Here is an incredible gathering of royalty. Most interesting is the King of Spain, who shows himself to be an excellent dashing horseman. He was first in Bavarian uniform, which did not suit him well, he looks much better in Spanish. He is a small elegant gentleman with a little Jewish type. The King of Serbia, taller and rather fat, does not look very distinguished. The Empress looks very well. She has grown stronger, which suits her well, and attends the maneuvers in the carriage. During the rain, she blithely stops in the open carriage without an umbrella and lets herself get rained on, as does the Emperor, who defies all the rigors of the weather in youthful freshness. In addition, there are a lot of royalty and royal highnesses swarming around, of whom one has never heard before. Dining is in the splendid halls of the spa house, where in earlier times the bank was held. The castle is small and unattractive, in general Homburg is a small, not very beautiful place. The surrounding area is pretty, with in places beautiful views of the Taunus range, the soil extraordinarily fertile. The red and white border posts of the Hessian territory touch one in a peculiar way. Uncle Helmuth is in excellent condition.

Homburg, 24 September 1883.

Yesterday, after the officers' race, I drove with our host to the ruins of Saalburg Castle, half an hour away on a mountain saddle. Interesting in the highest degree. It is the remains of an ancient fortified Roman camp, built about 30 B.C. and occupied for over three hundred years. The whole is built in the shape of a rectangle, surrounded by a high rampart, with a brick breastwork and a double ditch. Four gates lead in, each flanked by two towers. All the foundation walls are still completely preserved. One can see the drill house, the officers' quarters, military hospitals, kitchens, storehouses, a small amphitheater and a bathhouse, in which one can still see the complete heating devices, which were led in tubes under the floor. About five minutes before the camp, the ancient Roman border ditch, which they had built against the Germanic tribes from the Sieg across the Taunus to the Danube, is still clearly visible. The camp is said to be unique in its kind and owes its preservation to the fact that it was located in the middle of the forest. Only recently has it been uncovered and partially excavated, and a number of interesting finds have been made, which are exhibited in a museum in the local spa house.

Ragaz, 7 August 1884.

Now we are happily here. We did not encounter much worth telling. The first day we suffered very much from an unbearable heat and arrived half-fried and dust-covered in Prague, where we experienced the first travel woes by arriving at the state railway station and having to leave again the next morning from the western station, which lies at the opposite end of the city, so that any combination concerning leaving our suitcases at the station remained impossible!

At the hotel, where they were apparently not quite sure of Uncle Helmuth's identity, we were given two ghastly rooms and immediately went out to see the city. We walked across the historic Nepomuk Bridge with its numerous statues of saints, looked thoughtfully into the rushing waters from the railing where an inset metal cross marks the spot from which St. Nepomuk was plunged into the Vltava, but could not notice anything special. Perhaps the water, which roared just below us, was the same that once entered the mouth and nose of the saint, and now, returning in the eternal cycle, after it evaporated in the sea, rose as a cloud, was absorbed by plants, floated around in all kinds of animal and human bodies, fell as rain for the thousandth time, now just flowed past here again. Who knows!

We walked up to the venerable Hradschin, then turned left, lost ourselves in innumerable alleys and little streets, and finally reappeared at the Chain Bridge, which leads further upstream across the river back to the old city. Here we were embarrassed when we were asked to pay a *kreuzer* bridge toll per person and did not have a *kreuzer* of Austrian money. A fifty-penny piece I offered was rejected, and we would have had to walk all the way back if the noble Czech who acted as collector, too proud to stain his hands with German money, had not been as magnanimous as he was national and let us pass for nothing. This strange proof that there are big-thinking people even among the Czechs reconciled us to the remark we had made on our walk through the city that the German element is disappearing more and more from Prague, that almost all the inscriptions are Czech and only now and then, as if half-pityingly furtive, the German translation stands behind the Czech hieroglyphics. A nation that, as I have said, counts such great-thinking men among its own as that tax collector, is definitely entitled to push out the Germans, who once brought it culture, but who have now sunk so low as to want to buy their way across the Chain Bridge with fifty pennies, and to be masters in their own country!

In the middle of the bridge, which is built over an island, we discovered below us a garden with a large dance hall and garden music. So we climbed down, the entrance guard was less scrupulous here and exchanged us a *thaler*. We then sat in the midst of the people, apparently small craftsmen and burghers, maids etc. in front of a Czech music program that was completely incomprehensible to us, and drank a bottle of Pilsen beer.

The next day we drove to Regensburg. We stopped at the "Golden Cross" just as Emperor Charles V did. The city is very interesting. The old town hall with the unchanged hall, in which the Reichstag of the Holy Roman Empire of the German Nation used to meet, many old house fronts, towers, gables etc.. The most beautiful ornament of the whole, the magnificent cathedral, begun in the fourteenth century, is now completely finished. In the purest Gothic style, it is hardly inferior in beauty to Cologne Cathedral.

Unrecognized and in the deepest incognito, we left the old Reichstag city the next morning, but Uncle Helmuth was already reconnoitered at the train station, and as we arrived in Munich, the station inspector was on hand in full dress, a special room ready and a saloon car offered. Uncle Helmuth, meanwhile, declined everything with thanks. After an hour, we drove on to Lindau, where we arrived in the afternoon and took up residence in the "Bavarian Court," ruthlessly setting aside any incognito. The next morning we drove across the lake to Rorschach and from there by train here, where we arrived at noon 2 o'clock. I was very right to advise Uncle Helmuth to go here and not to Gastein. Mr.

Kinberger's joy at Uncle Helmuth's arrival was really touching; he confided to me that his heart had been beating with joy at seeing Uncle Helmuth, and the gardener Joseph, a famous personality, had literally jumped for joy. It was very amusing how Uncle Helmuth appeared in the evening at 7 o'clock for the *table d'hote*. There is a whole colony of Frenchmen here, some of whom have fled from the cholera, and with unfeigned interest Uncle Helmuth's personality was marveled at by them.

Ragaz, 12 August 1884.

Yesterday we took a tour into the mountains to an old ruin, the Wartenstein, near which a speculative entrepreneur has stuck a restoration on an overhanging rock. Uncle Helmuth went up by train, and I walked, arriving at the top a quarter of an hour before him. Then I walked another half mile to get to the so-called natural bridge, i.e., the place of the Tamina Gorge where the same has completely closed at the top, so that one can walk across it. To get there from the road on top of the mountain, one descends an almost vertical rock face on a kind of staircase that has more than four hundred steps, partly carved into the rock, partly made of fir trunks. It is the pure chicken staircase that descends in the sharpest zigzag. Once at the bottom, one stands on some mighty boulders that lie across the opening of the Tamina Gorge, which is only about two meters wide here. One looks down as if through a chimney into the dark depths, at the bottom of which the Tamina rolls down its grayish water boiling. In the old days, when there were no elevators, no bathing hotels and no railroads, the sick were let down on a rope to the healing spring, which steams out of the side wall of the gorge. Above it, on beams hewn into the rock walls, hovered the old bathhouse, where the sick had to stay during the three weeks of their cure without ever seeing the sun, only to be hoisted back into the daylight like a collie after the use of the bath had ended. After thinking myself sufficiently into a gruesome mood, I climbed the four hundred steps again and went back to our restoration, where I arrived like a poodle retrieved from the water for its master, for we had 28 degrees of heat. Then we had lunch and afterwards walked back here, where I arrived full of admiration for Uncle Helmuth, who at eighty-four is still capable of such footwork.

Ragaz, 18 August 1884.

Today there is a long article about Uncle Helmuth in the "Figaro", which we read with much pleasure and which contains the most unbelievable things. Among other things, the author shares the most interesting news, especially for Uncle Helmuth, that Uncle Helmuth is currently terminally ill on his Creisau estate, where he only receives visits from his nephew Burt, who, like him, is descended from one of the numerous small Mecklenburg noble families, and his departure is expected with concern. The article seems all the more drastic because it is written from Interlaken, the same country to which Uncle Helmuth gives tangible proof of his well-being by his presence. The author raises the credibility of his communications beyond all doubt by taking them from a conversation with a colonel of the Prussian General Staff, whom he has conclude the above-mentioned communication with the words: The will of God be done! – He also owes the new information to this smart colonel, that Uncle Helmuth is lame on one leg and drags it only with difficulty, and that at parades he prefers to wear a carriage that floats on him like on a skeleton, while Bismarck always rides in front of him and, by stabling his horse in front of him, tries to push him away from the Emperor, whom Uncle Helmuth would like to get close to, etc. The bathers present here also seem to enjoy this farce, at least the "Figaro" passes incessantly from hand to hand.

Yesterday I made a very beautiful, though rather strenuous tour. At 9 o'clock I left for Chur, from where I walked up the charming valley of the Rabiusa to Passug, from there on to Churwalden, where I had lunch, and then, as the post office did not leave for another hour and a half, with which I intended to return to Chur, I set out, tired of waiting so long, and walked back to Chur, where I arrived at the same time as the post office. Thus I had marched a good four miles on paths, some of them quite steep, and as I arrived at the station in Chur at 4:30, I was heartily tired. At 7 o'clock I was back in Ragaz and found Uncle Helmuth flown out. No one knew where he had stayed. Tea time came, but no Uncle Helmuth. It got later and darker, at 9 o'clock he was still not back. You can imagine how scared I was. I was about to call in the entire hotel staff to investigate, when suddenly he came marching up all cheerful. Where had he been? In Chur! – Probably thinking of meeting me there. Since he had not come to see me at the station when my train left, but had gone for a walk outside the city, we had "incomprehensibly" missed each other! Now he came back with the evening train and did not understand at all that I could not have guessed that he had been in Chur!

Ragaz, 20 August 1884.

Today's "Figaro" brings a supplementary addendum to its recent article, of which I wrote to you, by telegraphing from Berlin: Field Marshal Moltke is afflicted with paralysis of the brain, he can no longer walk and take food only with difficulty, he is dying of old age and has only a few weeks ahead of him, – I have translated literally! An excellently taught sheet!
    Since Uncle Helmuth gave me the fright the other day, where he had gone to Chur, I don't move away again for a whole day. He is already starting to study the return trip from the course book and has obviously had more than enough of his stay here. I also can't deny that my need for mountain air is completely satisfied. I long properly to mount a horse once again.

Ragaz, 25 August 1884.

Uncle Helmuth has again made me a few charming stories, which I will share very briefly, because I lack time and peace for longer writing. First: A few days ago, we were sitting in the garden in the morning, when he told me that he would like to go up to the Wartenstein ruin. Since it is a bit strenuous to climb, we could walk slowly up the footpath crossing the causeway leading up there, and on the way catch the mail that goes up at 10 o'clock.

Then he gave me money, with instructions to change it. So I go to the bureau, he remains sitting on the bench. When I come back ten minutes later, he is no longer there. I was not really surprised because, knowing him as I do, I did not expect to find him still sitting in the same place. So I resignedly set off in search, roaming the garden, the reading room, looking for him in his room, nowhere a trace of him. So I think he may have already gone upstairs, so I walk at high speed up the steep footpath, don't find him, think he can't possibly be that far, turn around, search the whole area again, ask the porter and waiter, no one has seen him. In the meantime it has become almost ten o'clock, I think to myself, if he still wanted to catch the mail, he must already be far up there, so I run like a deer, cutting off the curves of the sidewalks, directly uphill, high above me the post office is already driving along, in fifteen minutes I was up at the Wartenstein, never in my life have I sweated so much, the water ran down my whole body, but I still arrived a little before the post office at the top. Uncle Helmuth is not in it! – Now I had to give up all hope, turn around and, once home, change from head to toe. At 1 o'clock, Uncle Helmuth arrives quite happily. Where has he been? Across the garden through to Magenfeld, which lies just in the opposite direction of Wartenstein. Here he had looked at an old castle and then, as he told me with much pleasure, wanted to give a tip to the owner, who showed him everything and whom he thought was the gardener, and only realized his mistake when he indignantly rejected the donation!

Secondly: Yesterday, as I am still busy with my toilet at 8 o'clock, Uncle Helmuth, as he always does when he wants to go for coffee, knocks on my door with his cane as he passes. I follow in about five minutes and find him already finished drinking coffee. I say good morning, he says good morning, sits for a moment while I drink coffee, and then goes out into the garden. I drink quietly finished and go after. No uncle Helmuth to find. I go through the whole garden, no trace.

By chance I return to the corridor of the hotel, where the porter tells me: "Your Excellency lets me tell you that he has gone to the station to take the train to Glarus, if there is still time." So I go after him and catch up with him. He is furious and tells me, "Of course we are late, you could have gotten up earlier." I say, "Yes, if I had only known a word about going to Glarus!" After a few steps he says, "I suppose you could have taken the *Baedeker** with you and inquired whether we have a connection back."

I declare that I want to catch up on both, turn around, run to the hotel, get the *Baedeker* and run after him again. I don't realize that I don't see him until I finally spot him very small in the distance on a wrong path. But now I calmly went to the station and waited for him. He arrived five minutes before the train was due to leave, half-dead from asthma and still angry with me for having prepared so inadequately for this journey, of which I knew not a word. The thought that arose in me: "Why, when you knocked on my door, didn't you say a word to me?" I didn't say! By the way, he is always delightfully amiable, and when we were happily sitting on the train with a first-class return ticket, certain that we would have a connection for our return, his good mood soon returned.

Benrath, 17 September 1884.

We participated in our first day of maneuvers yesterday, which went very nicely. We arrived here on Monday evening and found very good quarters with Mayor Josten. We left the next morning at 7 o'clock by train for about an hour via Düsseldorf to Bedburg, where the horses were ready. I got an Ulan horse, which goes excellently, although it is a bit small for me. Uncle Helmuth rode very dashingly on the excellent going mare, so that he aroused general admiration. The troops were excellent and made a very fresh impression despite the great heat and rather strenuous marches. The Crown Prince was indefatigable, riding the entire maneuver field and approaching all the individual battalions. Very fine was a charge of the cavalry division, which put the armed guard of the VII Corps out of action. The approach was very skillfully laid out using the terrain, the appearance completely unexpected, and the deployment quick and orderly. The infantry

---

* Publisher's note: A travel guide published by the Karl Baedeker firm.

was seized directly in the rear and ridden over before it had time to maneuver. At 12 o'clock the maneuver was ended after a general attack by the VIII Corps against the VII, which was victorious. Then the Crown Prince delivered a very pertinent short review. He spoke very prettily and aptly, praising and rebuking rather sharply, something quite unusual, since the Emperor always speaks only in praise.

San Remo, 30 March 1885.

Today we have been here just fourteen days and our departure is imminent. No path and footbridge around San Remo that we would not have walked, no viewpoint that we have not visited. Now it goes first to Bordighera, how then further, I do not know yet.

The French newspapers are again quite childish in announcements about Uncle Helmuth. Soon it is said that he is in Nice, where he is being closely watched by the police. Uncle Helmuth said, "That may be a nice guy they're watching there, I hope he doesn't steal any silver spoons!" – Soon, reflections are made as to why Uncle Helmuth is living in a private home. But the correspondent can explain this, because he has come to know that in this house there is only a maid who speaks only patois, so she can't tell anything about the strategic works that are made in Uncle Helmuth's room when she cleans up there! Then we are told that the German consul is busily bringing in maps and statistical material for the field marshal – (in fact, he has sent him some booklets of "Flying Leaves" for his entertainment) – and the most alarming thing is that there are a lot of German officers here who appear with such magnificence of means, contrary to all German custom, that they are obviously general staff officers equipped by the state. So the matter is clear, Moltke is here with part of his general staff, and the purpose of their presence has not escaped the attention of the clever reporter: it is aimed at Corsica, which is to be made a German colony. It is really amusing to read these inane combinations, one believes to have private correspondences from the lunatic asylum before oneself!

Nervi, 17 April 1885.

Who would have believed that after all the saber-rattling, England and Russia would finally come to a peaceful agreement? Right now, they give me the impression of two dogs snarling at each other with grim snarls and then parting with bristled backs because neither dares to take the first bite.

Rapallo, 24 April 1885.

We are still very much at home in beautiful Rapallo, in whose surroundings we discover new beauties every day. The area here is so much lovelier because all the valleys are overgrown with mulberry trees, poplars, elms and oaks, all trees that have shed their leaves and are now clothed in the juicy young green of fresh leaves, which also gives the northern forest its own golden spring magic, which is so sorely missed here among the evergreen southern trees and plants. Also beautiful are the fig trees, which were still completely bare when we arrived on the Riviera, but now their mighty, large leaves are almost visibly unfolding more from day to day, completely hiding the unsightly polyp-like shapes of their branches. Wonderful mighty pines lift their spherical crowns from the light blue sky; an exclamation mark, set down by the Creator as he wrote down the glorious work of this nature, dark cypresses stand out from the colorful play of colors, and as in a mighty crystal-cut mirror the sky beholds its radiant glory in the clear depth of the steel-blue sea. From the rocky headlands, grave gray ruined forts look down into the depths, reminding us of a time when the sea was the road by which robbery and destruction approached these shores, where the ships of the Saracens brought death and imprisonment if the watchful eye of the tower keeper did not see them in time, or where later the perpetual wars of the citizens among themselves made a mockery of the peace that God's hand spread over this sunny land. Meanwhile, the darkly yawning gun ports of the mighty walls have long since ceased to tremble with the bang of cannons; here and there an Englishman has settled on the platform, built his cottage up there, and now, surrounded by all the comforts of the life he brought with him from his foggy homeland, gazes gleefully over land and sea.

Ivy climbs up the cracked ashlars, and from the corner towers, from which the Arquebusian once sent down death and destruction to the attacker, countless roses now nod down in greeting. Nature covers everything with her eternally young, driving life, and above the crumbling structure of man's hand she waves triumphantly the green flag of her blossoming, fragrant existence. With a low murmur the waves chatter between the rocks, as if they wanted to tell fairy tales, gracefully cradling the fishing boats on their backs, whose peculiar Latin sail shapes, blown by a gentle wind, shimmer as luminous dots on the water and lure the eye far out into the seemingly unlimited distance. At the very back, wedded by the softest fragrance, the seemingly rising surface melts together with the dome of the sky, one believes to see the sky lowering itself to the earth, and that indefinable longing which lies in every man's breast, when his feeling penetrates upwards and forwards, touches the heart with wondrous ringing.

How all this blossoms and smells! From the luxuriant grass of the meadows thousands of open calyxes struggle up, as it were one climbing away over the other, blue, red and yellow flowers are fragrant towards the sun, it is a formal struggle of the most exuberant luxuriance; from the waysides nod crowded bellflowers, and where a pleasing wind has gathered a handful of earth between stones, there has also nestled a little flower, which, grateful of the home it has found, adorns with fragrance and color its gray surroundings. How the chest expands when inhaling these streams of light and fragrance, the pure breath of nature flows comfortably through all veins and awakens in all fibers the feeling of infinite well-being.

And when the sun sinks, as it were hesitatingly, as if it were sorry to say goodbye to its spoiled children, then everything lights up once again in the most glorious blue inks. The slopes of the mountains stand out sharply and clearly from the twilight of the valleys, their towering peaks stand as if chiseled, not a leaf stirs on the trees and bushes, and the Hail of the numerous bells rings up through the still air like a prayer of thanksgiving to the Lord!

Rapallo, 26 April 1885.

Now it seems that the Anglo-Russian war is really getting serious. God may know how far this flame will spread and whether Bismarck's statesmanship will succeed in steering the German Reich through it without it beginning to smolder. Here in Italy, public opinion is already very agitated, especially since it really seems as if the state wants to take over England's dubious inheritance in the Sudan and militarily occupy Suakiu, if the English garrison should be withdrawn from there to face the Nordic enemy in India. If Italy thus becomes more or less engaged, even poor Turkey, sitting between the hammer and the anvil, will not be able to remain neutral. This may be a war which will reshape the whole relationship between the states and which will be a matter of life and death for England, for India is the lifeblood of England, without which she can no more live than a man without a stomach. However, war has not yet been declared, and I think Mr. Gladstone would gladly give up his little finger if he could get out of this mess in a decent way without being forced to strike. I wonder if Bismarck will take to the thankless office of mediator. He probably won't, but the Emperor might want him to.

Strasbourg, 11 September 1886.

Now I am here in the old, much disputed city. It is a special feeling that comes over you when you come to these places that have been reclaimed from the German Empire after centuries of alienation. How much blood has flowed before the ramparts of the hitherto impregnable fortress, of which it is already said in the old German song: "O Strasbourg, O Strasbourg, you beautiful city, therein lies buried many a soldier." And indeed, the city is beautiful, like a finger stretched out in warning, the slender tower of the magnificent cathedral beckons to the lands on the right bank of the Rhine, as if to say: "You German people, who founded and built me, won't you lead me home to you again?" – and as a representative of the heeded admonition, at this moment the various German troops march out from under my window to parade before the Emperor, Prussians, Bavarians, Württembergers, Saxons, a colorful sight in their flashing parade uniforms. I live on the banks of the Ill, which joins the Aar a hundred steps away in the middle of the city, numerous bridges swing across and in the background the new imperial palace, still under construction, stands out with its beautiful facade against the blue sky. On the left, towering over all the houses, is the cathedral, as if woven of stone filigree, with its thousands of spires and columns; through the high windows of the tower, which swings slightly upwards, the light sky is blue, the stone rose of the spire trembles in the sunlight. The faces of the inhabitants are unadulterated German and, where one walks, one hears only the broad Alsatian German, but above the stores are the French inscriptions, which no one has changed.

Yesterday I went to dinner with Uncle Helmuth at the Kaiser's. A lot of princes are gathered here. In the evening, the cathedral was illuminated, a truly fairy-like sight, the whole tower to the highest point filled with lamps. Since in the darkness one could not see the lower building, which was not illuminated, it seemed as if a magic castle carried by spirits was floating in the air, it was indescribably beautiful. The city had also pretty much continuously illuminated and is also otherwise rich and beautifully decorated, the mood of the population a quite animated. In many cases, one sees people with the cornflower in their buttonhole, and Uncle Helmuth was greeted with tumultuous cheers wherever he appeared. The greeting of the Emperor was almost enthusiastic. In the evening, there was a great tattoo, with thousands of people standing in front of the palace and cheering the Emperor standing at the window. Again and again the cheers resounded through the silent night, an outbreak of the ancient Germanism that two centuries of foreign rule had not been able to eradicate. In an hour we are supposed to go out to the parade. The sky is slightly cloudy, the heat has abated somewhat, there is no wind, a beautiful Kaiser weather.

Strasbourg, 12 September 1886.

Today we have an eventful day behind us. It is in fact Sunday, a day of rest, which we used to look around in and outside the city.

We went first through all kinds of streets to the Orangerie, a large public garden, to the Citadel, a work still built by Vauban, the master fortress builder of Louis XIV, with which he fortified the city after having occupied it in the middle of peace. The powerlessness of the then German Empire was such that no serious attempt was made to regain it, and the two old provinces of Alsace and Lorraine were lost to Germany from that time on. The citadel, an immensely strong work according to the state of the siege means at that time, is still imposing today by its massive constructions, even if, since it is mostly uncovered masonry, it is no longer durable in the long run against today's attack. However, it is also now inside the ramparts and is no longer exposed to such an attack.

Then we drove along a whole section of the new fortifications, also climbed the rampart and then visited the famous monument of Duke Moritz of Saxony in the Lutheran church. From there into the cathedral, where we were led around by a very polite priest, because of the crowd counting in the hundreds, which surrounded uncle Helmuth, but could see little. In general, wherever Uncle Helmuth appears, he is greeted with tumultuous cheers and everyone runs after him.

Strasbourg, 14 September 1886.

Yesterday was corps maneuvers, which went very nicely. The Kaiser was out in the wagon. Uncle Helmuth rode very briskly and we saw everything very well, two large cavalry charges of twelve cavalry regiments against each other. There are one hundred and fifty French officers registered at the local commandant's office, and as many may well still be here unregistered. In any case, these gentlemen must receive the impression that the sentiments of the local people are well German. Everywhere the towns are richly decorated, large gates of honor are erected, and the Emperor is greeted everywhere with great enthusiasm. Likewise Uncle Helmuth, whom everyone knows. Wherever you pass through a village, the people stand in front of the doors with water, wine and beer, which they hand to the passing troops. The officers of the front say that they can hardly save themselves from the kindness of the farmers with whom they are quartered. It is a beautiful folk beat here, many peasants can be seen in white pants, high boots, short jackets and their wide-brimmed felt hat on horseback on the maneuver field.

Strasbourg, 16 September 1886.

The Emperor's trip to Metz is still quite undetermined. The doctors would like to dissuade him, as the matter is likely to be very strenuous for the old gentleman.

This morning Uncle Helmuth and I took a trip to Fort Moltke, seven kilometers outside the city, and inspected it thoroughly inside and out. I was very interested to see a fort constructed according to the newer principles.

General Staff Berlin, 24 April 1887.*

Uncle Helmuth has still not said anything about what he actually intends to do. Whether and when he wants to leave and whether he expects my company is completely unknown! – Of course, I would prefer to stay here until you return, but heaven may know where I will move to after I resign my command on May 1. We now have only three days of drill left. On Monday and Tuesday we will drill in the battalion at Tempelhofer Field, and on Wednesday is the battalion presentation. It will be wonderful for me to stand there again without any connection to the troops, who have grown very close to my heart during the months of my service.

General Staff Berlin, 30 April 1887.

Prince Wilhelm was also present at yesterday's presentation of the Fusilier Battalion. At this presentation I had the opportunity to

---

* Assigned to service with the 2nd Guards Rgt. 136.

report immediately to all my superiors. This afternoon I am now handing over the company to its old boss G., whose hopes of becoming a major have not been fulfilled after all.

General Staff Berlin, 1 May 1887.

Yesterday was a banquet of love and at the same time my farewell to the regiment. The colonel said many nice things to me, and everyone seemed reluctant to lose me. Most of all the non-commissioned officers of the company, who bid me farewell with tears in their eyes. After the table I went through all the rooms of the company, where some of the people had already gone to bed, and said goodbye to them.

General Staff Berlin, 3 May 1887.

Yesterday I was invited to G.'s table at 4:30. I found Mr. and Mrs. v. W. furthermore Mr. and Mrs. v. B.. After dinner we all went together to the Concordia to see the hypnotic productions of the Danish mesmerist Hansen. These performances are really interesting, inexplicable and partly uncanny. About thirty gentlemen and two ladies came forward from the audience, all of whom were seated in chairs and each given a small glass prism to hold, with instructions to look at the same keenly. Meanwhile, Hansen went from one to another making mesmerizing strokes. After five minutes, half had fallen asleep, and the other half were dismissed as useless. Hansen now had complete control over those who had fallen asleep. He forced them to get up by the mere look and, attracted like the magnet by the iron, to run after him. He made them spin like tops, laid one with his head and feet on two chairs and stood on his stomach, then bent him together like a pocket knife and set him on the ground like a log of wood. There was decidedly no humbug involved here, but an as yet inexplicable force, which one cannot interpret, but also cannot deny.

General Staff Berlin, 10 May 1887.

Yesterday, I and Uncle Helmuth accepted an invitation from the board of the Wagner Society. I have never been able to make friends with the enterprise of detaching Wagner from the stage and transplanting him into the concert hall. One can just as well lift an oak out of the ground in which it is rooted and place it in the room. It will dry up, lose its leaves, and soon all that will be left of the magnificent, wind-swept tree will be the skeleton of its branches, interesting to those who want to study trees, but something dead and rigid to those who have come to rejoice in the beauty of primordial nature.

I find it incomprehensible that Wagner admirers make these daring experiments with the works of their idolized master, and it seems to me that no one has understood Wagner's intention in his sense, who himself has repeatedly emphasized that the music of his works is only the garment that envelops the living form of the drama; he himself does not call his works operas, but musical dramas. I hardly believe that he would agree if one took off the skirts of his mighty striding figures and hung them out like in a junk store.

Szczecin, 13 September 1887.

Just now we come back from the parade, which went very nicely in the most wonderful weather. Uncle Helmuth led his regiment by very nicely, came galloping well and truly and looked good. The Emperor very fresh and soulful about the many soldiers.

Szczecin, 14 September 1887.

The corps maneuver was completely rained out today. Since 7 o'clock it poured, at 9 o'clock it rained, at 10 o'clock there was fog and at 11 o'clock the sun was shining. The Emperor did not go out, sent Count Lehndorff and asked Uncle Helmuth not to go out either, since he could easily catch a cold. Uncle Helmuth, who is now in Zug, did not like this at all, he would have liked to go out at 10 o'clock. So we had to stay at home, took a walk through the city and then out to the large Vulkan shipbuilding plant, which we visited in great detail under the direction of the director. Very interesting, between four and five thousand workers. An armored corvette, close to completion, we visited inside and outside.

Creisau, 29 May 1888.

I set up a kind of painter's studio and started copying one of the landscape pieces. I am also cultivating my cello, so I live completely in the arts.

General Staff Berlin, 16 June 1888.

At 10 o'clock, Uncle Helmuth and I drove to Potsdam, where Uncle Helmuth wants to report to the young Emperor. Now we are back from Potsdam, and I have also seen this dead Emperor like the previous one. But how different was the impression. At that time, peace and tranquility, the conclusion of a life that had lived itself out and was quietly fading away; here, the traces of a terrible suffering, which in the midst of his fullest strength took away a man who seemed destined by nature to continue working for a long time.

I would never have recognized these sunken features as those of the man whom I had last seen in flourishing strength and health. The nose quite sharp and prominent, the eye sockets deeply sunken, the cheekbones protruding. Around the mouth clearly recognizable, despite the beard, between the contracted eyebrows a train of deepest pain, nameless pain. Something quite strange in the yellowish pale, emaciated face, from which the mustache protruded almost shaggy. The hair on the broad forehead had become thin, the chin beard shaded grayish. From the whole appearance spoke eerily, almost devilishly triumphant the demon of the cruel illness. This dead face told a shattering story of nameless painful wrestling with the strangling angel of death. It was as if the latter had trampled the struggling human strength underfoot until it broke with a groan, wailing, heartbreaking. The big strong hands, emaciated to the bone, almost translucent pale, crossed over the chest, held his heavy cuirassier *pallash*, which lay long and bare across the bed. It looked as if he was pressing his own executioner's sword to his chest. Under the bedspread, the long rigid figure stood out.

I cannot tell you how painfully all this impressed itself upon me, what nameless misery spoke from it all. How terribly the poor Emperor's condition has been lied about, for the end did not come to him suddenly and unexpectedly, one can see that only too well, slowly and gradually, step by step, it tortured him to death; and when he had to represent and when it was said of him: he had had a good night, he sleeplessly counted the strokes of the clock, each of which, as it died away, brought him a span closer to the end, the end of nameless torment, which he may have longed for and implored, God only knows how hotly.

Poor Emperor, with his breast filled with plans for the exercise of a power for which he had to wait beyond the best creative years, with his warm heart for the welfare of the people with whom he fought and contended in hard, yet so heroically fresh, beautiful times, how cruel has been his fate. Is it not as if he had atoned for all the sins of this people, he, the pure, the ideally thinking prince! Can the relatively short agony on the trunk of the cross have been more terrible than this month-long dying, than this cruelly enforced renunciation of everything that fills heart and mind, of the preparatory work of a whole life? Poor Emperor, shaken to the core, we turn away, like a painful numbness it lies on head and senses. I hardly know how we came back, but I had to communicate the impression I received, and I know you will feel with me.

General Staff Berlin, 17 June 1888.

Today at 1 o'clock, Uncle Helmuth swore in the general staff officers. You will have read the young Emperor's beautiful decree to the army in the newspaper. A significantly different wind is blowing in everything now. The young Emperor is in constant activity, has been conferring all day, issuing orders, completing signatures. Already the day before yesterday the first cabinet order with the signature of *Emperor Rex* came to us.

General Staff Berlin, 18 June 1888.

We have just returned from Potsdam, where we escorted the blessed Emperor to his final resting place. As we were in the hall of the City Palace, Prince Heinrich arrived and sought out Uncle Helmuth to deliver to him a small case containing the orders *en miniature* which the Emperor Frederick used to wear for civilian life. The widowed Empress Victoria sent the same as a souvenir to Uncle Helmuth. The young Emperor had had the case in his pocket to give it to Uncle Helmuth himself, but since he had not found an opportunity to do so, he sent Prince Heinrich after Uncle Helmuth in search of it.

General Staff Berlin, 19 June 1888.

God bless the young gentleman! Thereby he had written all proclamations himself, no foreign pen in it, rejected all suggestions and did the thing himself.

General Staff Berlin, 25 June 1888.

On our return yesterday evening from Ratzeburg, we found the program of the ceremonial opening of the Reichstag, which is to take place today. Uncle Helmuth was not mentioned at all in it, nor in the program of the funeral service. He was rightly deeply offended and at the first moment declared that he wanted to leave immediately, wanted to take his leave, said that he had been put in the skat, and so on. All quite true. This morning he wrote a letter to the adjutant on duty in which he said: Since he, as the oldest field marshal, Chancellor of the Order of the Black Eagle, etc., could have expected to find a place in the entourage of His Majesty, first of all behind the Imperial Chancellor, but was not mentioned in the program at all, and also did not find it compatible with his military dignity to appear as a deputy, he asked to inform His Majesty that he feels compelled to stay away from the ceremony. Of course, all the blame lies with the courtiers, who think, let the old man go, and rather turn to the new stars! Hopefully, it will rain something on their faces, and in the future, when the Emperor's eyes have been opened, Uncle Helmuth will be treated accordingly to his position.

General Staff Berlin, 26 June 1888.

That was a very beautiful, solemn act yesterday, which we were allowed to witness. At 12 o'clock we – Uncle Helmuth, Goßler and I – drove in an open car, accompanied by the continuous cheers of the people standing closely in the streets, to the castle, where we attended the service in the chapel and heard a very beautiful speech by Kögel. The given text was: "By God's grace I am what I am." The Emperor, who entered with the King of Saxony on his right and the Regent of Bavaria on his left, looked very beautiful and dignified. After the service, the whole company, the entire Reichstag gathered in the White Hall, Bismarck, who led in the members of the Federal Council like a flock of lambs, looked splendid in his cuirassier uniform, the whole arrangement made a splendid impression. The marching in of a company of the Castle Guard in step with rifle on, with officers stepping in with rapier drawn, made a great impression. The throne with large draperies of yellow velvet, the red-velvet *estrada* for the Empress, the armchairs for the princes to the right and left of the throne, all very solemn. As everything gathered, Bismarck went to report it to the Emperor. Then the court took its entrance. First pages in black *escarpins* with crape on the knees, then the imperial insignia.

Uncle Helmuth had been given a special place of honor, walking all alone behind the insignia bearers and immediately in front of the Emperor. He looked very handsome in the great red velvet coat of the Black Eagle, with his marshal's baton propped on his hip. The Emperor, again with the King of Saxony and the Prince Regent on his right and left, like all Knights of the Black Eagle, in long flowing purple cloak, looked immensely majestic and deeply serious. Almost majestic, as he stepped with sure step on the skin pas of the throne and greeted the assembly with solemn inclination of the head.

Then, after everything had fallen into order and silence, he had another very beautiful moment, when the chancellor handed him the Speech from the Throne, he seized it, put on his helmet with an energetic jerk and threw back his coat, in order to let his gaze glide upright over the silently waiting assembly. Then he began to read. I paid close attention and saw that the paper in his hand did not tremble. Nevertheless, the voice was at first whirling and indistinct. The sentences came out jerkily and with difficulty; he could hardly be understood in spite of the dead silence. Gradually, however, the organ lifted, the speech became fluent and as he got to the point: "I am minded to keep peace with everyone, as far as it lies with me," he emphasized the word to me so loudly and beautifully that it went like an electric spark through all the listeners, there was so much in it, the full consciousness of the ruler's power, there was, as it were, the affirmation in it: "but woe to him who should dare to come too close to me," an immense strength and certainty lay in the one word, so that spontaneously everything broke out in loud enthusiastic applause. He spoke the last sentences of the speech in a beautiful, penetrating voice, every trace of self-consciousness had disappeared and he stood there, firm and proud, the powerful, self-confident ruler of a mighty empire.

You cannot imagine how pleasant it felt to have a young, strong Emperor who knows what he wants. It was a beautiful, magnificent act. Afterwards, as they were leaving, Bismarck approached Uncle Helmuth, and the two sat side by side for almost half an hour in the otherwise completely empty picture gallery, shyly avoided by everyone who came in. I don't know what they negotiated, Uncle Helmuth is as silent as the grave, but I believe that Bismarck told him that he could not possibly take his leave, and Uncle Helmuth must have understood that, he is quiet and solemn today.

General Staff Berlin, 27 June 1888.

Yesterday, the Emperor sent his extraordinarily well-made life-size bust (plaster) to Uncle Helmuth through Lieutenant Colonel v. B. with a handwritten letter in which he said something like the following: "Esteemed Field Marshal! In memory of yesterday (opening of the Reichstag), which we were allowed to celebrate through your deeds in the Seventies War as an achievement of the same, I ask you to be allowed to present you with my bust, admittedly for the time being only in plaster, until the same is completed in ore. In loyal friendship, your well-affected Wilhelm". The bust is made by Schott and shows the Emperor in hussar uniform with a very beautiful, immensely bold look.

Today the swearing-in of the Emperor to the Constitution takes place, in the same solemn manner as the opening of the Imperial Diet.

In the printed program that arrived yesterday, Uncle Helmuth is listed personally, and he is again assigned the place directly in front of the Emperor. In the grouping around the throne chair, Uncle Helmuth stands on the dias behind the throne, all alone, while everything else stands to the right and left. It has thus had the most charitable consequences that he once showed his teeth, and the court marshal's office will probably not forget him again so easily. As I heard later, the Emperor was quite beside himself as a result of Uncle Helmuth's letter; he immediately sent a wing adjutant to Bismarck and asked whether it would be possible for him to let Uncle Helmuth go together with the princes, to which B. replied, yes, that would go very well. Uncle Helmuth, however, declared in the palace that no, he did not belong there and chose his own place behind the crown insignia in front of the Emperor, which is officially assigned to him again today.

All of Berlin, and as it seems from the newspapers, pretty much the whole of Germany of all party colors, is delighted and enthusiastic about the appearance of the young Emperor; everything breathes a sigh of relief, as if released from heavy pressure, and a feeling of calm and security asserts itself everywhere. Foreign countries, too, received the speech from the throne very sympathetically; the calm assurance and the fully conscious power of it impressed everyone.

Creisau, 26 July 1888.

As much as I would like to leave you the unabridged enjoyment of your vacation, I must ask you to return as soon as possible. Things can't go on here without you. Since you no longer feed him, Uncle Helmuth is getting more miserable by the day, he eats almost nothing and is a terrible hypochondriac. To keep himself busy, he works five to six hours a day in the bush and sinks more and more. The *whist en trois* is downright devastating for all concerned. Please telegraph me when I can expect you.

General Staff Berlin, [*] *28 October 1888.*

This morning I had inquired by telephone whether and when Uncle Helmuth could report to His Majesty. The answer came back: His Majesty asks the Field Marshal to have breakfast with him at 1:30. – I wanted to use the opportunity to report immediately to the Emperor, and therefore went along in my parade suit. Arriving in Potsdam, we drove across the Lustgarten and out to the Marble Palace. Here we were led into a small room and asked to wait, since Her Majesty still had a lecture. After a short while, the Empress came in alone without any ladies, said hello to Uncle Helmuth in a very friendly manner and sat down with him. A somewhat halting conversation now began, the Empress a little embarrassed, which suited her charmingly, very amiable and cordial, and when she speaks, with an extraordinarily winning feature in her face. She looks very well, very comfortable and fresh. She has very beautiful hands, and her movements are all full of grace. She immediately asked about you and the children, and after the first embarrassment was overcome, she chatted very prettily and harmlessly.

---

[*] Major on the General Staff.

Then came the Emperor, who first greeted Uncle Helmuth and then approached me, who had pressed myself into a corner. I now immediately jumped into his face with my report, reported myself: "By Your Majesty's grace promoted to Major", while he held me by the hand during the whole time. Then he said: "My God, you're already a Major too? One grows old when I think how I still knew you as a very young badger in the regiment. Well, I congratulate you." We then went straight to the table. The table was served in a small hall whose open French doors across a terrace afforded a magnificent view of the deep blue lake and the opposite shore. It was splendid weather, warm, windless, and quite bright sunshine.

The Emperor sat facing the open door, the Empress opposite him, to the right of the Emperor the Countess Brockdorff, then me. To the left the Countess Keller, then Bissing. Uncle Helmuth to the left of the Empress, to her right Colonel v. Villaume, military attaché in Petersburg, who had come with us. Then Lyncker and on the other side the wing adjutant His Majesty v. Scholl. That was the whole round table. The Emperor was very lively and animated, talked a lot. He looks very well. The face has become more marked and manly, the big blue eyes even bigger than before. Toward the end of the meal, the Empress says, "You, Wilhelm, I suppose the boys could come and say good day to the Field Marshal." "Yes, of course," replies the Emperor. Then to me, "Tell me, Julius, the field marshal has a cap with him, doesn't he?" "Yes, sir." – It is brought; we get up and go to the terrace, where a little table with cigars is set down and coffee is served.

Then the boys arrive! Four in number. The three oldest in velvet suits with little helmets with tufts of hair on. Baby Wilhelm August in a little white dress and bare legs. Lovely healthy children who shake hands with all of us and then immediately group around Uncle Helmuth. The oldest has his father's eyes, a fine little face, a little pale; the second with his curly head is prettier, and so is the third, but the most splendid is No. 4, who is very spoiled by his brothers. Mama thinks that it is too cold for his legs, which, by the way, are tight, and immediately there is a race to find a hat and coat for baby, from which the eldest emerges as the winner, very proudly wearing both things, still quite out of breath. Baby is now dressed by his mother, the brothers want to button him up, he is knocked over, falls on his nose, makes a crooked mouth, but is immediately put back on his feet by the brothers, patted down and comforted. There is neither a nanny nor any servant spirit to be seen. The boys are completely alone with their parents. The Emperor is standing there laughing with a cigar in his mouth and is very happy about the boys! It is a charming family scene.

Suddenly the whole company rushes up to the Emperor, "Papa, may we get our rifles?" Permission is given, and now they arrive with solemn seriousness and rifles on in line march. Baby does not yet have a rifle and tries to keep up without it, but is put aside by the brothers as a guard, which renders him harmless. Now Uncle Helmuth has the three elders line up and make turns, which are conscientiously executed, then they march under the command of Bissing, who as a cavalryman gives cavalry commands and is rectified for this by the little crown prince. Then guard is posted and the request is made to the Emperor, "Papa, pass once so we can step out." Finally Villaume is arrested, one going in front, one behind with his rifle cocked. He bolts, the two after him, he is wounded in the head (faked, of course) and has to bandage himself with his handkerchief. Then he is placed against the wall and two chairs in front of him, so he is trapped in the sign house. "You can't smoke as a prisoner," says No. 1, he has to throw away his cigarette. The Empress looks with a blissful smile at her pretty children, whose cheeks glow and whose eyes shine with pleasure.

Time goes on like this until I suddenly see a footman waving energetically at me. It is time to leave. I avert Uncle Helmuth, who does not want to leave until the Emperor comes to his aid and bids him adieu. "It was very kind of you to come out." He shakes my hand at least three times: "Adieu, dear Julius, greet your wife beautifully." The Empress also shakes my hand and tells me the same: "Give my warmest regards to your wife."

Uncle Helmuth is in a cheerful *dejeuner* mood, mistakes Frl. v. Gersdorff for the Empress, wants to kiss her hand and then asks, "Where is the Princess?" At this, the Empress stands a step behind him and says: "Here I am." – But all this does nothing, everything is taken harmlessly, and we depart.

The footman is in all states, for the train leaves in ten minutes. I try to get Uncle Helmuth to hurry a little more, but he starts another long conversation with Major v. Scholl on the vestibule, lights his cigar again, and declares that we still have a long time. Finally we get into the car, which now drives off with us like mad. We have to pass through the whole of Potsdam, we still have two minutes before we reach the Lustgarten. I call out to the coachman, and Uncle Helmuth declares with the greatest composure, "We'll certainly be late."

The train is about to depart as we stop in front of the platform. Uncle Helmuth is recognized, the royal equipage had already been seen, and, since all coupées are full, another carriage is attached, into which we climb. As soon as we are seated, off we go, and Uncle Helmuth says, "We've just timed it right!"

General Staff Berlin, 12 August 1889.

At 5 o'clock we, Uncle Helmuth and I, drove with Count Waldersee to the Tiergarten train station, where soon after us the Emperor arrived in Austrian uniform, which does not dress him at all. He looks downright bad in it, otherwise very blooming, all brown and burnt, extraordinarily healthy. He greeted Uncle Helmuth, who reported to him, very warmly and talked with him for a long time. Prince Heinrich was also there. Then came the Emperor of Austria, very handsome, with a blooming complexion and elegant figure, the Duke of Este also excellent looking. We then drove up the linden trees under the usual cheers to the castle, where Uncle Helmuth signed in. Tonight we are to go to the taps, tomorrow at 7 o'clock to the dinner, the day after tomorrow to Babelsberg.

General Staff Berlin, 13 August 1889.

We were at the castle last night for the concert, which was wonderfully pretty and extraordinarily happy in all its parts. The Emperor of Austria told Uncle Helmuth that he had made him head of the 71st (Austrian) Regiment. I was standing too far to be able to understand exactly, but heard that there was talk of regiment, etc., and also saw that Uncle Helmuth made one of his doubtful bows, which he always makes when he has not quite understood. The Emperor of Austria stood in front of him for a while with a somewhat embarrassed face and then went away. I now asked Uncle Helmuth if the Emperor had not awarded him a regiment, and he answered me indifferently, "Yep." – "Which one then?" "Yes, I didn't understand that." So I inquire with the Austrian wing adjutant, and he tells me it is the 71st Regiment, a very fine Hungarian regiment. The Austrian military officer now goes to Uncle Helmuth and congratulates him and says he is so happy to welcome Uncle Helmuth now as a member of the Austrian army. Uncle Helmuth looks at him wildly and says, "What do you mean?" He repeats. Uncle Helmuth stands up and says, "Me? What do you mean?" Steininger says, "Excellency, His Majesty the Emperor has awarded you the 71st Regiment, after all." – "To me? Don't even think about it."

Finally it comes out that he understood that the Emperor of Austria had told him that he had awarded a regiment to our Emperor. Uncle Helmuth is now quite distressed that he has not said a word of thanks. I ask Count Wedell to inform the Emperor that the Field Marshal has misunderstood him and that he asks to be allowed to lay his thanks at the feet of His Majesty. This is done. The Emperor stands up once again and goes to Uncle Helmuth, who now duly thanks him. This act of mercy on the part of the Emperor towards his old adversary and defeater is truly magnificent, all the more so since it is a very rare case in Austria that a foreigner and not a prince is given a regiment. The Austrian gentlemen, who all make a very pleasant impression, are full of combativeness. Bismarck, on the other hand, is said to be blowing the peace shawm from all keys. He was also at the reception, but looked pale and miserable.

General Staff Berlin, 18 November 1889.

Today at 11 o'clock, I was present with Uncle Helmuth at the parade ground of the 2nd Guard Regiment at the swearing-in ceremony of the recruits of the Berlin garrison, on which occasion

Uncle Helmuth reported to the Kaiser. It was quite a solemn act. The drill house was decorated with flags and shields, in the center under a purple canopy a field altar was erected, from which first the Protestant, then the Catholic garrison priest held an address. All the generals of the garrison and all the flags were present. The Emperor looked very fresh and well. One got an aftertaste of our torn political conditions when the various oath formulas were read out. First the Prussian subjects swore a) to the Protestant, b) to the Catholic religion. Then the Brunswickers, then the Württembergers, then the subjects of the other small federal states, finally the Alsace-Lorraineers, all took their special oath!

General Staff Berlin, 24 November 1889.

Yesterday we heard a rather mediocre performance of *Lohengrin*. E. with a completely failing voice as Lohengrin and a Mrs. P., whom I judge from her horrible pronunciation to be English or American, gave the Elsa. It was pitiful. This lady had a huge mouth, which she opened so wide when she sang that one could see the back of her palate with opera glasses over an enormous tongue. As soon as she began: "My poor brother!" her tone snapped, in all her movements she was ungraceful, mannered unnatural and unattractive, she had no idea of the essence of the role, it was really terrible. The orchestra sometimes dragged, sometimes in such strength that one heard nothing of the singing on the stage, only saw the opening and closing of Elsa's huge mouth, if she did not just in moments of excitement, which she illustrated by disappearing with her whole head between the raised shoulder blades, so that one saw only a red wig more, deprive the audience of this enjoyment as well. No, our opera is really downright hair-raisingly miserable.

General Staff Berlin, 27 November 1889.

Uncle Helmuth and I are going to Prutz tomorrow. We have quite an interesting read now, *The Establishment of the German Empire by Wilhelm I* by Heinrich von Sybel. Nicely and interestingly written and compiled from the state archives.

Kiel, Royal Palace, 3 April 1891.

This morning at 10 o'clock was parade of the Sailors' Division and Sea Battalion and a battalion of 85s. After the parade march, the Emperor assembled the officers and expressed his appreciation of the parade. Then he continued as follows: "I have decided to give the Navy a new proof of my benevolence in order to honor it and to give it a new incentive for ever renewed striving and never tiring activity and work. General Field Marshal Count von Moltke has always taken a lively interest in the navy, and the mighty army commander has not disdained to show his goodwill and sympathy again and again to our little numerous and still nascent fleet. In order to honor the Navy by bringing His Excellency the Field Marshal into an even closer relationship with the same, I hereby place His Excellency *a la suite* of the 1st Sea Battalion, and I beg Your Excellency to give your orders for the battalion."

Uncle Helmuth was very surprised, but fortunately, since he was standing next to the Emperor, had understood what he was saying and did his job very well. The battalion presented, Uncle Helmuth had the officer corps introduced and walked down the front, then he approached the Emperor and thanked him for the new proof of his grace. Hereupon the Chief of the Admiralty, Admiral Goltz, stepped to the front and told the battalion in a resounding voice what had happened, concluding with a hail to the Kaiser, in which everyone joined, including the audience crowded by the hundreds on the roofs and in the windows of the surrounding houses (the parade took place in the navy barracks yard). Then followed a combat drill by a company of sailors with blanks, which banged tremendously in the courtyard surrounded by tall barracks, and finally a breakfast in the Navy mess hall, at which the Kaiser made a long speech. Admiral Goltz then let Uncle Helmuth speak, recalling a remark he had made on occasion of the construction of the Kiel harbor fortifications: "You shall fly out, gentlemen, so that you can do so, we will build you a safe home to

which you can return."
    We sat at table for about two hours, after which we returned to the castle. In the afternoon, Uncle Helmuth tried a walk with me on the promenade running from the castle along the harbor, but had to give it up again very soon, driven away by the cutting east wind and the crowds of curious people following us.
    Uncle Helmuth is very well. He eats with a huge appetite and is interested in everything.

Kiel, Royal Palace, 7 April 1891.

Yesterday, unfortunately in bad weather, cold wind and persistent, though not heavy rain, we made a tour to the Kiel Canal under construction. First we went by wagon to a small place located near Holtenau, where three small steamers were ready to take us. The Kaiser arrived five minutes after us. Uncle Helmuth was in the uniform of the naval battalion.
    We embarked and set off first on the old Eider Canal. In front was a small police steamer, then the steam launch with His Majesty, Prince Heinrich, Chief of Admiralty Goltz and Minister of State v. Bötticher, who had come from Berlin for this trip. Then the rest of us followed on a larger steam launch. The old Eider Canal, built by the Danish government about a hundred years ago, is quite a magnificent work in its way. If one considers that at that time the work had to be done without the help of the machines of the present time, that all the earth-moving, some of it considerable, was accomplished only with the spade and the wheelbarrow, only with human hands, then one can well say that this work, measured by the measure of its time and its circumstances, is not much inferior to that now undertaken by us. The old canal mostly follows the course of the Eider, which has been dug out and deepened, and in many places also straightened. It climbs over the watershed with three locks and offers only smaller coastal vessels the possibility of passage. It is often sinuous and curved and avoids cutting through significant ground elevations as much as possible.
    The new canal partly follows its course, but cuts off the curvatures everywhere and presents itself as a fairly straight line,

on the whole somewhat curved towards the north. It begins at Holtenau in the port of Kiel and flows into the lower reaches of the Elbe near Brunsbüttel.

The work has progressed very differently, some sections are completely finished, others have only just begun. The canal will have an upper width of ninety-five meters, i.e. one hundred paces, so that two ships can pass each other everywhere. It is quite an enormous work, which at present employs seven thousand workers and a myriad of machines, mainly ground and dry dredgers. Very interesting is a stretch where the canal cuts through a liquid bog. Since here the embankments would keep subsiding and filling the depth again if they were simply cut out, huge sand and gravel embankments are first poured on both sides in the width of the projected cutout. The material is taken from other places where high land is cut through. Temporary railroad tracks are laid on both sides, on which the excavated soil is driven by small locomotives. The excavation is usually done with dry excavators, which dig the soil and pour it directly into the railroad loris. When a wagon is fully loaded, the whole excavator, which also goes on rails, pushes itself one wagon further and thus loads a train of twenty wagons full in about ten minutes. The train now travels to where the embankment is to be poured, whereupon all the wagons are opened at the side and overturned. The dam thus formed sinks into the liquid mire, which rises completely out between the two dams, from the pressure of the same, and then between the dams thus first poured the actual channel is cut out, the banks of which now stand.

At another place we saw a so-called spray dredger. It works as follows: It lifts the soil from the bottom under water, brings it to the top, where it is mixed with water by the same machine, which at the same time moves a water pumping station, to form a very thin slurry, which then in turn flows off through a pipe to a marshy terrain off to the side. The water accumulates here, settles the soil it carries, and in turn flows out again through a weir. In this way, not only is the transport of the excavated material saved, but at the same time an unusable piece of land is transformed into good cultivable soil. I had to think of the second part of "*Faust*" during all this great work.

At another place, from the embankment of a pierced bump, one looked down on a piece of excavated canal that still lay dry, as if into a deep valley. Ant-like, people worked down there, locomotives wheezing and whistling and dry dredges groaning. All these excavators are as big as houses, and all of course work with steam power. There are about seven million cubic meters of earth to move. The entire route is divided into so-called lots, which are awarded to contractors. One of them has four million marks in working materials alone. Each lot is under a construction official who controls and directs the work. Barracks made of corrugated iron have been built for the workers, small, individual cottages with two rooms each, bright and friendly. Catering for this army of workers is managed by the canal construction inspector. The man has housing, morning coffee and lunch bread for 60 pfennigs a day, he gets 3 marks wages, so that he can spare 2.40 marks a day after paying for his needs.

Of course, to see all this, we had to get off and on repeatedly, which was not pleasant with the fine rain that was beginning to fall. Uncle Helmuth, however, survived everything very well and is quite well.

At the town of Rendsburg we went through the lock of the old Eider Canal, which was occupied on both sides by hundreds of people, and went out quite a distance on the Lower Eider, then turned around and at 5 o'clock got on the special imperial train waiting at the Rendsburg station to take us back to Kiel. This morning Uncle Helmuth and I were at the 1st Sea Battalion, where he visited the barracks and had breakfast with the officer corps, and also had his picture taken with the gentlemen, to their greatest delight. Then we went for a walk and returned to the castle at 1 o'clock for breakfast. After breakfast we went to the "Moltke", which was commissioned this morning, where we inspected the entire ship in detail, which is to go to sea in three days. It is a beautiful proud ship with 3 masts and 2 screws, painted all white, carries 12 heavy guns and 430 crew. Under the bowsprit is Uncle Helmuth's head in huge size and the crew wears the name "Moltke" on their caps.

*Neues Palais,** 15 May 1891.*

The Emperor was very gracious and kind to me; I still had to tell him a lot about Uncle Helmuth.† Likewise the Empress.

Berlin, 7 November 1891.

At 5 o'clock, the Emperor had announced his intention to dine with the Reich Chancellor, and we left for Berlin at 4:15 by special train. I ate for the first time in the rooms in which the spirit of the mighty predecessor seemed to me still to be blowing. What a lot these rooms had experienced! The Emperor's memories also came flooding back, and as we drove away, he once again spoke to me with great frankness, full of bitterness and right heartbreak about the dismal experiences he had had with blatant ingratitude. I felt so sorry for him, because hardly anyone understands how deeply he is touched by the rift with Bismarck and how inwardly he feels the break.

Wartburg, 23 April 1892.

The Grand Duke restored the castle, which was in a bad state of disrepair, with great reverence. Everything that could be preserved has been preserved and the new has been added exactly according to the old masters. When you pass through the low arched gate and step into the courtyard formed by the rock, you think you are in the middle of the Middle Ages. This is how the castle stood when, under the reign of Landgrave Philip and St. Elizabeth, the minstrels from all the German territories came up to it to fight out the war of the singers with song and harp playing in the festival hall. These are the thresholds that Heinrich von Ofterdingen, Hartmann von

---

* Serving Wing Adjutant to H. M. the Emperor.

† Publisher's note: Helmuth von Moltke the Elder had died on April 24, 1891, at the age of 91.

der Aue, Walther von der Vogelweide and Tannhäuser crossed, this is the same hall in which their songs resounded and awakened echoes as far as the German tongue could sound. This is the woman's chamber in which St. Elizabeth lived, there stands the old chest in which she kept the bread and wine for her poor, which turned into roses in her basket when her husband was hard on her for her lavish mildness. Still the same columns bear the vaults that arched over her then, and on the battered *Estrieh* her foot has walked. Unfortunately, my time is not sufficient to describe everything. However, the Grand Duke told me yesterday: "Tell your wife that I invite her to visit me at the Wartburg together with you. Give her my best regards."

Weimar, 10 October 1892.

I used the few free hours I had left to visit the Goethe House and the library he had set up. The death chamber, a small room facing the garden, in which a bed with coarse sheets, the reclining chair in front of which Goethe died, his very small washstand with the simplest wash bowl and a brown earthen water vessel stand, is completely preserved as it was. A solemn feeling comes over one when one enters this little chamber, in which there is not even a stove, and contemplates this unadorned, almost poor room, in which one of the greatest spirits detached himself from the earthly shell. The study next to it shows the same simplicity. Stiff straight furniture without any ornamentation, without any comfort. The richly animated spiritual world, in which he lived, probably did not let him attach any importance to the outward appearances. I would have liked to spend hours in these rooms, where all the collections he had made and arranged himself are kept, but time was short and I had to be content with a cursory wandering.

Berlin, 15 December 1892.

I know that you have an open mind for the beautiful old memories of which Weimar is so rich, and I can imagine your holy dread with which you enter the places over which a breath of the great spirits still hovers, who lived there and – as you think – suffered. Certainly they suffered, otherwise how could they have created so great things. As man is born with pain, so also his best spiritual creations come out of suffering and pain, and what he himself has suffered becomes a benefit for his fellow men. The external environment of these spiritual heroes was plain and simple, they built their temples inside, the man who could feel and express a "fist" is also not imaginable in the midst of the comforts of our modern life.

CABINET ORDER.

I have today promoted you to the rank of Lieutenant Colonel and it gives me pleasure to announce this to you.
Berlin, 27 January 1893.
Wilhelm R.
To My Wing Adjutant in Service, Major v. Moltke.

CABINET ORDER.

I hereby appoint you Commander of the Castle Guard Company.
Potsdam, 9 February 1893.
Wilhelm R.
To My Wing Adjutant, Lieutenant Colonel v. Moltke.

Urville Castle, 3 September 1893.

We have a fully grafted time behind us, and it will yes continue for another fortnight. The lighting of the Rhine in Koblenz on September 1 was wonderfully beautiful. We didn't see much of Trier, just rode through it, including the famous *Porta Nigra*, one of the most beautiful buildings of ancient Roman times. This morning we rode from Koblenz to Metz, where there was a big field service. Then we rode with the Emperor at the head of the entire garrison into Metz to the Esplanade, where the Emperor had the troops march past him under the monument to the old Emperor

Wilhelm.

One has a magnificent view from up there of the Moselle valley and the imposing height of Mont St. Quentin behind it, a great panorama. The participation of the population in Metz was moderate, there were not too many people on the streets. The windows were thinly occupied, almost nothing to be noticed of the rural population, yet I was told that the turnout was a much more lively one than during the last imperial visit.

From Kurzell to here to the castle one drives no ten minutes. The whole causeway was densely packed with schools, clubs, etc., all with German flags and little flags, but of course all delivered goods. A larger part of the rural population had also gathered here and spontaneously participated in the homage.

Urville Castle, 5 September 1893.

Today we had the first day of maneuvers. The exercises are very interesting. It sounds strange when the Emperor passes by a group of countrymen and they enthusiastically shout "Vive l'Empereur." – The fresh and beautiful appearance of the Emperor visibly affects the people. Everything here speaks French, and the people look like stock Frenchmen, blouses, jabots and white pants.

Urville Castle, 8 September 1893.

It is 4 o'clock in the morning, I am sitting by the lamp with saber and sash to wait for daybreak. Today the Emperor is leading the two cavalry divisions united into one cavalry corps, and we are spectators today, since he has a cavalry staff. We are very *matinous* these days, up at 3 o'clock every morning and not to bed before 11 or 12 in the evening. The Emperor led the XVI Corps yesterday. Our horses, squadron horses, are very driven off, the ground is immensely difficult for them, rock hard with large solid lumps and boulders, always going up and down hills. I am often amazed at the performance of the horses, some of which come to the bivouac only at dusk and are saddled again at 2 o'clock in the morning to stay under the saddle all day without food and watering.

Karlsruhe Castle, 12 September 1893.

The day after tomorrow is the last day of maneuvers here, then come the two days in Stuttgart, and then the maneuver will be over, I can say. I feel as if we have only just started the maneuver; I have hardly ever been so interested in a maneuver as I am in this year's maneuver. The physical exertion, which is not insignificant, is excellent for me; I feel good and fresh and could last for weeks like this.

Visit of Prince Bismarck to His Majesty the Emperor in Berlin on January 26, 1894.

On Friday, January 26, 1894, at one o'clock in the afternoon, the Headquarters of His Majesty the Emperor and King were ordered to the Berlin Palace, Portal 5, in order to be present there at the expected arrival of Prince Bismarck. Present were the commander of the headquarters, General v. Plessen, the wing adjutants Captain v. Arnim, Lieutenant Colonel v. Scholl, v. Arnim II, v. Moltke, Major v. Jakobi. Colonel v. Kessel, commander of the 1st Guards Regiment, had also been ordered to the reception by His Majesty. In addition, the heads of cabinet General v. Hahnke, Admiral v. Senden, Privy Cabinet Councilor v. Lucanus.

In order to preserve the military character of the reception, His Majesty had ordered the officers to appear in service dress, epaulets and high boots. The Wing Adjutant, Major Count Moltke, whom the Emperor had sent to Friedrichsruh three days before with a handwritten letter inviting the Prince to come to Berlin as his guest, had been ordered to attend the Prince and was awaiting the Prince's arrival at the Lehrter station with His Royal Highness Prince Heinrich of Prussia, the Commandant Colonel v. Natzmer and the Governor, Colonel General v. Pape. I was commanded to replace Count Moltke, who was on II Service with His Majesty. I arrived at the palace at 12 o'clock. In front of the Brandenburg

Gate and Unter den Linden, a densely packed crowd was already awaiting the Prince, and new crowds were constantly arriving on the Charlottenburg causeway and from the side streets. Everywhere one saw happy, expectant faces. The weather was fine, the public buildings had flown their flags by order of the Most High, and many private houses were festively decorated.

When I arrived, a deputation of the 7th Cuirassier Regiment, consisting of the regimental commander, Count Klinkowström, Captain v. Zitzewitz, a lieutenant and six non-commissioned officers in parade dress with bustle, was standing in the entrance of Portal 1 in the palace, which His Majesty had summoned, since he intended to appoint the Prince as the head of this regiment. I went up to the adjutant's room, where Captain v. Arnim, who had the 1 Service, was present. As early as 12:30 p.m., the bodyguard reported to us that His Majesty was about to go through the nuns' corridor to the terrace apartment at Portal 5, which had been kept ready for the Prince. We hurried after him and met the Emperor on the stairs of the theater. His Majesty was wearing the uniform of the *Gardes du Corps*, blue tunic, high boots, epaulets, helmet and sash. The Emperor was about to ascend the stairs when we reached him and Arnim pointed out to him that, on the contrary, he would have to go down to get to Portal 1. He was obviously nervous and agitated, gave no answer, turned around briefly and quickly went down the stairs while we followed him. On the way Arnim tried a couple of times to obtain an order from him as to when the deputation of the 7th Cuirassiers was to be brought forward, etc., but received only short, dismissive and unfriendly answers in an impatient tone.

As we entered the apartment, chambermaids and footmen were still busy arranging flower baskets and huge bouquets, which had been delivered from many sides for the Prince, in the rooms. The house marshal v. Lyncker ran from time to time and sped up the work. The carpet was swept and tables wiped, general unrest prevailed, which was increased when the Emperor ordered all flowers to be taken out of the sitting room and into the anteroom, as the smell was too strong. The smell was indeed deafening, and the windows had to be opened. Outside, in front of the ramp, the crowd stood head to head, the muffled roar of crowding people sounded in, one could hear the stamping of the horses of the mounted guards on the asphalt. The center of the palace square was kept wide open, under the windows of the apartment stood a company of the 2nd Guards Regiment with flag and music in parade dress as a guard of honor. The Emperor walked restlessly through the rooms. Around him servants dragged the flower baskets and girls walked with dust brooms and wiping cloths to clean the carpet and furniture. We huddled in a corner and watched the hustle and bustle.

Finally order was established and people were chased out. One by one those ordered to the reception arrived. They shifted back and forth, no one knew where we should line up, and everything whispered quietly. The Emperor spoke hastily to this and that, but had no peace, broke off briefly and went again into another room. Suddenly he strode quickly toward the exit and went out through the portal onto the palace square. Arnim and I followed. The Emperor approached the right wing of the honorary company, bid them good morning, and walked down the front. Then he returned to the palace just as quickly and without saying a word. Then he ordered that a section of the castle guard should occupy the ramp and not let anyone up on it. This was done. No one had been on the ramp before. Now the Marshal-in-Chief Graf zu Eulenburg arrived, as did the heads of the cabinet, and last, as usual, General v. Hahnke. The Emperor had already repeatedly asked each of them if they were not yet here. In the meantime, it had become 1 o'clock, and everyone was assembled.

The day before, the Emperor had ordered that the two eldest princes be picked up from Her Majesty the Empress by a wing adjutant and, after the Prince's arrival, be escorted down to greet him. General v. Plessen had appointed Lieutenant Colonel v. Scholl for this purpose. The latter now approached the Emperor and asked when His Majesty would order that the princes be fetched. The Most High Lord became very indignant and said that he would order in time what should happen, whereupon Scholl silently withdrew. In the meantime, the Marshal-in-Chief made the closer arrangements. The headquarters were to line up in the anteroom to greet the Prince first; the Emperor had ordered General v. Plessen to introduce us all. His Majesty remained in the anteroom. The Prince was to join him here alone. On a table in the anteroom lay a large album, on the cover of which was printed in gold letters: "The New Lord." It contained a collection of photographs of a series of scenes from this play, and must have been there for years and years. I opened the album and looked at the picture. It was the scene where the chancellor, Count Schwarzenberg, was kneeling in front of the Elector, who, standing tall, was standing in front of him. I drew Count Eulenburg's attention to the album, which was here so little *a propos*, and he carefully placed it in a drawer.

At 1:10, General v. Plessen, who had been on the train to receive him, arrived with the message that the Prince had arrived, that in his company, in addition to Dr. Schwenninger and Dr. Chrysander, who were expected, there was also Count Herbert Bismarck, who was not expected. This was obviously unpleasant for the Emperor. He ordered Count Herbert to remain in the anteroom and not to come in with the Prince. The court marshal's office was in great agitation as to how to deal with this unexpected *fait accompli*. The prince could arrive at any moment now. We had taken up our positions in the anteroom and were looking through the window in eager anticipation. Now we could hear roaring cheers coming up from the linden trees. The crowd piled up in front of the palace began to move, everything was pushing and shoving forward, all heads were turned towards the palace bridge, over which the escort was coming in a slender trot, with cuirasses flashing in the sun, behind it the large, closed gala carriage in which the Prince was sitting with Prince Heinrich. Arriving in front of the guard of honor, the escort swung off, the carriage stopped, supported by Prince Heinrich, the Prince got out and walked towards the right wing of the company. The latter presented, and in the whooping acclamations, the roaring cheers of the crowd, which waved hats and waved scarves, mingled the sounds of the band playing the presenter's march.

While the Prince walked down the front of the company with his slow, dragging step, we pressed our noses to the window pane. In the next room, the doors of which were closed, the Emperor was alone. What may have passed through the soul of the monarch at that moment, as he saw the man who had so bitterly hurt him and whom he had so magnanimously forgiven, striding along at the front of his guards, tossed about by the enthusiasm of thousands. Four years of rancor lay between them, and in a few minutes they were to meet eye to eye. After the prince had walked along the front of the honorary company, he, supported by Prince Henry, again mounted the carriage, which after a few moments stopped under the portal of the palace. The doors were opened, and on the arm of the Prince, the Prince entered the antechamber. We all bowed deeply.

The mighty figure of the old chancellor, who towered over his careful guide by head's length, seemed unbroken, straight and erect, the round head with the enormous eyes, brushed over by thick brows, was of a pale color. He passed over us with a quick glance and accepted the introduction by General v. Plessen, who called our names. He greeted each of us with a friendly wave of the hand. To Colonel v. Kessel he shook hands and looked inquiringly into his face. "Kessel?" he said in a questioning tone. "It seems to me that you have grown smaller since then." As General v. Plessen mentioned the name of Geh. Kabinettschef v. Lucanus, who seemed somewhat embarrassed and held back a great deal, the prince made a stiff bow and said, "I have the honor from before."

After the performance was over, a footman took the Prince's coat. He had on the dark tunic of the cuirassiers, long leggings, and was calmly buttoning his gloves. His hands trembled a little, and he was obviously tense and excited. Prince Heinrich now approached him and said, "Will Your Serene Highness now come in to see His Majesty." The Prince bowed silently. The double doors were opened and he stepped over the threshold. The Emperor, who was standing in the middle of the room, quickly approached him with his hand outstretched, which the prince, bowing deeply, grasped with both hands. Then the Emperor bent down and kissed him on both cheeks. The doors closed, the two were alone. Outside stood head to head. The crowd was crowded up to the ramp and shouted their incessant cheers, hats were waved, scarves waved, and again and again the shouts were renewed. Finally, one of them began to sing "Germany, Germany above all," others joined in, and soon the song resounded in many hundreds of voices, interrupted by repeated cheers as soon as someone showed himself at the window.

After about ten minutes the Emperor opened the door again and ordered that the two oldest princes be fetched. Then he beckoned Prince Heinrich inside. While Scholl went to fetch the princes, we remained in the anteroom talking with Dr. Schwenninger and Herbert v. Bismarck. Then the princes came in, dressed in the uniform of the I Guard Regiment and wearing the ribbon of the Order of the Black Eagle. They remained in the Prince's room for about five minutes and were then escorted back by Scholl. After another ten minutes or so had passed, the Emperor opened the door again to dismiss us. His face was bright and cheerful, there was on it like the gleam of a great joy. While the other gentlemen were escorted out to breakfast by the court marshals, Arnim and I went to the adjutant's room to have breakfast as well. Then we changed our clothes for riding. The Emperor had ordered the riding horses at 2:30. In the portal I still stood, now for over two hours, the deputation of the 7th Cuirassier Regiment. Only after breakfast had ended had the Emperor presented the Prince with the cabinet order appointing him chief of this regiment, and had the deputation presented to him. The Prince is said to have been deeply moved and grateful.

In the meantime, the Prince had gone up to Her Majesty the Empress with the Emperor and Prince Heinrich to greet her. Breakfast was taken by the two Majesties, Prince Heinrich and the Prince alone.

It was 3:30 before we rode off. In front of the palace and on Unter den Linden, the crowds were still surging back and forth. When they saw the Emperor, they cheered endlessly. Everyone pressed toward him. The guards tried in vain to hold back the people who broke through all the barriers. "Up! noble Emperor!" "Long live our magnanimous Emperor!" "Hail! beloved Emperor!" resounded from all sides. We had to ride to the right and left of His Majesty to keep him reasonably clear. All down the Linden the cheers accompanied us, flowing directly from the heart of the enthusiastic people. On the Charlottenburger causeway, where the Emperor, using the bridle path, began to trot, people ran breathlessly beside us and accompanied us with their shouts, a whole motorcade drove on the causeway beside and behind us, and the occupants tirelessly waved scarves and hats. At last, only the boys held out, until one after the other of them, exhausted, stayed behind, giving up the run with a gasping "*Adieu*, beloved Emperor!" We rode to the Hippodrome, where we cantered off our four thousand meters. Then we galloped back after the Brandenburg Gate through the Tiergarten. The Emperor was in a very elevated mood. He spoke animatedly and joked with us. He told how he had served the Prince some of his best Rhine wine at breakfast and how it had pleased him. The enthusiastic ovation, of which he had become the object, had obviously deeply moved him, and he rejoiced in the victory he had won over himself, the most difficult that a man can win. From the moment we approached the Brandenburg Gate, where a dense crowd was already awaiting the Emperor's return, the same jubilation again surrounded us. It was almost dark when we arrived back at the palace.

At 6:15 a small dinner was held in the Prince's rooms. As we went downstairs, following the Emperor, the Emperor gave me the order to order a company of honor to the armory for tomorrow, his birthday, to issue the parole. I went up to our room to execute the order. As I come down again, a footman opens a door for me, I enter and find myself face to face with the Emperor, who is in conversation with the Prince and Prince Heinrich. I report on duty that the order has been carried out and stand at attention next to the door. The Emperor says to the prince: "This is Lieutenant Colonel von Moltke, who was the adjutant of the late field marshal for a long time." The prince nods in a friendly manner and says, "Oh, I know Herr von Moltke, and have already greeted him." On this the Emperor says: "The two of them" (by which he means Cuno von Moltke and me) "are namely cousins." As I was about to go back to the room I had so unexpectedly stumbled into, the Emperor said to me: "Why don't you tell Count Eulenburg that we are hungry and would like to eat?"

The table set in the anteroom had eleven place settings. Prince Heinrich sat to the right of the Emperor, the Prince to the left. Also present at the dinner were: Herbert v. Bismarck, Count Eulenburg, Count Klinkowström, Lieutenant von Niesewand of the 7th Cuirassiers, who was in command as an orderly officer, v. Arnim, Prince Heinrich's adjutant, v. Colomb, Cuno v. Moltke and myself.

The conversation was animated and informal, the intercourse between the Emperor and the Prince cordial and without any genes. Again it gave the old Rhine wine, to which the prince added vigorously. In his quiet, halting voice, he told stories of the Empress Augusta, and how his old dog Tyras had once almost grabbed the Grand Duke of Weimar, who was visiting him. There was much laughter, and His Majesty also told lively and animated stories. As we were roasting, His Majesty was informed that Count Wilhelm Bismarck was outside, whereupon the Emperor ordered that another place setting be placed on the table and that he be called in. In the meantime, however, the count had already left and was brought in by the messengers sent after him shortly before the end of the dinner. Coffee and cigars were served at the table. The prince smoked a cigarette as did the Emperor. The Emperor had drunk with the Prince and likewise with the two Counts Bismarck.

At 7 o'clock we drove ahead to the Lehrter station, where again the whole headquarters was assembled. The Emperor accompanied the Prince in a gala carriage, preceded by a squadron. As the carriage stopped in front of the station building, Prince Heinrich, who had gone ahead, assisted the Prince to alight, then the Emperor followed. Entering the station hall, the Emperor gave the Prince his arm and led him down the steps. Thunderous cheers from the crowd gathered on the platform greeted them both. In front of the salon car, the Prince took leave of his Imperial Lord, who kissed him again on both cheeks, he bent over the Emperor's hand and brought it to his lips. His eyes were moist. As he got in and was still standing at the open window, the Emperor said to him, "Now, dear Prince, I hope you will sleep well after your tiring day." And then he added: "When I go to Wilhelmshaven in February, I will ask once in Friedrichsruh if I can visit you." – Then the locomotive whistled and the train drove slowly out, while the Prince stood at the window waving his hand. The vault echoed with people's cheers as we turned to return. We had been in a wedding mood all day.

Written for Liza by Helmuth.
Berlin, 28 January 1894.

St. Petersburg, 17 November 1894.

It all happened so quickly and unexpectedly, the news of Papa's death and our departure, which could no longer be changed. Now I have stood at the bier of another dead man, at a bier around which all the pomp and splendor of the earthly will once again unfold before the quiet man who rests on it will be buried in the tomb, and at the same time the other quiet man lies in Sweden, probably still on his simple bed, and what difference has now remained between the two? They have become equal before the Almighty Equalizer, they have been removed from human activity, and the Lord God will weigh them without regard to what was the difference between them in life.

Here the chants of the priests resound, clouds of incense rise to heaven, and a whole people lies on its knees to pray for the dead – there perhaps just now the simple country priest speaks a simple prayer. How rapid was the change of events also for me, the baptism under the fresh impression of the news of the death, then immediately afterwards the departure, the next day with the crossing of the border, the many strange impressions, the arrival this morning in Petersburg, immediately afterwards the visit to the catafalque, where we laid the wreath brought by the Emperor, then in the course of the day two masses for the souls at the open coffin, in between an endless journey with registered mail etc., all in a gray, steaming fog in which the giant buildings of the city look ghostly. The dead Emperor lies in his magnificent sarcophagus in the cathedral of the Peter and Paul Fortress, a sky of silver brocade and ermine stretching over him. The Emperor's cloak covers his figure. The head is free. The face is haggard and sunken, the complexion almost brown, the hair on the head thin, the features sharp, furrowed with suffering. It is as if even the otherwise powerful forehead has slumped, the head looks small, as if trying to hide in all the splendor that surrounds it. The air is filled with incense and the litany of the praying priests resounds incessantly. The people flock to the coffin and kiss the image of the saint lying on the dead Emperor's chest, and outside the sad sky weeps over the city and over all Russia.

St. Petersburg, 20 November 1894.

The funeral of the late Emperor took place today. It was a moving ceremony, only a little monotonous due to the length of the action. The ceremony lasted two and a half hours. At 10:30 we gathered in Peter and Paul Cathedral, in the center of which the sarcophagus with the body is laid out. The church is not large and the thousands who attended the ceremony were crowded together, unable to move during the whole time. The numerous clergy in magnificent white silver brocade robes surrounded the coffin. The famous choir sang in the most moving manner, never have I heard more beautiful singing, the basses of the depth of an organ and in between wailing soft soprano voices. Incense fills the room and rises in blue clouds to the high vault. Again and again the priest raises his deep voice to implore God for peace for the deceased, and rhythmically the choir falls into the closing words.

Finally the family takes leave of the deceased. First the Empress-dowager, then the young Emperor, then all the grand dukes and grand duchesses approach the coffin and kiss the dead man on the forehead. Then the coffin is closed and lifted off the sarcophagus by the Emperor and the Grand Duchesses and carried to where it is to be lowered into the tomb. The Emperor himself puts the ermine cloak over the coffin, and slowly it sinks into the depths. The crowd at the exit was terrifying.

In the afternoon we had the imposing spectacle of the return of the crown jewels to the Winter Palace, fifteen four-horse carriages, all gilded and lined with scarlet velvet, led the jewels back. All the carriages were harnessed to white horses with rich golden harnesses and led by four people in long, gold-embroidered scarlet coats on golden reins. The procession is opened by a squadron of the Chevalier garde, all mounted on horses, with the steed and the flying double eagle on the golden helmet. The same squadron closes the procession. The densely packed people let this fabulously beautiful procession pass by in silence. The unfolding of the splendor here is indescribable. All dimensions are gigantic. The width of the streets, where palace follows palace, is in harmony with the size of the open spaces. You can get an idea of the Winter Palace, where we live, if I tell you that among other things there is a hall here where three thousand people can dine at small tables during large festivities. Above all these huge masses lies a dense, gray fog that prevents any distant view. We remain here until after the wedding, which takes place on the 26th.

St. Petersburg, 21 November 1894.

We went to the church again today for a big ceremony, this time held at the closed tomb. It was the last one and I can say: thank God. In the long run, these ceremonies are tiring and start to seem theatrical. The essence gets lost too much under external pomp and pretense. A silent prayer would be more uplifting.

This afternoon I came for the first time a little into the city, but I didn't get a proper impression yet. It's all too massive and large, and everything is shrouded in the eternal thick fog that even London couldn't exhibit more beautifully.

St. Petersburg, 23 November 1894.

We used today to see two sights of Petersburg, St. Isaac's Church and the Stables. The former is a marvel building in its own right. It is situated on the most beautiful open square in the city, which it towers high above with its gilded dome. Since the whole of Petersburg stands on marshy ground, it has been necessary to create a firm foundation for all the buildings by driving innumerable tree trunks into the ground. To support the magnificent building of St. Isaac's Church, a whole forest of mast trees must have been necessary. Wide granite steps lead up to the platform on which it rises. The two main entrances to the north and south are formed by two peristyles supported by columns. These columns are fifty-six feet high and seven feet thick, and are each composed of a single block of granite polished to the smoothness of marble. They rest on bronze bases and support a bronze Corinthian capital. Throughout, the entire church is built of granite, marble and ore, unlike most of the rest of St. Petersburg's colossal buildings, almost all of which are built up of brick. Massive bronze doors with rich skin relief work lead into the interior of the church, which in its whole arrangement is reminiscent of St. Peter's in Rome. Only there the dome is twice the size as here. In accordance with the Byzantine style, here the dome is narrow and high in relation to the substructure, in hemispherical form. Its windows, placed at height, allow only a subdued light to enter the room; the eye must first get used to the semi-darkness, and in this mystical light, which, by the way, is loved in all Russian churches, the splendor of the material used is not fully appreciated. As prescribed by the Greek rite, the Holy of Holies is separated from the rest of the church by the iconostasis, which narrows the space. In the iconostasis, two colossal columns of polished lapis lazuli stand first of all at the imperial gate, and next to them six such columns of malachite. Between them are representations of saints in the most beautiful mosaic that I remember to have seen. A sacristan, who immediately took possession of us and shone a burning wax light in front of us, also led us into the Holy of Holies itself, where a model of the church, six feet high and made of gold, stands. The background is completed by a window painting depicting the Greek Christ in the prescribed posture. The Blessed Sacrament is treated as such only during the celebration of Mass; once the service is over, it loses all claim to special consideration, usually used by the priests as a checkroom. Worthy of admiration are the many church chandeliers, made of solid silver, which stand all around the nave, some of them far above man-height. The whole building, executed by Emperor Nicholas I, is probably the most beautiful Greek Catholic church in existence.

In the Marstall we saw an endless row of gilded splendid carriages, mostly from the time of Catherine II, partly painted by Boucher and Pesne and richly decorated with precious stones, then the ceremonial carriages for the transport of the regalia, ten of which are quite the same, formed of heavily gilded silver sheet and red velvet. In the midst of this golden splendor, truly beguiling, stands the simple coupe of Emperor Alexander II, the entire back of which is shattered by the bomb that crept under the carriage without injuring the Emperor, who fell victim to only the second bomb. A serious reminder for all future rulers!

St. Petersburg, 24 November 1894.

We visited the local riding school this morning, to which we arrived after driving astray for almost an hour. The footmen assigned to us are the most stupendous thing imaginable; mine has never once put me in the right place. Horses and coachmen are treated with great ruthlessness here. No one attending a diner or an evening party thinks of sending the carriage home, it simply stops in the street, the coachman, wrapped in his long fur, sleeps on the buckboard by leaning his head against the edge of the carriage box, and the horses stand motionless with their heads bowed.

Of the draconian severity with which the police are handled here, I have experienced an example. One fine day I had a new coachman, and when I asked about the old one, my footman simply replied that he had been sent away. The next day I read the following in the newspaper under the heading: *Daily order of the city captain*: "The temporary driver of the stables office Ivan etc. was found drunk at night in the stables building. When confronted, he gave an impudent answer. He was punished with fourteen days of arrest, eight days of which were to be served with bread and water, and he was forbidden to stay in Petersburg for two years. The haulier who provided this coachman is to be fined fifty rubles." – I have no doubt that this Ivan was my coachman, who so criminally misused the free time I left him.

Today, as I said, we drove around for almost an hour, my footman took me to all kinds of riding tracks, just not the right one, we ended up at a wooden yard, but finally arrived at the riding track after endless questions. Here we saw a detachment of officers commanded there riding in the very beautiful, spacious track. The performance was, in our opinion, quite poor. The horse material was pitiful. The jumping over hurdles and stone walls was poor. Not a single horse went over the obstacles in a smooth jump, almost all of them stumbled and made restrained jumps. The tempos were unbalanced, the distances were not kept at all, the riders' seat was loose, no influence of the thighs was noticeable at all. Then we saw the Cossack officers riding, all of them riding the high Tatar saddles, on which the rider hovers over the horse standing in the stirrups. The bridle is the simple snaffle, as a result all horses walk with the nose in the air and step under themselves at a trot. The walk, where the horse lets go, is spacious, canter is not ridden, only walk, trot and careen. Again, jumping over the low hurdle was highly deficient. Often the horse clipping in front of the obstacle had to be brought over by lashes with the leather Cossack whip that every rider carries on his fist strap. Then another frame was brought into the track, on which finger-thick willow rods were pinned. The officers rode past the frame one by one, starting from the spot on the right, and it was a matter of cutting one of the rods with the saber as they rode past. Most succeeded in this maneuver, some of the rods were smooth as if cut with a razor. The commander of the riding school, who only a few weeks ago returned from Hanover, where he had attended a course at our riding school, told us that he had had eighteen horses with their ears cut off last year. If the hair-sharp saber is not wielded very skillfully, such a mishap is easily explained. We then saw a few, probably specially selected people, vaulting on old school horses. They did their thing very well, one of them could have immediately appeared in the circus as a jockey rider.

After the performance was over, I drove to the Kazan Cathedral, famous for its immense wealth of sterling silver. The church, like St. Isaac's Cathedral, built in the Byzantine style, is located in an open square on Nevsky Prospekt, the largest street in Petersburg. It is flanked on both sides by an open semicircular colonnade, an imitation of the great colonnade of St. Peter's in Rome. Inside, the Russians' predilection for columns has been satisfied, which is also evident everywhere in the private and public profane buildings, the majority of which show column arrangements, admittedly made of brick and plastered with lime. Inside this church there are some forty granite columns of one piece. Since there was no room for them, and although there is nothing for the columns to support but their own capitals, they were placed in a double row.

I saw the famous image of the Mother of God of Kazan, covered with jewels and precious stones, in front of which there are always some people on their knees, with their foreheads touching the tiles of the floor. On the columns hang a number of conquered French flags, also the captured marshal's baton of

Marshal Davoust and a number of keys of conquered cities. On a side wall there is a simple tomb of Field Marshal Kutusoff. The iconostasis decorated with magnificent images and of immense size, is made almost entirely of chased silver. A massive silver barrier, long and high enough for a moderate bridge, separates it from the inner church space. Tall, silver church chandeliers stand all around, with wax lights burning on them from the thinness of a pencil to the thickness of an arm. The faithful place them there and measure the strength of them according to the measure of their means and – according to the greatness of their request to the Holy Mother of God.

In order to take advantage of the few hours, which with a pale glow indicate the short Petersburg day, I gave up breakfast and went to the Hermitage, the largest sight in Petersburg. Probably in no other place in the world are so many and valuable art treasures united in such a small space as here. Here the most famous masterpieces of painting and sculpture of all countries are distributed in an immense series of rooms and halls, each of which is itself a work of art in beauty and taste. There is no famous painter who is not represented here by his most exquisite creations. Rubens, Raphael, Titian, van Dyk, Ruisdael, Teniers, Wouwerman, Corregio and Murillo fill entire halls; unfortunately, the lighting is so poor that almost none of the uplifting masterpieces can be fully appreciated. At 2 o'clock it was already so dark that almost nothing could be seen, the foggy, gray sky suffocating all light. I did not see the part of the collections that includes the antiquities, the mosaics, jewels and cut stones, I could not get away from the pictures. The excavations of Kerch in the Crimea, where Greek culture flourished four hundred years before Christ, until the wave of the Scythians and the Tatar hordes washed it away, are also said to be very strange.

CABINET ORDER.

I have promoted you to Colonel today and it gives me pleasure to announce this to you.

New Palace, 18 August 1895.

Wilhelm R.

To My Serving Wing Adjutant, Lieutenant Colonel v. Moltke, Commander of the Castle Guard Company.

Szczecin, 7 September 1895.

We have just come from the castle, where we had maneuver meetings. This life, tiring as it is, agrees with me extraordinarily well. It always seems to me as if my strength only develops when greater demands are placed on it, and that comforts me again with regard to the future; I still hope to be able to stand my ground when the time comes.

On board S.M. yacht "Hohenzollern," 14 September 1895.

On October 15, I will be back on duty, and then I will start traveling again immediately. To Urville near Metz, where a church will be consecrated, and to Wörth, where a monument to Emperor Frederick will be unveiled.

Rominten hunting lodge, 27 September 1895.

I am writing you just a few words to tell you that I am leaving for Petersburg tomorrow morning. The Emperor sends me with a handwritten letter to the Emperor of Russia.

St. Petersburg, 2 October 1895.

I arrived here on September 29th. Since the journey came as a complete surprise to me and I had no belongings with me, I had requisitioned my uniform and passport by telegraph from Berlin. The items arrived on the same train as I was traveling on and were handed over to me at the train station in Trakehnen. At the Russian border station Wirballen my arrival was announced, I was received very politely by the chief of the customs office and let through without any difficulties.

The same gentleman had reserved a sleeping *coupé* for me, which, as he told me, had already been sold, but from which the owner had been put out without further ado, a procedure which, while very pleasant for the one who benefits from it, must be equally unpleasant for the one who has to suffer from it. Since the evictee was and remained unknown to me, I slept with a fairly calm conscience on the comfortable sofa bed of the wide carriage, which provided an excellent resting place given the very slow speed of the Russian train. I left Rominten at 9 a.m. and Trakehnen at 11:30 a.m. The next day at 12 noon the train arrived in Petersburg with a one-hour delay according to the schedule. At the station I found our ambassador, Prince Radolin, and the "military attaché," Captain Lauenstein, who had been waiting for me for a full hour. The former told me that I had been accommodated by the Imperial Russian Court Marshal's Office in the Hotel d'Europe as a guest of His Majesty, and that court carriages and footman had been placed at my disposal.

I now drove to my hotel, where I found a nice apartment consisting of an anteroom, salon and bedroom ready for me, – then to our Embassy to pay my visit there and to stay there for breakfast. In the evening I went to the opera with Lauenstein. The huge house, just newly restored, makes a splendid impression, it is decorated in white and gold, curtains and draperies of blue damask. The ballet *Copelia* was given, and since the Russians are particularly fond of ballet, great importance is attached to equipment and personnel. Never have I seen a more appreciative audience. Every performance was greeted with storms of applause, and many solo dances had to be repeated.

On September 30, the following day, I was scheduled for an audience with His Majesty the Tsar at 11 o'clock in the morning. I had already telegraphed the day before to the adjutant of Grand Duke Vladimir, the only member of the imperial household present here at the moment, and asked to be allowed to report to His Imperial Highness after my audience. Highness after my audience. The Grand Duke lives in a special palace, also in Tsarskoe Selo, where the Emperor resides. I left on the train that left here at 10 o'clock. It takes thirty minutes, as from Berlin to Potsdam. At the station, the Grand Duke's aide-de-camp, Count Versen, received me and told me that His Imperial Highness wanted to see me and asked me to come to his residence. Highness wanted to receive me and asked me to have breakfast with him. Now I drove to the small Alexander Palace, located about ten minutes from the station, where His Majesty lives, while the large palace, built by the Empress Catherine in the Baroque style, is empty. I was immediately received by the court marshal Count Benckendorff and immediately led through a series of rooms, halls and corridors to the Emperor's antechamber. As we passed through a narrow corridor, at the entrance of which two huge, pitch-black Moors in oriental costume and armed to the teeth stood guard, a door opened just as we were passing, and the Emperor appeared in a white piqué jacket, about to reach the opposite door. As soon as he caught sight of us, he quickly pulled the door closed again, and we made our deep bow to the doorway!

Now we reached the anteroom, in the middle of which, just as in the adjutant's room in Berlin, stood a billiard table, and in which a short, fat gentleman with a large roll of drawings under his arm was waiting for the moment when he would be admitted to the lecture. He was introduced to me by the court marshal as the Minister of the Navy.

After a few minutes of waiting, I was announced to His Majesty by a valet, whom Count Benckendorff had commissioned to do so. There was neither a general nor a wing adjutant to be seen. The Emperor is said to live pretty much without any military surroundings; I heard that in the palace, apart from the Court Marshal, only the Chief Stable Master and the commander of the guard are present.

I now entered, rather burdened, His Majesty's study. I was, of course, in parade dress, had the helmet and saber in one hand, the letter from our Emperor in the other, and under my arm a rolled-up picture, executed according to our Emperor's design by Professor Knackfuß and reproduced in lithography. I was to hand over this picture at the same time as the letter. The Tsar immediately approached me with an outstretched hand and told me: "I am glad to see you here, we already know each other." – After I had concentrated, not without difficulty, all my belongings, to which the removed glove of the right hand was added, in the left, I was able to accept the hand that was graciously offered to me.

I then handed over the letter and then gave an explanation of the picture, which His Majesty himself helped me to roll up on a table. The picture shows a group of female figures in ancient costume, in the manner of the Valkyries, standing on a rocky outcrop and looking out over a plain covered with flourishing cities, rivers with ships and tilled fields. They represent the European states. In the foreground Germany, closely nestled to it Russia, to the side France, behind Austria, Italy, England, etc. In front of them stands, with one hand pointing into the distance, the flaming sword in the other, the cherub of war, above the group hovers, surrounded by rays, the cross. Behind the flourishing landscape, which symbolizes trade and commerce, European culture and morality, one sees the smoke of a burning city. The plume is threatening in thick clouds that gather into the shape of a dragon. From the smoke rises the image of Buddha, who looks with stare, cold eyes at the destruction.

The meaning of the whole is the existential struggle of the white and yellow race dawning in the future. The idea for the picture came to His Majesty when, at the time of the conclusion of the peace preliminaries between China and Japan, there was a danger that the immense mass of the Chinese Empire, over whose development Japan was seeking to gain a decisive influence, might be organized and brought into ferment by this active country striving for expansive development, and that the surge of the yellow race would then pour over Europe with devastating effect. Under the picture, written by the hand of the Emperor, are the words: "Peoples of Europe, preserve your most sacred possessions." – I did not fail to add, after giving the explanation, that this danger was for the time being restrained by the wisdom of the policy and joint action of Russia, Germany and France. The Emperor took a lively interest in the drawing, and I had to explain to him all the details. I pointed out how, in the silhouettes of the cities, the dome of the Orthodox church stood out next to the tower of the Protestant cathedral, and when the Emperor, pointing to a city, asked if that was to be Moscow, I replied that, although I did not know whether His Majesty, my most gracious Lord, had had that very city in mind, Moscow would certainly be as threatened as any other European city.

After inspecting the picture, the Emperor had the grace to dignify me with a longer conversation, and then gave me the order to return the letter of reply to our Emperor. After the Emperor had bid me farewell in the most gracious manner, he said to me: "You would certainly like to see the Empress, so let me announce you to her." As I was serving my way backwards out of the door, I lost a glove, which was brought to me by the valet. A superstitious person might have seen in this an omen, which God and all the saints want to prevent.

I now had myself announced to Her Majesty. After a short time, I was led to the Empress, who received me all alone. There was no lady present here either, and the registration was also done by a valet. The Empress looked splendid. She had fresh colors, radiant Madonna eyes and looked like a true Empress in her wrinkled mourning dress. She talked to me in a very friendly manner, I had to tell her about the Emperor from Rominten, about the Empress and the children, and as she gave me her hand in farewell, I took it to my lips with the feeling that the Russians can be grateful to their Orthodox God that he has called such an angel of light to the throne of the Tsarist empire.

From here I drove to the palace of Grand Duke Vladimir, where Versen received me and immediately led me to His Imperial Highness, who greeted me most kindly and talked with me for about half an hour. We then went to breakfast, which was attended not only by the Grand Duke, Versen and myself, but also by a Russian with an unpronounceable name. His Imperial Highness is a very passionate hunter and knew all the hunting grounds of Germany, had often shot deer in Rominten and the Schorfheide in the past and could not suppress a quiet regret that these times were now over. He also had the antlers of the last deer he shot brought in, which I could sincerely admire, since they were indeed capital.

After breakfast, at which only German was spoken, the Grand Duke dismissed me with the words: "I hope to see you before you leave. That he was serious about this is proven by a telegram that has just been brought to me: "*Voulez-vous venir diner chez moi* *demain jeudi par trains sept heures.*[*] Overskirt, cap. Vladimir." – A few moments later I received a telegram from Court Marshal Benckendorff : *"L'Empereur vous recevra demain jeudi a onzes heures. Train a dix heures."*[†] – So tomorrow, Thursday, I will receive my letter of reply, and can leave here tomorrow evening at 12 o'clock.

After returning by train from Tsarskoye Selo, I went to our embassy, from where I addressed a two-and-a-half-sheet telegram to our Emperor, on which the cipher writers had to work for over two hours. On Tuesday I went again to Tsarskoye Selo to accept an invitation from Count Versen to breakfast. We had a very nice breakfast, and then he let loose and drove me on an almost two-hour tour of the magnificent parks of Tsarskoye Selo.

A tremendous amount of effort has been expended on the creation of the extensive grounds. The terrain is swampy throughout, only on individual solid islands, which lie in the marshy meadow soil, grow beautiful groups of trees, which admittedly had already lost their foliage almost throughout. All paths (and they are miles long wide roads, flanked by double oak avenues) are filled up. As soon as you get off the path, you sink into the swamp.

Nevertheless, the whole, to which many extended water levels give variety, makes a scenic picture. One passes many larger and smaller castles, the barracks of the guard cavalry regiments, Chinese building complexes where revenge-blocking dragons sit on the roofs and old retired generals in the cottages eating the mercy bread of the Tsar. The focal point is the grand palace of Empress Catherine, who, like Peter the Great had stomped Petersburg, in turn had stomped Tsarskoye Selo out of the swamp. The front of the mighty palace is probably twice as long as that of the New Palace. The low roof is supported by thick white columns, between which enormous caryatids, all gilded, in the form of the

---

[*] "Would you like to come to my house for dinner tomorrow Thursday by seven o'clock train."

[†] "The Emperor will receive you tomorrow Thursday at eleven o'clock. Train at ten o'clock."

atlas supporting the world, bend under the weight of the window ledges. Two massive, soaring pediments interrupt the elongated line of the front, which runs out on either side into circular wings, one of which is adjoined by the Greek church with its many onion-shaped domes and tall, blue-painted windows. The domes, studded with thick gold bronze, gleam in the sun, and the sky-blue windows emerge somewhat indiscreetly from the marble-white walls. All window and door surrounds of the castle are baroque curved and gilded. Thus the whole thing lies there in massive power, like a ukase turned to stone of the autocratic Empress who created it.

From there we drove to Paulowsk's Palace, built by the unfortunate Emperor Paul, who had to breathe his last under the throttling sash of General von Benningsen. This palace, built in an almost closed circle, is just as simple, almost timidly bent together, as that of the mother challengingly demanding, broad and straight unloaded. The surroundings are also quite different. If there wide areas spread out, straight roads open radiant views or cross each other mathematically at right angles, the palace of Emperor Paul lies in the middle of a tall spruce forest. No hand has modeled this forest floor; it bears its tall trunks and its sprawling undergrowth as nature's gardener instructs it, and right through the middle of this forest, soft but well-maintained paths nestle against the undulating ground elevations to which the terrain here rises. It is a delightful ride through this primeval forest, sometimes along quiet forest lakes, sometimes over modest wooden bridges that skillfully lead over rushing water. In their way, these comfortable paths that lead through the middle of a forest, in whose darkness and tangle it is almost impossible to cross, are as surprising as the fjords of Norway, on which one drives smoothly and comfortably right into the middle of the high mountains.

The oldest railroad in Russia leads from Pavlovsk via Tsarskoye Selo to Petersburg. It is the fourth railroad ever built in Europe and is unique in that its track width is even wider than that of the other Russian railroads. The wooden station buildings, the wooden platforms, the infinitely wide carriages equipped with rickety windows and dirty, tattered sofa seats give the impression that nothing has been changed or repaired since the construction of the railroad. And yet this is the busiest railroad, for in the summer half of Petersburg flocks out here every afternoon to stroll along the dry paths under the dewy old trees or to sit in front of the huge wooden bandstand where concerts are given daily by the best bandmasters. It was five minutes to 3 o'clock when we stopped in front of the station building, which looks something like a Polish oxen stable. At 3 o'clock the train left, taking me back to Petersburg.

Yesterday evening I had another dinner of our embassy lords, but this time we were among ourselves. Count Pückler, you know him, and Herr v. Romberg have rented a dacha together on the islands on the other side of the Neva, in whose small rooms they lead a comfortable summer life in peaceful marriage. The constantly good weather allows them to stay outside, although the season is long over. Both of them had invited me to dine in their hut in the evening, and in addition to me, Lauenstein and the first embassy councilor, a Herr von Tschirschky, were there. Lauenstein picked me up, and we drove out in my court car. In spite of the insane speed at which everything travels here, and especially the imperial carriages, it took us over half an hour to get out. The islands lie enclosed by the many-armed Newa estuary and are kept park–like throughout. Between the trees are scattered the small dachas, where in the summer everything that has the means to do so settles. Here, on the long, bright summer evenings, the parade of the Petersburg world takes place, which culminates in everyone driving to a certain point, a wide traffic circle, which forms the western tip of the last island. Here, wagon after wagon stops crowded together and everything looks out over a wide expanse of water framed by trees, and on one side of which a dumpy wooden house draws a melancholy silhouette in the desolate landscape, and everything waits for the moment when the ball of the sun, having made its long journey across the northern summer sky, has disappeared behind the shining expanse of water. As soon as the last spark has faded away, the tangle of wagons twirls apart and everyone drives dully home.

This morning I went to the Peter and Paul Cathedral and laid a wreath on the sarcophagus of the late Emperor Alexander III. I had a wreath made entirely of laurel leaves with a large black and silver ribbon, on one of which I had a W made of laurel leaves and on the other a crown. *De la part de Sa Majeste l'Empereur d'Allemagne** – as I told the commander of the fortress. The church was full of people who stared at me in amazement in my Prussian uniform.

Report on the farewell audience with His Majesty the Emperor of Russia on 3 October 1895.

St. Petersburg, 3 October 1895.

On the morning of October 2, I received a telegram from Count Benckendorff, Marshal of the Supreme Court, informing me that His Majesty the Emperor intended to receive me in Tsarskoye Selo on the following day, at 11 o'clock in the morning.

I went with the so-called court train leaving Petersburg at 10 o'clock on October 3 to Tsarskoye Selo, where a carriage was waiting for me. Again – as in my first audience – I was led by Count Benckendorff to the anteroom of His Majesty when I arrived at the Alexander Palace and was immediately announced to the Most High. In the antechamber I found the Minister of the Interior and some generals who had been ordered to speak and to whom I was introduced by Count Benckendorff. After a few minutes, I was ordered to come in to see His Majesty.

The Emperor met me in the most gracious manner, shook my hand and asked me how I liked Petersburg. Then the Emperor asked about His Majesty and was told about His Majesty's stay in Rominten. After the conversation had turned to hunting for a while, I had the opportunity to inform His Majesty that I had been to the Peter and Paul Cathedral yesterday and had laid a wreath there on behalf of His Majesty on the tombstone of the Blessed Emperor Alexander III, which obviously touched His Majesty in a pleasant way.

Then the Emperor, using the French language, while until then He had spoken German, said: "*Maintenant j'ai encore quelques*

---

* "On behalf of His Majesty the Emperor of Germany."

mots a vous dire, mais il me faut parler francais, parce que en allemand je ne peux pas exprimer ce que j'ai a vous dire."* His Majesty then sat down at the desk in His study and invited me to sit next to Him on a chair.

The Emperor then said something like the following, which I noted down immediately after the end of the audience: "Your Majesty is concerned about the presence of my Minister Lobanoff in France. He had asked me for leave to go to the baths and telegraphed me from there asking whether I would allow him to attend the revue, which interested him very much. I answered that I had nothing against it. When he left, I had given him the order to have a calming effect on the French. Now that I have seen and have been reminded by Your Majesty's letter that, on the contrary, French chauvinism has been vividly aroused, I have again ordered Lobanoff by telegraph (and at the last word His Majesty energetically struck the tabletop with his forefinger) not only to refrain from any demonstrative appearance, but also to cool down French chauvinism where it comes up against him. I have also ordered him to seek an audience with Your Majesty the Emperor on his return journey, and I leave it up to him whether he wants to receive him. If he receives him, he will hear from his mouth the same as I am telling you now. I was not sufficiently aware of how easily the French catch fire. Had I known and been able to foresee this, I would not have given Lobanoff or Dragomirov permission to go to France, and I shall be more careful with my masters in the future."

His Majesty then spoke about the French press, commented on how much mischief the press had already caused in the world, and then continued: "I suspect that during the silence of his hunting stay, when none of his ministers were with him, His Majesty was aroused by the reading of the newspaper clippings, and I can fully understand this. Reading the news from France only in this form, I can imagine that the news from there must be alarming. I myself have forbidden myself the newspaper clippings, which one also

---

* "Now I have a few more words to say to you, but I have to speak French, because in German I can't express what I have to say to you."

wanted to present to me at first. I am afraid that through them I will only get knowledge of a certain direction, which is in the hands of the one who selects and prepares the clippings. Instead, I read a German newspaper (I think it is the *Kölnische*, which I at least saw lying in His Majesty's room), a French one – the *Temps* – , an English one and a Russian one, – the latter not gladly, because they are all useless, and by listening to the different voices, I try to form my own judgment. But I don't attach too much importance to the newspapers, because I know how they are made. There sits some Jew who makes his business by inciting the passions of the peoples against each other, and the people, mostly without their own political judgment, stick to the phrase. That is why I will never release the Russian press as long as I live. The Russian press shall write only what I want (and at this His Majesty again poked the table with his index finger), and in the whole country only my will may prevail."

His Majesty then explained how the Russo-Turkish War was only due to the agitation of the press, and how this is also now spoiling relations between Germany and Russia and France and embittering feelings, and then said: "There has been no war between Germany and Russia for a hundred and fifty years. Germany has fought with about all her neighbors except us, and it is also an absurdity to think of a war between Germany and Russia, since these two countries have no conflicting interests at all."

Then His Majesty told that he was constantly receiving reports from the German-Russian border districts, from which he was pleased to see that the relationship between the troops on both sides of the border was excellent. The officers were visiting each other, inviting each other and maintaining good comradeship. All news about which he was sincerely pleased. Here, at least, there was no sign of the animosity that was spreading in the press.

I now remarked: "Your Majesty will graciously allow me to come back to the fact that, according to the sentiments expressed by Your Majesty, we certainly have no reason to be concerned about Russia. What we must fear, however, is the easily excited temper of the French nation, which is naturally heated still more by the presence of the Russian generals and statesmen." The Emperor replied, "I know it, but tell the Emperor that I will maintain the peace! For the time being, the French have Madagascar on their hands. They can't help doing this thing for the sake of honor. They must demand new credits and send new troops. This will certainly keep them busy for another year, so long they can think of nothing else. And when the year is over, I guarantee Your Majesty that they will be calm and will continue to be calm. It is extremely important to me that we (Germany and Russia) maintain good relations with each other. We are still far behind you, have infinitely much to do in the interior. We produce mainly grain, you industrial goods, which we must exchange. A war between us would bring infinite misery to both peoples."

I said: "Your Majesty knows my most gracious Lord well enough to know that He sees nothing else in His life's work than to enable His people to develop peacefully." The Emperor replied: "I know that, and I can assure you that I, too, do not want to know anything about war, and will strive to maintain peace until the end of my life. I will continue in the peaceful policy of my late father."

Returning to Your Majesty's letter, the Emperor then said: "Your Majesty thinks that, as a result of the war, I will not know anything about war. Majesty thinks that, as a result of the year of mourning, I would have no opportunity to orient myself sufficiently. Quite the opposite is the case. Precisely because I can live so quietly, I have been able to occupy myself in detail with all the circumstances of my empire and politics, and I believe I can give myself the testimony that I have worked diligently and, above all, have striven to form my own unbiased judgment. I know what we still lack, and I want peaceful work in the country; I do not want war and will never admit it. I have also explained all this to His Majesty in my letter, but I am anxious that you repeat it to him verbally as well."

I replied that, after all that His Majesty had had the grace to tell me, I considered myself very fortunate to be able to convey the sentiments expressed to His Majesty, my Lord and Emperor.

His Majesty then rose and, returning to the German language, offered me the warmest greetings to Your Majesty and also those of the Empress to both Majesties. Thereupon, Their Majesties took leave of me with a strong handshake.

The audience had lasted a little over half an hour.

In deepest reverence I remain as
Your Majesty's
most subservient
v. Moltke,
Colonel and Wing Adjutant.

Visit of H. M. the Emperor to Prince Bismarck in Friedrichsruh on December 16, 1895.

On December 16, 1895, Se. Majesty the Emperor left Kiel in the morning for Altona, where the Blohm & Voß shipyard was visited, and then had breakfast with the Commanding General of the IX Army Corps, Count Waldersee. At 4 o'clock in the afternoon, His Majesty departed again from Altona, and at 5 o'clock the special imperial train stopped at Friedrichsruh. Prince Bismarck awaited the arrival of His Majesty. In overcoat and helmet, without a topcoat, the rangy figure of the Chancellor of the Old Reich stood on the platform. The Emperor quickly got off the train and greeted the Prince with a hearty handshake, he made him put on his coat, and after a short greeting of the entourage and the gentlemen who had appeared with the Prince, Count Rantzau and Professor Schwenninger, we all walked toward the house. Countess Rantzau was standing in the doorway and her two youngest sons in the anteroom.

The Emperor had brought Wislicenus' illustrated work on the German fleet for the Prince, and while he opened it to explain the drawings to the Prince, we retired to the next room. The monarch and the chancellor of the old empire remained alone. They sat opposite each other, each in a large armchair at the round table of the small salon, the large folder with the drawings of the ships lying between them. We heard nothing of what was said there for about three quarters of an hour; we soon got into lively conversation with the Countess Rantzau. So the time passed quickly, until at 6 o'clock it was announced that dinner was served. The Emperor gave Countess Rantzau his arm to lead her into the adjoining dining room, where we all followed. There were twelve of us at the table. At its head sat the Emperor, on his left the

Prince, on his right the Countess Rantzau. Then followed, on the side of the Prince, General von Plessen, Admiral von Senden, Kalckstein, Schwenninger, on the side of the Countess, Excellency von Lucanus, Lyncker, Dr. Leuthold, myself. At the lower end of the table sat Count Rantzau. The dinner was good, the wines excellent. The conversation revolved around everyday topics. Now and then the Emperor addressed one of the gentlemen sitting below or drank to one of them. As the champagne was poured, the prince said that he had once spoken to Frederick William IV about his ministers at the time and had told the king that the ministers drank too little champagne, that they had too little rocket fuel in them. For dessert, a white Italian wine was given, somewhat reminiscent of Château d'Yquem in taste, which the Prince said he received as a gift from Crispi every year. He then added : "He never forgets me a year, we are both such old buccaneers."

After the table was lifted, we gathered again in the small salon, cigars were served, and the Prince spoke with various gentlemen of the entourage. The Emperor had presented him with a bouquet of lilacs and lilies of the valley on his arrival, which the prince now took in his hand again, smelled it, and expressed his delight at the fresh flowers. He then spoke of the Emperor's appearance, saying that he looked a little affected, and then said, "Your Majesty must have been annoyed with his ministers. After all, a king could live much more quietly if he had no ministers, but sometimes it is quite good when the tide comes in and when there is a dike like that." He then turned to Colonel von Kalckstein and asked him where he had stood during the campaign, and when he learned that Kalckstein had been with the i . Garde-Landwehr-Regiment, he asked how the people had been, whether they had gone willingly, and how they had done in battle. He recalled with pleasure the splendid apparitions of the Guards-Landwehr who had stood guard at the Seine bridge and to whom the little Frenchmen had looked up with shy amazement.

In the meantime, the Prince's long *meerschaum* pipe had been brought, he sat down in an armchair at the table, took the large amber mouthpiece between his lips and lit it on the match that Professor Schwenninger had ready. The Emperor, who was sitting in the sofa on the other side of the table, said to me that I would like to sit down next to the prince and tell him something about the Tsar. I now sat down on a chair opposite the Prince and told him that His Majesty had sent me to Petersburg some time ago to present the picture of Professor Knackfuß to the Tsar, and that I had found that the Emperor had developed very much to his advantage. The Prince very soon interrupted me with the question: "What kind of a man is the Tsar? I mean, would he be able to make up his mind to pull off the leather?" At this he made a hand gesture as if he were about to draw his sword. I replied that in my opinion the Tsar was mainly a man of the mind, whereupon the prince said: "He will not keep his company in order with that. Does he at least have the will to be a ruler?" I then told how, on occasion of the conversation which the Tsar granted me, the conversation had come to the press, and how the Emperor had said: "I will not release the Russian press as long as I live. A free press does the greatest harm. The Russian press shall write only what I want, and in the whole country only one will shall prevail, and that is mine." The prince then said, "I like that, and he does very well to do so, for if he first permits public discussion, he will soon face a shoreless sea. For the Russian peasant the Tsar, the little father, must remain a demigod, almost a god. I know Russia and its people, I have been there for full three years and have looked around. If you wanted to alienate the sixty million Russians from their Tsar, they would soon go mad."

After I had said that I feared the Tsar would not be the man to impose his will ruthlessly, the Prince asked about the Tsarina, whether she had any influence on him. I said that the Tsarina had made the best impression on me, that she had a decisive influence on her husband and that it was to be hoped that he would have a firm support in her. The prince then said: "I have also heard only good things about her."

Hereupon the prince came without transition to the Emperor Napoleon III. While the sentences came out of his mouth jerkily, in the manner of an engine expelling steam, he sucked violently at the pipe that kept going out in the intermissions. The powerful head was sharply illuminated by the lamp, and the enormous eyes gazed fixedly before him. He turned to no one in particular, but spoke straight out. The whole company was crowded together, all eyes were glued to his mouth, all senses were under the spell of his personality.

"I remember that when I was in Paris in 1856, – the Emperor Napoleon once summoned me and put to me the question – whether he should rule absolutely or constitutionally. I said to him: – 'As long as Your Majesty has the Guard, you can allow yourself the luxury of this experiment, – but when the flood comes, – then it is quite good to have a dam standing between you and the people. But as long as the guard is there, you can do the experiment.' – With the fifty thousand men of the Guard, Paris could be dominated, and with it France. These were all selected troops, tall, handsome people, who had put on the hat for Quer and who knew that they ruled Paris. The people were in a good position, – they could only lose if there was a change, – they could not be better off. When they walked in the street, they didn't avoid anyone, they always walked in twos – and didn't avoid a loaded wagon." The Emperor asked, "Who was in command of the Guard Corps at that time?" The prince replied, "It doesn't matter at all. The Emperor could rely on them under all circumstances. Who commanded them, – that does not matter at all. I remember that when I went to the lecture in those days, I sometimes used a forbidden way. When one of the little Frenchmen from the south stood at the post, I simply said: *'Le ministre de Prusse'*,[*] – but if one of the guardsmen was standing there, he would say to me: *'Cela m'est tout à fait égal'*."[†] – Everyone laughed, and the prince himself laughed heartily, his eyes wide open, his mouth just a little agape, as if amazed that he had made a joke.

The prince then continued: "Yes, – well, – as long as he had these fifty thousand guards, I told Napoleon, he could do the experiment. But it would be good if he had a wall of ministers around him to absorb the first blow. Otherwise the people would blame him for every bad weather, *c'est l'art de regner!*[‡] The

---

[*] "The Minister of Prussia."

[†] "I don't care about that at all."

[‡] "It is the art of governing."

Emperor was then already sickly, – he had no more right energy, – and then he felt also pressed by the predominant intelligence of the Empress. She was the most beautiful woman I have seen." The Emperor said she was still a beautiful woman, with all white hair and, despite her age, of impeccable, slim figure. Bismarck replied: "Yes, she was an energetic woman – much more energetic than the Emperor – I spoke to him as one speaks to a healthy, energetic person, – but he may not have quite believed me, – he was sickly and felt inferior to his wife." – I interjected that he must have done so wrongly, to which the prince replied, "If he had been unmarried, he would never have started the war against us."

Someone asked if the Emperor spoke German, to which the Prince replied, "He is said to have spoken it very well, but with me he never spoke a word other than French, and even if he once had to intercalate a German word, he pronounced it affectedly in French, for example, the word *Kreuzzeitung*."*

In the meantime, it had become 7:30, the departure had been set for 7 o'clock, and Count Rantzau reported to the Emperor that the time had already elapsed.

His Majesty stood up. The sabers were strapped on and farewells were taken. Someone asked the Prince about a charming plaster design for a Bismarck monument for Rudolstadt, which was on the table in the next room. On a pedestal the prince is depicted sitting as a student. The lithe figure leans casually in an armchair, one knee crossed over the other; his lowered right fist holds the bat. Youthful boldness coupled with assured energy speak from the figure. A large dog strives from below the pedestal up to its master, – the prince mentioned the name of the artist and told how he had been moved by this mainly to the assumption that the dog on the collar bears the name Ariel, – "and," he added, "that was the name of my dog at that time. At my age," he then continued, "one must endure the floods for better or for worse."

When someone told him that he could put up with the good ones, he said: "No, you can defend yourself against the bad ones,

---

* "*Cross Newspaper*." A Berlin-based newspaper with the emblem of an Iron Cross. (Publisher's note)

but you are powerless against the good ones."

The Emperor now took leave of the Countess Rantzau and, guided by the prince, went to the train. After repeatedly shaking hands with the old man, he boarded the train, which immediately began to move.

The prince stood tall, with his hand on his helmet in a military salute.

Palermo, 2 April 1896.

The old Count Roger of Normandy, who plunged his Nordic sword into this soil and made it sprout all the wonders of the noblest art, is now as familiar to me as if I had lived with him, and a few days ago I had no idea that he existed. What an appalling piecework is our knowledge, and how much precious time is wasted that would be better used to orient oneself in something about the times that created great things and the men who accomplished great things. Only then the true interest in a country, in a place, awakens, when one can think of it as the scene of events, imagine it as the great theater where the great drama of life has taken place. Then the old stones begin to speak, palaces and churches are rebuilt out of decaying walls in their long-since sunken glory, the gaze that encompasses the beginning and end of an epoch sharpens for the traces left by the course of mighty events, and the old princes, their satellites, their artists and scholars emerge tangibly clear from the darkness of the past.

Syracuse, 7 April 1896.

It is a horribly run-down generation that dwells on the sites of ancient glory. It must have been a different one then, because only powerful people could have been able to create such great things.

If Jehovah once said to Moses, "Take off your shoes, for the ground on which you tread is holy land, what shall we say of this harbor, of these rocky heights in which the history of the world has carved its imperishable traces!

Moscow, 18 May 1896.

Now we happily arrived here in pouring rain. The trip was very nice. For the rest, the tour itself is incredibly dull, one drives for thirty-six hours through swamps and stunted wood, sees wretched huts on flat terrain and could think that one is always in the same place, so much does one part of the vast landscape resemble another. Since this morning, when we passed Smolensk at 5 o'clock, it has rained, and in places a little snowed.

In Warsaw – yesterday morning – the honorable officers, a General Count Pushkin and an Admiral Prince Sharavskoy reported to Prince Henry. We changed trains here, because from there we got on the broad-gauge Russian railroad. The Russian special train, which was provided for us from there on, was comfortable and well furnished, but had terribly bad axles, so that we were terribly jolted. Now we are in our quarters, a pretty house owned and rented by a rich merchant. We live here: General v. Villaume, General v. Bülow, Klinckowström and myself. None of the owners is here. The prince lives diagonally across from us. Apart from water and dirt, I have seen nothing of Moscow so far.

Moscow, 20 May 1896.

We went to the Petrofsky Palace yesterday afternoon to report to the Emperor. It takes almost an hour to get there. The palace was the residence of Emperor Napoleon when he was in Moscow. The Emperor and the Empress both received our entire deputation. She has become much stronger, she looked very beautiful in a simple gray dress. The Emperor looked very miserable, pale and attacked, it may also be an exhausting time for him. Both majesties spoke to each one of us. Opposite the palace is the immense training field of the garrison, where at present the grenadier and part of the guard corps are in summer camp in barracks. In the evening there was to be a parade through the camp, in which we wanted to take part, followed by a great tattoo. But when we came out, everything was canceled because of the bad weather, so we went back without having accomplished anything.

Klinckowström and I used the free evening to quickly drive up to the Kremlin, from where one has a magnificent view of the much-curved Moskva and the city with its hundreds of church towers. This view is overwhelmingly beautiful, large and peculiar. It is only here that one sees what Moscow actually is. The Kremlin itself is a city of its own, with palaces and churches, gigantic in scale, as is only possible in such a giant empire as Russia.

Moscow, 22 May 1896.

You will have read about the ceremonial entry of the Majesties from Petrofsky Palace to the Kremlin in the newspapers long before this letter comes into your hands.

Fortunately, we had wonderful weather. It is as if summer arrived here in one fell swoop, beautiful warm sunshine and mild air. The splendor of the move-in was magnificent and imposing. We had to go out to Petrofsky as early as 11:30 in the morning, because later all the streets were closed. Life in the city was tremendous. Whole streams of people flooded through the streets and jammed in all the places where the train was to pass. The troops, about fifty thousand men, formed a line all the way to the Kremlin, eight kilometers long. Outside in the palace all the suites gathered, forming a retinue of about three hundred horsemen. We had to wait almost three hours before the procession started to move. At last the horses came on which we were to be mounted.

Now the golden carriages for the Empress and the Empress-Mother, decorated with precious stones, drove up, each drawn by eight white horses, and then the Emperor sat down on horseback. He also rode a white horse. Since we had to join the princes who immediately followed him, we saw only a part of the procession, so it was all the more interesting to see the troops and the people riding by. The former looked very good. The beautiful uniforms of the Chevalier garde, the *Garde a cheval*, the Grenadiers on horseback, the Cossack Guards wearing long scarlet skirts, the Ural Cossacks dressed in sky blue, with blue lances and ditto saddle pads, shone in the sun. Then came the Paulovsk Grenadier Regiment, with grenadier caps, in which, in memory of the

Emperor Paul, only people with blunt noses are recruited, finally the Preobratschenske Regiment, corresponding to our 1st Guards regiment.

The whole long street was thickly strewn with sand, on both sides stood the thousands who had flocked to watch. All the trees were full of people, it looked as if they were covered with huge caterpillars. All the people stood bare-headed and shouted a rolling hurrah to their little father. The enthusiasm shone from the people's eyes. Truly imposing was the view of the city street after we had passed the *Porta triumphalis*, where the Emperor was served bread and salt.

All windows full of people, everywhere erected large stands occupied by ladies in bright toilets, like giant greenhouses of white azaleas. All the houses in rich flag decorations, between which the shining procession moved slowly, but without stagnation. Twenty-four golden carriages, lined with red velvet, all harnessed with white horses, gold-glittering uniforms, a fairy-tale splendor. In front of the churches the clergy stood in overloaded splendor, steaming incense, in the center the great golden image of the saints of the church, flags and gold monstrances in their hands. It is impossible to describe all the pomp of this procession. In front of the gates of the Kremlin, the Metropolitan, surrounded by the highest ecclesiastical dignitaries, awaited the Majesties, who received the blessing here on the purple platform.

In the meantime we rode through the gate into the wide castle courtyard, where all the deputations from the wide empire were lined up. There stood Samoyeds from the icy climes of Finland, Kirghiz from the Urals, Tatars from the Don, from the Sea of Azov and the Caspian Sea the tribes had sent their delegates, from the steppes of Siberia they had come, the whole immense empire was represented here in a small space. The community leaders from the interior stood in long parted hair, broad peasant faces next to the brown, mischievous merchants from Kazan, it was an exhibition of the most diverse races of people, such as probably cannot be seen again in the world. The Emperor rode down the long front, then through the Holy Gate, where everything bared its head, into the interior of the Kremlin.

Here they dismounted from their horses, and now the Emperor

and Empress entered the two inner churches one after the other to perform a short devotion. This was the end of the ceremony for us. In the evening we went to the opera and then took a tour of the illuminated city. What illuminate means, I got to know only here. Thousands upon thousands of colored glass lights cover the buildings. Entire churches, built of light up to the highest spire, rise into the dark night sky, a fairy-like sight. We drove through the middle of the densely packed crowd. One hears no loud word, no shouting, no scolding. Everything makes way for the court car as a matter of course, many people take off their hats and make deep bows, while our car pushes them aside!

Moscow, 25 May 1896.

Now we have started to look at churches, galleries and other sights. I try to record my impressions, even if only in sketchy form, in my diary, but they come at me in such masses that it is difficult for me to bring order into them. We have seen at least part of the interior of the Kremlin. The Kremlin is a city in itself, with two large castles, barracks, arsenal, five or six churches, three monasteries, cavalier houses, stables, etc. The whole thing is surrounded by high, circular walls. The whole enclosed by high, cremated wall with five gates. Here is the Holy Gate, the Sspassky Gate, through which no Russian may pass with his head covered. In front of it there is always a crowd of pilgrims, poor people who come from all over the Tsarist empire to worship in the holy Moscow, and who cross themselves devoutly even in front of the Victoria on the gate. The men in rough coats, the women with felt-wounded legs, the pilgrim's stick in their hands, the bundle on their backs.

The great palace in the Kremlin has the most beautiful halls that perhaps ever saw a man's eye. Next to it the oldest part with the small, narrow chambers of the old Tsars, preserved and restored with historical fidelity.

Then we went to the most beautiful church in Moscow, the Church of the Redeemer, built to commemorate 1812, which took fifty years to build and cost a capital of fifty million marks. From its height, which we climbed, I was able to take the first comprehensive look at the city, of which I had no understanding until now, although we had been driving around in it for days. From up here you can clearly see how the city has crystallized around the Kremlin. Like the annual rings around the trunk of the tree, the districts of the city wrap around the height of the Kremlin. The streets are drawn in a circle around this center, intersected by radial streets. However, even from up here, one cannot get a clear overview. In order to see and recognize Moscow completely, one would have to float in a balloon a few hundred meters above the city. Endlessly stretching out on all sides are the green roofs of the mostly low houses, which again lie individually in gardens and between free, green squares, and out of the tangle of the whole, immense picture rise innumerable domes and towers of the forty times forty churches and chapels of the city. They shine as golden bulbs or colored deep blue, as pinnacles and spires in a bewildering mass, quite impossible to count. In the background lie the darkly wooded Sparrow Hills, from which Napoleon once looked down on the city that was to become so fatal to him; monasteries enclosed by walls shine across into the farthest distance. The sound of bells incessantly pervades the air, and the streets are crowded with hackney carriages, three-and four-in-hand vehicles, all with horses walking side by side.

This morning, the famous Li-Hung-Chang had an audience with the prince. We were all present and were introduced to the great Chinese. The conversation went by interpreter. I was particularly interested in him because of Uncle Helmuth. He looks extremely interesting, a clever, witty face. He was wearing the famous yellow jacket. Afterwards we visited the cradle of the Romanovs, the old Boyar house, where the progenitor of the now ruling dynasty was born, most interesting. Then the most desolate spawn of architectural imagination, the Church of Vasily Blashenyi, built by Ivan the Terrible. Furthermore, we saw a painting gallery, where only Russian artists are represented, with an interesting portrait of Tolstoy.

1896

Moscow, 27 May 1896.

Yesterday the coronation took place in the most glorious weather. The Russians are really lucky with these events. Just like the day of the move-in, it was the most glorious weather yesterday on the coronation day. The sun burned with almost southern glow from the cloudless sky. In case of rainy weather, the coronation could not take place at all, since the whole procession with all its pomp moves for the most part under the open sky.

We had to drive out to the Kremlin as early as 7:30 a.m., where we had seats on a grandstand erected in the wide palace courtyard. At 8:30 the solemn act began with the churchgoing of the Empress-Mother, who, under a golden canopy adorned with ostrich feathers, with the brilliant crown on her head and the ermine cloak worn by ten cavaliers around her shoulders, strode from the palace to the Uspensky Cathedral, where the coronation would take place.

We had a very good place from which we could overlook the whole palace courtyard. In the same, two paths for the elevator were made crosswise of planks covered with red cloth. One led from the great staircase of the palace to the cathedral, a few hundred steps, the other cut across the courtyard. A third one led in the walk from the Coronation Cathedral to the Ivan Veliky, from it to the Archangel Cathedral, from there to the Church of the Annunciation and from there back to the Grand Staircase. After the coronation the Tsar has to go this way and to perform a devotion in each of the mentioned churches, which are situated around the palace yard.

The whole wide courtyard was filled head to head with the deputations of the entire people, all peoples united by the Russian scepter were represented here, from the turbine-wearing Bukhar to the fur-clad Finnish. The *Chevalier Garde* in helmet and cuirass formed a guard on one side of the courtyard, the people of the imperial Caucasian convoy dressed in long scarlet skirts on the other.

At about 9 o'clock trumpet blasts announced that the procession was starting to move. All bared their heads. A rolling hurrah rose from the hundred-language throats of the masses, who thronged in excitement. The whole wide courtyard, surrounded by numerous tribunes, on which the bright toilets of the ladies gleamed, between them the bright uniforms of the trellis-forming troops, the whole surrounded by the gold-covered towers and churches and by the high front of the old Tsar's castle and flooded by glowing sunlight, made in itself an enchanting impression. And now, on the red plank road leading through the middle of the maze, the coronation procession passed us in all its oriental fairy-tale splendor to the cathedral, at the portal of which the Metropolitan of St. Petersburg, surrounded by the high clergy, stood with the holy image of the Mother of God to bless the entrance of the imperial couple.

It took almost a quarter of an hour for the whole procession to pass. First came a detachment of chevalier guards, then the pages, the masters of ceremonies, the syndicates of the whole empire, the municipalities, delegates of the nobility, the bourgeoisie, the merchants, the artists, then endless chamberlains in uniforms overloaded with gold, the representatives of the universities, the ministries, the delegates of the various Cossack tribes, the noble marshals, the General Synod, the senators, the Council of State, heralds, the castle guards, then in solemn pomp the imperial regalia, the imperial flag and sword, crown, scepter, apple, mantles, etc., a peloton of the Empress's Chevalier Guards, the High Court and Court Marshals, and finally the Emperor and Empress under a golden canopy with ostrich feathers carried by twenty generals. According to ancient tradition, the Empress walked under the same canopy behind the Emperor.

Then followed the long procession of all the Russian Grand Dukes and all the princes gathered here for the coronation, then the long procession of the court ladies, ladies of honor and palace ladies in the Russian court costume, the red velvet overdress, the *kokoshnik* on the head, again a section of *Chevalier Garde* and then a lot of generals, winged adjutants, representatives of the hereditary nobility, etc. All this passed us by like a fairy tale and disappeared in the cathedral. The ringing of all the bells, the thunder of the cannons and the roaring hurrahs were indeed a picture of indescribable impression.

The ceremony in the church lasted from 9 to 1:30. After the end of the ceremony, the procession came out again for the ceremony. Now the Emperor wore the heavy brilliant crown, the mantle and in his hand the scepter, at the tip of which sparkles the largest diamond in the world, the Orloff, and the imperial orb, a sight one usually sees only on picture sheets. He had crowned himself and then the Empress, had received the holy anointing and, as the highest ecclesiastical head, had enjoyed the Lord's Supper in both forms. Only now did he appear before his people as the rightful Emperor in all the splendor of his enormous power.

There is something great in these celebrations, the tidings of which will be carried out to the endless steppes of the empire by all the deputations who attended them, who will tell how they saw the White Tsar in all the splendor of his power, followed by hundreds of subject princes, blessed by God who made the sun shine for him and blessed by the clergy, cheered by all the people, covered with the treasures of the earth, a supreme being in whose hand lies the weal and woe of untold millions. This people and this empire need such an external display, and one does wisely to maintain it in all pieces according to ancient sacred rite. Religion and world domination are so intimately fused here that neither can be separated from the other without both bleeding each other to death. One must have seen all this to understand why in Russia the Orthodox Church is often conducted with draconian severity, to understand how it is possible to sum up and maintain in one thought this endless empire which reaches from the eternal ice of the north to the eternal summer of the south. Only absolute power, supported by the universal Orthodox Church, can govern Russia, and any crack between these two basic pillars would bring down the whole huge edifice.

After the coronation procession passes all the churches, the Emperor and Empress climb the red-covered flight of steps to the castle. Arriving at the top, both turned and greeted the people with three bows. The two majesties looked splendid, the noble stones on their heads flashed in the sun, the figures flowed around the wide folds of the ermine coats, it seemed as if heaven breathed a blessing kiss over them, and all the thousands who had lain on their knees outside while their Emperor was being anointed in the church cheered up to the ruling couple, one felt surrounded by the flood of blessings, the enthusiasm and the monarchical loyalty of a whole people.

That day about three thousand people were fed on the Kremlin; in tents, in halls and halls the endless tables were arranged. We escaped the crowd and drove to the house, where we arrived at about 5 o'clock. The whole ceremony had lasted nine hours!

The Empress looked lovely. The fine face pale from excitement and exertion. She wore a dress of silver brocade. The imperial crown, made entirely of diamonds, which the Emperor had placed on her in church after crowning himself and touching the forehead of the woman kneeling before him with his crown, sat on her rich hair like a ray of heavenly light. The Emperor also wore the heavy crown with imperial decorum. It must be terribly heavy, for it too is made entirely of diamonds. The top is formed by a ruby the size of a chicken egg, in which the sunlight broke with a bloody red glow.

In the evening Moscow was illuminated. What that means is difficult to describe. The whole Kremlin shone with electric light. The towers and gates were built up of millions of lamps, from the foot to the highest tip of the cross. They stood there like apparitions of another world. The whole eight kilometer long surrounding wall was covered in its cremation of lamps. This whole sea of fire ignites the hand of the Empress. She grasps a bouquet, and in an instant everything flares up. From the terrace of the Kremlin we looked down on a city of fire. Blue, red, green, the houses, bridges, towers shone in flashing sparks. Garlands of lamps stretched along the banks of the Moskva as far as the eye could see. It was such an indescribable splendor that we were completely stunned.

It is also quite impossible to reproduce the impression. Let your imagination wander into the unmeasured and you will not reach the reality for a long time. Here every thinking stops. Even if you see this illumination, you think it is impossible. You touch your forehead and ask yourself if you are in your right mind or if you have feverish fantasies. And three evenings in a row this spectacle should be renewed!

Moscow, 30 May 1896.

The hustle and bustle of the last few days was great. We were constantly on the road from morning to night, without a break. We had a big congratulatory ceremony that lasted for hours. Individually passed by with two bows. The Empress gave me her hand for a kiss, I have never kissed the hand of a princess with more joy! – Yesterday we were in camp with Prince Heinrich. We drove in the morning to the Petrofsky Palace, where we got horses from the stables. It was interesting to see the camp, where there are three infantry and one cavalry division as well as two brigades of artillery. The people are housed partly in wooden barracks and partly in tents. We rode through the camp for about three hours.

In the evening there was a gala opera. The huge house looked magnificent. The ranks were filled with ladies adorned with jewels, the first floor with officers. Roaring hurrahs and national anthems greeted the majesties, who, followed by all the grand dukes and princes, entered the great court box. An act from the opera "Life for the Tsar" was given. The splendor of the costumes was tremendous, as in general the luxury that is developed here leaves behind everything that I have seen so far. At the end, the national anthem was played again, and the entire chorus of the theater, united in a shining gold and silver group, sang along. We arrived home at 1:30.

Today is great folk festival, where a hundred thousand people are fed in the open air. Everyone takes home his dishes and a cup with the image of the Tsar.

Moscow, 1 June 1896.

Since I last wrote to you, we attended a mass party at the French Embassy. The strangest thing about this party was that we managed to get out without being crushed. We were almost like the poor thousands of the people who were crushed to death. According to official reports, 1365 people were killed and 320 wounded. One cannot think of anything more gruesome than a people crushing each other and trampling under each other's feet. About a million people are said to have gathered in the huge square.

Berlin, 1 September 1896.

Now it is generally said that I will get the Alexander Regiment after the maneuvers. That is also likely, because His Majesty likes to arrange such things on the last day of the maneuvers. The fact that I have been named as a candidate for the Alexander Regiment is probably connected with my Russian connections. I am looking forward to getting out. It is necessary for my future that I return to the front after a long, twenty-year break. The thought of growing old and outdated at a post and finally being dragged along only out of mercy, like a worn-out horse that is reluctantly given a reprieve, would be unbearable to me. Then rather go before by itself. Thus I have the confidence in myself that I will pass my exam as regimental commander well and thus acquire the right to continue climbing the military ladder with a clear conscience as long as strength and health suffice.

Breslau, 6 September 1896.

Yesterday morning at 6:30 drove to Brieg, where we waited until the Russian special train arrived. We were stowed in a very nicely appointed saloon car, where we made the acquaintance of the Russian escort. After half an hour, the Emperor and Empress appeared to greet us. The Emperor was dressed in the uniform of the Alexander Regiment, which did not clothe him particularly. He looked pale and sickly, was very amiable and spoke to each of us individually. At the station in Wroclaw there was a great reception, our Emperor and Empress were standing on the platform. The welcome was very warm, – guard of honor, a throng of princes, princes, generals, etc. We went to the State House, where we had an hour to get ready for the parade. This took place in fine weather. The Russian Emperor led the Alexander Regiment past twice very nicely. In the evening, parade dinner and then great taps.

You will have read the Emperor's address at the dinner in the newspaper, it was very good, measured and yet warm. The answer of the Tsar, according to the Russian newspapers, is somewhat softened, he really said: "*Je remercie votre majeste et la ville de Breslau pour le bon acceuille qu'elle a bien voulu me preparer. Je partage sincerement les relations traditionelles, qui unissent nos deux pays. Je bois a la santo etc.*"* – In the newspaper this is changed to, "*Je partage les sentiments traditionelles, qui existent entre nous.*"† – This is a big difference and sounds much cooler. The amendment is surely a concession to Paris!

Görlitz, 11 September 1896.

Tomorrow we have our last maneuver day and at the same time for me the last day of a now closing period of life. The curtain falls, a new piece begins!

So let us go the new way as good, faithful comrades. In the beginning it will not be easy for either of us. We have become too unaccustomed to life in the troops for many years, but with good will we will soon feel the beautiful sides and we will, each in his own way, have a grateful sphere of activity. This is probably the last time that I will write to you as a serving wing adjutant of His Majesty. Today the Emperor led the V and VI Corps and, of course, won a brilliant victory.

CABINET ORDER.

I hereby appoint you, leaving you in the position of My Wing Adjutant and relieving you of the position of Commander of the Castle Guard Company, as Commander of the Kaiser Alexander Guard Grenadier Regiment No. 1.

---

* "I would like to thank your majesty and the city of Breslau for the kind welcome it has given me. I sincerely support the traditional relations between our two countries. I drink to your health etc."

† "I share the traditional feelings that exist between us."

Goerlitz, 12 September 1896.

Wilhelm R.
To My Wing Adjutant in Service Colonel v. Moltke.

Berlin, 14 September 1896.

You won't find me here anymore, I left for the maneuver area of the Guard Corps at noon to take over my regiment. I have just arrived for the big corps maneuver, I have two nights of bivouac, and at a stroke I am plunged into the practical life of a soldier, which I have not known for twenty years. I remained a wing adjutant. The Emperor told me on the last day of maneuvers that I had been given the regiment. He was very gracious, told me, "Well, I think the Tsar will be pleased with the new commander." – Not true, you see that I am right in having pushed a little "on the front." The Emperor did not resent me, I feel that well enough. It will be very wonderful for me when I draw my rapier for the first time in front of the regiment and forty-five officers and two thousand men listen to my command. I am very much looking forward to it and especially that I can lead in the maneuver right away.

St. Petersburg, 9 March 1897.

Through my dispatch you have seen that I have arrived here safely. I just had time to change my clothes and then immediately get back on the train and go to Tsarskoye Selo, since His Majesty the Emperor wanted to receive me that same afternoon. Today I was received by the old Grand Duchess Constantine in a long audience and then by her son, the Grand Duke Constantine and his wife, a princess of Anhalt – tomorrow the Grand Duke Vladimir invited me to breakfast.

St. Petersburg, 11 March 1897.

The week goes by so slowly, I sit here motionless and do not even know when I can come back at all. Yesterday at the Grand Prince Vladimir's, completely *en famille*, as if I belonged to it! I had to talk about Berlin as if it were the only city in the world! Then I was with the old Grand Duke Michael, who talked with me for about three quarters of an hour. It was like reading an old diary from the sixties, when Prussia and Russia still walked arm in arm through the world like two merry students, drinking sulks and bumping into everything that got in their way.

Petersburg is silent and does penance, goes to confession and communion, and has stripped off everything that could remind one of the pleasures of this world. No musical tone is heard, no theater is open, but the people crowd into the churches in droves.

I went to Peter and Paul's Fortress today, then I visited the little wooden house where the great Peter lived while the city that bears his name grew out of the swamps of the Newaufer, while he broke his window into the wall of savagery that then enclosed the Russian Empire, so that the light of European culture might fall into his vast empire.

Döberitz, 1 July 1897.

In the morning there is a drill. The whole training area is one square mile in size, alternating between forest and cleared areas. One can perform all kinds of battle formations on it and since one does not have to take into account any damage to the land, one is completely unhindered in all movements. The poor horses suffer a lot from the countless horseflies. The day before yesterday "Nyalka" got a colic attack. I immediately sent for a veterinarian, she was given half a liter of Hoffmann's drops, massaged and treated with Prießnitz's poultice. After a few hours the attack was over. The day after tomorrow I have regimental inspection, you can keep your fingers crossed for me, because of course I will be inspected on my own behalf, so that my superiors can judge how foolish I am.

Berlin, 3 July 1897.

My regimental presentation today went very well. The division commander and a lot of spectators were present. The criticism was very good and everything was satisfactory. I then bid adieu to my officers and left here at noon. From here I leave tomorrow morning for Travemünde. I still can't get over having to leave the regiment.

Norway, Odde, 12 July 1897.

Yesterday, Her Majesty was injured in the eye by a falling end of a rope, and that same afternoon Lieutenant von Hahnke, the son of the old General v. Hahnke, who was on duty on the "Hohenzollern," was killed. The sailors say that the whole misfortune is due to the fact that there is a pastor on board.

The Emperor's injury is quite insignificant, the matter will be over in a few days, he will be back on deck today. The accident with young Hahnke happened as follows. Some of the ship's officers wanted to take a trip to Lotefoß, twenty kilometers from Odde. Hahnke and a lieutenant v. Levetzow by bicycle, another officer with an official drove behind with Karriol. Lieutenant v. Hahnke was the first to ride ahead on the narrow road, which was partly blasted into the rock; about four hundred yards behind him followed Levetzow, also on the wheel, then the others. After driving for about an hour, they came to a place where the road is very narrow.

On one side steep rock, on the right the rocky bed of the Elf, which flows along with torrential force. The road here is about four meters above the river bed. Just here are strong rapids and eddies, the water boils between large boulders and forms deep whirlpools. Close above the spot, a narrow wooden bridge leads across the river to a farmhouse on the opposite bank of the road.

As Lieutenant v. Levetzow, who had dismounted and was leading his bicycle, since the road rises here, came to this place, two boys aged ten and seven, sons of the farmer living opposite, came running across the wooden bridge to meet him and told him that they had been standing on the other bank and had seen a man, who had been riding a bicycle, fall from the road into the river with his wheel. Fortunately, Levetzow understands Danish. He had not been able to see Hahnke, who, as I said, was riding about four hundred meters ahead of him, because of the bend in the road. Hahnke has since disappeared without a trace, the raging torrent has swallowed him up and not even a piece of his clothing, hat or anything has come out again.

The boys say that the gentleman drove very slowly along the road, on the side facing the river. As he was facing them, he pulled out his handkerchief to wipe off his sweat, the wheel began to sway, he quickly grabbed the bar with his hand, but the wheel hit a bumper in front, overturned and the gentleman fell head over heels. In the fall he had emitted a loud scream. A short distance downstream he emerged from the whirlpool, threw both arms in the air and let out another scream, at the same moment he disappeared. Since yesterday afternoon, the river has been searched by sailors with nets and grapnel anchors. Today one hundred and twenty men are at work, no trace of the casualty has been found. If it were not for the two boys, Hahnke would have disappeared from the earth without anyone ever knowing where he had gone.

The poor father, who is in Karlovy Vary for a cure, is informed of the misfortune by the eldest son, who was notified by telegraph. The Emperor, himself lying down, was deeply moved and wants to stay here until the body is found. Stahlheim, etc., has of course been abandoned, and deep dejection prevails throughout the ship.

Odde, 14 July 1897.

We stayed here for three days to make inquiries about the body of young Hahnke. One hundred and forty men worked day in and day out to find it, but without any results. The torrential mountain stream that swallowed him has released nothing. There are such deep eddies and undercut rocks in the rocky riverbed that they mock all attempts to get down with grapnel anchors, etc. The hope of finding it must be abandoned. So the hope of being able to prepare a grave for the corpse in German earth must be abandoned, the Elf holds him tight and rushes around him with its cool water in dark rocky chasm, a grave of somber majesty. Today we had a moving memorial service on board. The Emperor will have a memorial stone erected on the rock face at the site of the accident.

Norway, Digermulen at Lofoten, July 20 1898.

We passed the Arctic Circle at noon, sitting on deck, caressed by the warm sun that blazed down on the deck as hot as if we were deep in the south. We saw whales spouting their dusting jets of water, *pamorans* and eider geese skimming the surface, and spread wide to our right lay the mountainous shores of Norway in a thousand-fold variety of shapes and colors, for miles stretching between the purple mountain shapes the shimmering ridge of the world's largest snowfield, Svart Jisen. It is indescribably beautiful up here when the sky is clear. The vastness of the views draws the mind into infinity, the magnificence of nature, which seems to be made for its own sake and not for the sake of people, makes the mind feel solemn. Indescribable is also the changing play of colors, which pass from the deepest tones through delicate mediation to the lightest coloration. One cannot get enough of the panorama; wherever one's gaze turns, it encounters new beauties, and drunk with the sun's brilliance and clarity, it rushes over the infinite sea that melts into the sky in the endless distance.

Norway, Lofoten, 23 July 1898.

Very beautiful was the midnight sun, which descended under a bank of clouds to about thirty minutes of arc above the horizon, then stopped for about ten minutes, flooding the ship and the distant mountain peaks of Lofoten with a crimson glow, and then slowly rose again. The Prince of Monaco came aboard to show us the catch he had made with his trawl. He brought with him several large glass jars, in which were again a number of ghastly animals in spirit. There were large sea spiders, with legs as long as this letter sheet is high, sea cucumbers that look like ghastly, thick leeches, with an opening in the front and back so that the mud of the sea can flow through them. Etc. etc. In a word, a collection of horrors, but most interesting. One wonders what all these beasts exist for. What is the intention of creation with them? Perhaps, as a punishment for bad living, one is later turned into a sea cucumber and must now swallow the mud in deep darkness?

On the trip to Kiel, 1 August 1898.

The news of the death of Prince Bismarck arrived in Bergen yesterday morning, quite unexpectedly, because the dispatches that His Majesty had received about the Prince from Professor Schwenninger were quite reassuring. Thus we had no idea of what all Germany knew, that it was the end of the old warrior. The Emperor now ordered an accelerated repatriation. The Emperor's dispatch to Bismarck's son, in which he says that he wants to bury the Prince in the Hohenzollern crypt next to his ancestors, you will probably have already read in the newspaper. The sons answered with thanks that the prince himself had determined the place in the Sachsenwald where he wanted to be buried.

Berlin, 10 August 1898.

Today I was at the art exhibition to look at the large wall paintings by Prell, which are coming to Rome as frescoes after the German Embassy Villa Caffarelli. They are very beautiful, of great effect and in part of captivating charm. The motifs are taken from ancient Germanic mythology from the Edda. In the first picture, the young spring god Baldur has descended to earth to free the goddess of earth – Gerda – who has been bound by the ice giants. He is greeted by swan maidens. In the second picture he fights against the giants who are thrown back into the high mountains (summer). Thunderstorm. The old winter in its weakness, retreats to rough mountains. In the third, the sun sinks into the sea (winter). The abandoned earth goddess mourns her captivity. Baldur is slain, only the singer is left to sing of the beauty of summer. At his side is a nun who holds in her arms the child of Gerda, the future spring. You must see these pictures when you come.

Berlin, 12 August 1898.

In about eight days I will have to travel to Russia once again. On the 27th, the unveiling of the Russian national monument to Emperor Alexander III will take place in Moscow, and a deputation from the regiment is to go there.

Paris, 22 February 1899.

We had a very good trip, were treated impeccably at the frontier, and on our arrival in Paris were received at the station by a colonel sent specially *en parade* from the President's *Maison Militaire* and a senior civilian official. We found two carriages provided for us by the Elysée. About forty policemen were deployed, who formed an uninterrupted ring around us and immediately got everyone by the collar who only stretched his neck to look at us! Some whistles sounded from the crowded crowd, but otherwise everything remained quiet.

We want to go out now and also to the Dome des Invalides. In the afternoon we will be received by the President and the Minister of Foreign Affairs Delcassé. Tomorrow we are to take part in the whole procession, about eight kilometers. Following the example of Germany, all the other states have now also sent deputations, which are arriving head over heels.

CABINET ORDER.

I hereby appoint you, with promotion to Major General, as My General *à la suite* and Commander of the I Guard Infantry Brigade. At the same time I entrust you with the duties of the Commandant of Potsdam. It gives me pleasure to make this known to you.
Berlin, 25 March 1899.

Wilhelm R.

To My Wing Adjutant, Colonel v. Moltke, Commander of the Kaiser

Alexander Guard Grenadier Regiment No. 1.

TELEGRAM.

Colonel von Moltke, Commander Kaiser Alexander Guard Grenadier Regiment No. 1, Regimental Bureau, Alexanderstrasse 56.

I appoint you as My General à la suite and Commander of the 1st Guards Infantry Brigade as of April 1. In dismissing you with a heavy heart from your excellent regiment, which has been superbly trained under your proven leadership, I wish to express to you by this promotion My fullest satisfaction at the way in which you have understood how to fully comply with My intentions in your previous position and have thereby achieved such a brilliant result.

Signed Wilhelm R.

Döberitz, 29 June 1899.

On Monday I will hold the visits of the 3rd Guards Regiment, on Tuesday those of the 1st Guards Regiment. Then the brigade retreats begin under my direction, and on July 12 I and my brigade are inspected by the division commander. In this way, one always convinces himself of the other's achievements.

Potsdam, 19 July 1899.

The lonely height of the commander and brigade commander is quite boring. Yesterday I did long maneuver work.

Potsdam, 23 July 1899.

Now that I was in Berlin, I went to the exhibition, where I had not been before, and looked at the rather mediocre paintings for two hours. With the art it seems to me to decline rapidly, the best there are old known pictures, from the newer I found nothing remarkable.

Potsdam, 30 July 1899.

With great interest I read Bebei's book about woman, which I found among your books. God forbid that we and our children should live to see that state in which life will be a dreary monotony and the whole earth will be transformed into a great factory hall in which everyone will be equally unhappy, just so that some will not be happy.

Potsdam, 23 August 1899.

The canal affair is a rather distressing and serious matter. I fear it will have unpleasant consequences for the Conservatives' position toward His Majesty. That there will be changes in the Ministry I consider certain. In my opinion, it would not be a pity for a whole part of the gentlemen. How everything will develop, I do not know. The refusal was probably a great stupidity, because the canal will come after all.

Potsdam, 25 August 1899.

The Emperor sat down with me and talked at length about the canal proposal, etc. I did what I could to soften and conciliate. However, His Majesty's agitation was very profound, and I fear that orders had already been issued that cannot be reversed.

Potsdam, 5 September 1899.

Since I'm running the maneuvers myself, I have a lot to do and will have to be on horseback pretty much all day. I am curious myself how it will go, it is the first time that I have created such maneuvers myself.

Döberitz, June 14, 1900.

The day before yesterday and yesterday I visited the 1st and 3rd Guards Regiments in the presence of the Division Commander and the Commanding General. Everything went splendidly, and at the end I received praise from the Commanding General, who expressed his special appreciation for the handsome manner of my visit. He said: "I recommend to all of you, gentlemen, the warlike and interesting way of sightseeing, as the brigade commander demonstrated it to us."

Wilhelmshaven, 4 July 1900.

The "Hohenzollern" is scheduled to set sail this evening. The Emperor wants to see the armored division that is to go to China before it sails. I like Bülow very much, he is calm, clear and determined. His influence on the Emperor, it seems to me, is a favorable one. His task is not an easy one; his great cleverness and agility serve him well. Schlieffen arrived late last night, Hahnke is coming today.

I am tingling in all my limbs to join the China expedition. It must be enormously interesting, though I think the whole thing will amount less to an entry into Peking than to a protection of Shantung. I suspect that the latter will have become necessary by the time we can be there, for I do not think that the whole movement will be so quickly stifled. The political entanglements between the European powers will probably follow.

Kiel, 7 July 1900.

The political conditions seem to be favorable so far. The occasions for quarrels between the European powers will only occur later. In the meantime, the uprising in China seems to be spreading with rapid violence; in a few weeks, the entire monstrous empire will probably be in flames.

What one actually thinks with an enterprise against Peking is completely unclear to me and, I fear, to the "stage directors" as well. The few men we can get there (to Taku) will be useless against the onslaught of hundreds of thousands of fanatical hordes, and now a warfare of ten different contingents under a leadership to which no one will want to submit; the Frenchman will not want to be under German, the German not under Russian, the Russian not under Japanese supreme command, in addition no object of war, no legal government with which peace could be made even in the most favorable case, nothing but a causeless abyss of people in which the European little heaps will drown. No equipment with trains, etc., no base for more than five or six ships, no regulated supply of food, etc.

I regard this whole enterprise as a wild adventure and hope that the pressure of circumstances will save us from it and lead us to confine ourselves to the only thing we can do and, in my opinion, must do, namely, to protect our colony of Kiautschou, then to let the Chinese giant fire burn itself out and later to hold ourselves harmless by compensation.

What do we want in Peking? – We must hope that the time that must pass, thank God, before our first transports can arrive, will allow calm and deliberation to gain the upper hand among us as well. For the time being, we are exposed to an unexpected explosion of wills at any moment, which is completely unpredictable. The advisors have a hard time.

I look forward with apprehension to the inevitable coming reproaches in the press, which will come with the accusation that hasty action has plunged us into headlong warlike entanglements in the Far East, where we really have no business to be. That will surely come when we are advancing on Peking and lose our protectorate over it, when our little group in the giant empire gradually melts away and is consumed like a snowball on a stove, when we will then be compelled to bring in new forces, When the Reichstag, which is now being left completely aside, will have its say and the enormous means will have to be explained which we have used and still use to achieve a phantom which cannot be called anything else but...: Revenge. I look to the future with gloomy apprehension. But I am a pessimist, and perhaps everything will be better.

Kiel, 9 July 1900.

A complete turnaround has occurred here in the last twelve hours, and I am very glad about it, because the resolutions that the Emperor has now taken are completely in line with what I considered to be right. The revenge campaign to Peking has been abandoned. All troops on the way and still to leave are ordered to Kiautschou. A secure base will be established there and peace and order will be established or maintained. We are content with that for the time being, watch the development of things, let the fire in China burn out and keep watch only with the water hose in our hands that the fire does not seize our own house. This will get us out of all the political turmoil, we won't have to mess with Russia or England, and we can present our bill later. I have been advocating this position from the very beginning. Now the Emperor is completely won over to it, as I hope to God he will hold fast for the good of the fatherland. It was an exciting time, the most fantastic projects were made, and the future was often on a knife's edge. I am very glad that everything turned out this way. The Emperor spoke to me very nicely and I also spoke my mind unabashedly. Nothing has yet been decided about our departure. I still hope that it will not happen at all, but even if we go out now, I do so with a lighter heart.

Kiel, 10 July 1900.

I can still tell you that I had asked for the command in China to be given to me; yesterday Hahnke was here and had lectured on the matter, so I asked him once again to propose me to the Emperor, which he did, but without success. The Emperor did not let me go, not, as I think, because he considers me incapable, but because, as he says, he cannot spare me. A quaint idea, I also said that my brigade could be led by anyone and that I could be replaced with the greatest ease, but to no avail. I was quite disappointed, for I had already made up a great campaign plan and the old soldier's spirit, with its urge for danger and activity, had fully awakened in me again. Now I have gently put it to sleep again and will continue to cultivate my profession and otherwise feel quite superfluous.

Norway, Kopervik, 11 July 1900.

The composition of the troops going to China has probably been published by now. The supreme commander is General v. Lessel. That is the position I would have liked to have. But since I am "indispensable," I had to do without it. It is very funny to be so indispensable and to feel so completely superfluous. You certainly find my idea adventurous and yet, how I would have liked to lead the black–white–red flag against the yellow scoundrels who killed our compatriots.

Of course, it is not necessary to go into the actual motive of the whole expedition, because if we want to be completely honest, it is greed that has moved us to cut the big Chinese cake. We wanted to make money, build railroads, put mines into operation, bring European culture, in other words, make money. In this we are not one bit better than the English in the Transvaal!

Norway, Molde, 21 July 1900.

From China we have no new news of importance. After Tientsin was taken by the Europeans, there will probably be a standstill for the time being. Our troops have behaved well, as was to be expected. Medals upon medals are being sent down from here, I think no officer is undecorated any more. Captain U. has become wing adjutant, it is the usual excess in everything that always comes out again.

Potsdam, 28 July 1900.

Politically, I can't tell you anything, because I don't know anything. Bülow and the Reich Chancellor arrived as I disembarked, so I don't know what was agreed. But I think the situation is not unfavorable for us.

Potsdam, 2 August 1900.

The assassination of the poor King of Italy is one of the meanest acts of knavery that ever occurred. He was a true father of his people and did only good. The scoundrel who shot him down should be publicly staked. I often think with concern of our Emperor, over whose head the steel of murder always hovers, and who is so extraordinarily careless.

I do not understand why all anarchists are not simply put under lock and key as generally dangerous. If a lunatic goes around threatening human lives, one puts him away, but if these criminals publicly declare that they want to murder and also occasionally turn their words into deeds, one treats them as an equal political party. People are just struck with blindness and will not become wise even if the roof over their heads is set on fire.

Potsdam, 8 August 1900.

J. told me today that the dispatch of Count Waldersee to China was at the request of Russia, which had asked that Germany take over the definitive supreme command there. I consider this a very happy omen as proof of the union of Germany and Russia, which France will of course join.

Potsdam, 9 August 1900.

This morning I was in Berlin, where a high mass for King Humbert was celebrated in the Hedwigs Church. On me the whole action with the incomprehensible manipulations of the priests in front of the altar, the clouds of incense and the nasal singing made an almost repulsive impression. It is just like idolatry after all. I cannot imagine that Christ could agree with this kind of worship, he who preached his sermons under God's open sky and who rejected everything that reminded of the ritual customs of the old law and who himself said, when you pray, you shall not chatter like the pagans.

Döberitz, 19 May 1901.

Yesterday I was inspected. Everything went smoothly and well and I received congratulations from all sides about the good inspection. I am glad that this day went off happily, the only one in the year when one is demoted from teacher to pupil and has to show that one can not only tell others how they should have done it, but also knows how to do one's own thing. I have been lucky enough to solve all the tasks given to the brigade in a satisfactory way.

New Ruppin, 19 September 1901.

Tomorrow would look bad if it continues to pour, because tomorrow is the first corps maneuver day, where all troops must bivouac. I see in the newspaper that the Emperor has suspended the major maneuvers for a day because of rain. The layman will hardly have an idea of what this means for the maneuver management. All the dispositions are thrown over. The railroad transports, which had been agreed upon with the railroad authorities long beforehand, have to be stopped, everything goes haywire, and apart from all the difficulties, the feeling is aroused in the army as if the soldiers could not stand any more rain. Think of the consequences if such a violent intervention were to take place in an emergency.

CABINET ORDER.

I have appointed you today, with promotion to Lieutenant General, as My Adjutant General and Commander of the 1st Guards Infantry Division. It gives me special pleasure to announce this to you.
Berlin, 27 January 1902.

Wilhelm R.

To My General *à la suite*, Major General v. Moltke, Commander of the 1st Guards Infantry Brigade and charged with the duties of the Commandant of Potsdam.

Madrid, 16 May 1902.

I would have so much to tell you, but we are already in the usual rush and I don't know how far I will get. Therefore, first of all, I would like to tell you that I am in excellent health, that the journey is over happily, that we arrived here yesterday, on the 15th, in the afternoon, and that I am staying with two other gentlemen of the entourage in our embassy, where we are accommodated quite excellently.

So on the 13th, at noon, we left Berlin. In Braunschweig we reported in our traveling suits to Prince Albrecht, who drove along from there. We were ordered to the Prince's dining car at 7 o'clock in the evening and then sat together until we arrived in Cologne at 10 o'clock in the evening, where we changed trains and embarked on the luxury train Cologne – Paris. The next morning at 8 o'clock we had breakfast again together with the Prince and his gentlemen and at 8:30 we arrived in Paris, where the Ambassador Prince Radolin received us at the station. We now immediately boarded waiting carriages and drove first to the Palais de Justice, where we viewed the charming Sainte Chapelle with its old, wonderful stained glass windows and its magnificent mosaic and enamel paintings, which are old Venetian work. Then we saw the lower rooms, of which the most interesting is the small cellar hole where the unfortunate Queen Marie Antoinette spent the last year of her martyrdom. From there we went to the Louvre, through which we made a run, visiting the Venus de Milo and seeing the most beautiful pieces of the collection of paintings. Then a drive through the Place de la Concorde, the Elysées, across the Pont Alexandre II to the Embassy, where there was a large breakfast with all the members of the same. Paris was beautiful, the weather clear, everything green, I was yet again surprised by the grandeur of the city, which, since I last saw it, has been heightened by the two great palaces built in front of the Alexander Bridge on occasion of the World's Fair. Immediately after breakfast we went on the train. At 12 noon we departed, passing through Orleans, Bordeaux to the Spanish border station of Irun, where we arrived at 11 o'clock in the evening. Unfortunately it was already dark as we approached the Pyrenees, so we saw nothing of the most beautiful areas, San

Sebastian and Biarritz.

But the tour through France was wonderful, it is a wonderful country, wealth and culture show up everywhere, viticulture and carefully cultivated fields with clean villages. Everything is green and blooming, the first clover was already mowed, the grain already had ears and the cattle was on the pasture.

From Irun we had an extra Spanish train, which was set up as a princely train. In addition to us, Grand Duke Vladimir, Prince Christian of Denmark, the Crown Prince of Siam, Prince Eugene of Sweden, the Prince of Monaco, etc. were stowed in the same train – I was given a small coupe for myself, where I slept comfortably on the couch. The Prince's gentlemen were four to a compartment. Also on this trip, the most beautiful part of the night was lost to us because of. I woke up at 7 o'clock in the morning. We drove through barren, desolate land and it didn't get any different until we arrived in Madrid. Wide, barren, uncultivated stretches, bare mountain slopes, the fields indescribably sloppily cultivated, the grain as thin as my hair, now and then a flock of sheep or a troop of mules grazing among the stones. The houses were miserable, built of unbaked mud bricks, dilapidated, some without roofs. The population was ragged and dirty. In between, cowardly priests with greasy cassocks. A miserable country. Now and then some vineyards in the plain. All dwellings crowded into villages, on the wide stretches of land no house, no farm, no tree, everything beaten down. Later, some arid pine forests or balsam spruces, all with the bark cut open and under the wound a pot to catch the resin flowing out, it looked as if the game had peeled. Of course, all the trees go out with time. Almost no bird, no piece of game, desolate abandonment under the bright sun. Near Madrid some olive plantations, all gray. At the same time heavy, beautiful soil, where everything would grow by itself if the fields were properly tilled. It is sad to see this land heading towards decay.

At 4 o'clock in the afternoon we arrived in Madrid, already in our parade suits, changed in the train. Big drive up to the high, very beautiful castle, which is really outstandingly beautiful. On the wide staircase inside reception by the Queen, hatchets with halberds, music, fanfares. All very splendid and ceremonial. Solemn greeting of the successive princes arriving according to rank. Then general presentation of the entourage. We beat all others by head count and body length. The queen very amiable, the little king slight, delicate, still a child, but in good posture and of creditable assurance. Then we who live here go to our embassy, which is at the other end of the city, very beautiful, in the middle of a flowering garden, surrounded by blooming roses, acacias, chestnuts, in between tall dark cedars. It is the prettiest embassy I have seen so far, and we are excellently accommodated here. In the evening 8 o'clock big gala dinner in the castle. Splendid hall, electrically illuminated, with an abundance of flowers on the table. Everything first class.

Return home at 11 o'clock in the evening. On the 16th, trip with the prince to the Prado (museum) with its masses of masterpieces by Murillo, Velasquez, Titian, Raphael, wonderfully beautiful. At 3 o'clock in parade suit at the palace. The King has donned Prussian uniform and thanks the Prince for awarding him the regiment. Then visit drive. Towards evening drive in the large, beautiful park *Buen Retiro*. Hundreds of very beautiful carriages, in them painted Spanish women with glowing eyes and Semitic noses. In the evening big dinner at the embassy. To bed at 3 o'clock.

Madrid, 18 May 1902.

In the meantime, we are continuing to work. Yesterday at 1 o'clock we were on parade at the castle to take part in the grand ascension to the king's oath-taking ceremony. This took place with all the pomp that the court can muster. State carriages, gala harnesses, all the horses with giant plumes, all the troops in the streets as a trellis. We gathered in the hall of the Cortes, a relatively small meeting room where a podium was made for the court. While we were still waiting for the king, the news of an assassination was spread, great excitement. The President stands up and says that a madman or a scoundrel has attempted an assassination, high on the King. Finally he comes. Huge acclamation, clapping of hands, cheers. He looks quite amused and has a good posture. With a clear voice he reads the oath formula. Cheers. Returning after the church. Thousands of people on the street. All after the church, which is packed. *Te Deum*. Wonderful music, wonderful singing, it was the most beautiful of all. After the church it is hardly possible to get the prince into his carriage. Everything was in a mess. The most desolate disorder. No trace of any clearing of the streets or order in driving up. We are stuck in the crowd for almost an hour, without backs or stirring, in the burning sun. Finally we arrive at the castle. Here congratulations. Then all on the balcony. The troops marched past in front of the castle. Crowd head to head, a pretty sight from above. The troops very well dressed, very colorful and picturesque. Beautiful horses in all Spanish type. In the evening, grand ball at a Granden, where many beauties with painted eyebrows and some magnificent false jewelry. Great illumination. In the embassy, all the electric lights go out at once and cannot be seen the whole evening. We have to make do with stearin candles. Our hosts are very kind.

The nights are very cold, the days mostly very hot. Madrid is actually quite a modern city, houses very high, without characteristic style. A nice wide avenue where the embassy is located, and then the big beautiful park *Buen retiro*. Many acacias in the city, all perfumed by the sweet smell of their flowers. The Manzanares is a small watercourse in a wide bed. We are now to go to a polo match. At 4 o'clock laying of the foundation stone of the monument of Alfonso XII. Parade suit. In the evening gala opera.

Madrid, 19 May 1902.

We are constantly well, but we are in a permanent rush, so that I cannot come to write properly. Yesterday evening opera. A huge house with five tiers, three thousand people. Very nice restrooms and beautiful women. The house looked very pretty, though it was not decorated at all as is usual with us on such occasions. The performance – Don Juan – was quite good. Pretty voices. The *mise en scene* miserable, also here complete lack of decorative furnishings. The performance lasted from 9 o'clock to 12:30 with endless intermissions.

Yesterday's groundbreaking was again a comedy with crowds and ghastly disorder. No trace of any keeping clear or order in the columns of wagons, all driving wildly in confusion. It is always almost life threatening to get to your car, if you can find it at all. This afternoon 4:30 parade to be held in the streets of the city.

Paris, 24 May 1902.

Yesterday evening 11 o'clock we arrived here after a twenty-five hour trip from Madrid and stayed at the Hotel *quai d'Orsay*. We leave this afternoon 2 o'clock on to Berlin, where we arrive on the 25th in the morning.

Berlin, 25 May 1902.

I arrived at 9 o'clock this morning. Left Paris yesterday at noon 2 o'clock. I still hope to find time to write about one thing and another, especially about the great *corrida* we attended, in which nine bulls, some ten to twelve horses and two men were killed, then about our visit to the Escorial, the castle of Philip II, the father of the Inquisition. Now I can't get to it. I have just had two hours of lecture and at 7 o'clock I am to dine with Prince Albrecht, who was very gracious and kind. Tomorrow I have brigade inspection in Döberitz, on Tuesday examination shooting there. On Thursday I am to receive the Crown Prince of Siam in the morning and the Shah of Persia in the afternoon at the station in Potsdam, on Friday there is a parade here in Berlin, on Saturday a parade in Potsdam. So the week is full to the brim!

Berlin, 26 May 1902.

Until July I am very busy, and then comes the north country trip, and then immediately the double maneuver, then autumn is here and the wind sweeps over the stubble. So one summer after the other flies by, and the summer of our lives soon turns into autumn.

Berlin, 31 May 1902.

Now the second parade is also happily over, in blazing sunshine under the blossoming chestnuts of Potsdam's Pleasure Garden. I commanded the parade and everything went well. The Emperor was very pleased and especially praised the troops. Monday afternoon I have to go to Beeskow, where sightseeing is Tuesday. Tuesday afternoon to Lübbenau to the maneuver area. Wednesday evening back here.

Norway, Bergen, 15 July 1902.

In the morning Cuno, His Majesty and I took a long walk ashore, visited an old Schleswig-Holstein man who has a cute villa on a hillside with a beautiful view over the city's roadstead, and then his neighbor, an old Norwegian ship captain. We sat for a long time in the gardens climbing up the bluff and chatted with the people and their wives. On such occasions the Emperor is of a charming amiability, harmless as a child; it gives him pleasure to associate with these simple plain people without all ceremony, to hear their views of the conditions of their native land, and to be told their little joys and sorrows. These people are then always in a state of the most boundless enthusiasm.

Norway, Molde, 18 July 1902.

We went from Bergen on Tuesday to Gudvangen, where we arrived Wednesday. Here we made a game to Stahlheim, where was eaten, the same afternoon back on board. I rode with the Emperor in his chariot, which was harnessed to a brave little Norwegian horse. He drove himself, and I had some heart palpitations now and then when we encountered descending wagons that we had to avoid on the narrow country road, and he drove hard past the precipice at the bottom of which the water roared over the rocks, holding the reins with his left hand and taking off his hat with his right to return the greetings. But we arrived happily at the top. Down he let me ride, which was dear to me, because the little horse went like thunder and lay hard on the reins, so that I was again glad to be able to deliver him down without accident. He is always very nice and friendly to me, and the other day gave me proof of special trust by having me called into his study and read me a letter he had just written to the Crown Prince, and wanted to hear my opinion. He has actually never been so friendly as on this trip; I have never seen him at all so amiable and even-tempered. He now often discusses military questions with me and often wants to hear my opinion. At such moments, you can tell him anything, then he is charming, like a good comrade, and you can say what you mean quite freely, which I also made extensive use of.

Berlin, 5 August 1902.

I have invited her (E.) for tomorrow evening to "Old Heidelberg," so that she can have some fun for once. The little —— was also there. She is currently treating a man who has been blind for years and, in my opinion, has thus presented herself with an unsolvable task right from the start. Of course, like all Scientists, she has the best hope and claims that he already has the famous "glimmer" which all blind people who are treated scientifically infallibly get and beyond which – at least as far as I have experienced – just as infallibly no one has ever gotten before. We have talked for a long time about the subject of science, it has much more reasonable views than the genuine Scientists and sees itself that in the whole movement the germ of solidification in a new dogma is contained.

St. Petersburg, Palais d'Hiver, 16 January 1903.

We arrived here two hours ago safe and sound after a very pleasant journey. After arriving here, we went to the Winter Palace, where the Emperor and Empress greeted us. The latter looks extraordinarily well and has become even prettier than she was before. From there to the Empress-Mother, who also greeted us all.

We are all staying at the Winter Palace. The whole trip was very nice and harmonious. I feel as if I am coming back to old familiar areas after some absence. I now know almost the entire local court.

Palais d'Hiver, 17 January 1903.

Last night there was a big gala dinner, very beautiful and splendid. I sat to the left of the Grand Duchess Maria Georgievna, daughter of the King of Greece, to her right sat the Tsar. We had a very animated conversation, she speaks fluent German. Opposite me sat the Crown Prince, next to him the two Empresses. The poor Crown Prince was very excited about his speech to be given. Only after it was over did he become lively. After the table, the Empress-Mother talked to me for a long time and was extraordinarily gracious. So were the reigning Empress and Grand Duchess Vladimir. The Grand Duke Vladimir is unfortunately ill. He told me through the Grand Duchess that he would like to speak to me and that I would like to come to him one of the next days. The reigning Empress impressed again with her beauty. She has become a little stronger, which suits her very well. The Emperor looked more comfortable than in the morning. This morning we went to the Hermitage and unfortunately saw only at a great gallop the magnificent art treasures, which are unique in their kind.

Palais d'Hiver, 18 January 1903.

We went to the Lutheran church today, where we heard an excruciatingly boring sermon followed by an endless liturgy. Then breakfast here at the Palais. Last night at the French Theater, where a namelessly stupid play was given. After the theater I sat until 1 o'clock with the Crown Prince, who told me of his Russian impressions. He is very fond of being here and generally likes it. I think the whole trip will be very nice and harmonious and will have the good success of forming personal relationships.

Palais d'Hiver, 19 January 1903.

Today was the feast of the consecration of water. Since the Emperor's cold is not yet completely cured, he did not go out, and we were able to watch the dreaded second part of the celebration, which takes place outdoors with bare heads, from a window of the palace. The whole thing was most interesting. In the palace deputations of all the regiments of guards with the flags lined up through a long flight of halls. Beautiful people, brilliantly dressed. A veritable state of troops. Grand service in the Castle Church, then the celebration on the banks of the Neva, then marching past of the flags before the Emperor and then breakfast. The affair lasted from 10:30 to 3 o'clock. Yesterday there was a big gala dinner at the Embassy. In the evening at 10 o'clock we heard a wonderful concert by the imperial singing corps, eighty boys and forty men, the most ideal of singing imaginable, pure music of the spheres. Basses that sound like organs, and in addition the fine voices of the boys, who sing as if with angelic tones.

Letter from Moltke to one of his children.

Berlin, 29 January 1903.

Mom told me that you would like to hear something more about Russia, the country and its people, and as an obedient father who is good to his daughter, I hasten to comply with your request and tell you what I experienced there.

We were our seven who accompanied the Crown Prince, three regimental commanders commanding the regiments of which the Emperor Nicholas is the chief, namely Lieutenant Colonel v. Schwerin of the 6th Cuirassiers, Lieutenant Colonel v. Lyncker of the 8th Hussars and Colonel v. Schenck of the Alexander Regiment, also Wing Adjutant v. Friedeburg and myself, furthermore Colonel v. Pritzelwitz, the military governor of the Crown Prince and his adjutant Stülpnagel. On January 14, in the evening, we reported to him at the Friedrich Strasse train station, where the Kaiser was also coming to bid farewell to his son. There was a sleeping car reserved for us, in which each had his own compartment, I as excellency and the piece de resistance of the company had two! After a quiet night's sleep, we arrived at Eydtkuhnen, our border station, at about 10 a.m. on the 15th, from where our train was immediately transferred to the Russian border town of Wirballen, or as the Russians say, Wirballowo. Here the Russian honor guard awaited us and, not to be sneezed at either, an extra Imperial Russian train. The former consisted of the adjutant general, Prince Dolgoroucki, the cavalry captain in the *Gardes à cheval* regiment, wing adjutant Count Shuvalov, and the lieutenant of the *Chevalier garde* regiment, Prince Kantacouzeme; the latter of a saloon car with a bedroom for the crown prince, a kitchen car, a dining saloon, a meeting saloon, three cars with smaller living quarters and bedrooms for the entourage, three cars for the servants, and several baggage cars, all electrically lit. Two locomotives at the front for pulling and a third at the rear for pushing were to carry this train, which was the size of the Russian Empire, to Petersburg.

The Russian railroads, as is well known, have wider tracks than ours and travel significantly slower, not exceeding fifty kilometers an hour, both of which contribute greatly to the convenience of travel. The engines are heated only by wood, which gives a splendid fireworks display at dark, in that the whole train is enveloped in a sea of flying sparks that pass in long streaks in front of the windows like thousands of small, luminous comets. I was directed to a chamber that contained a wide bed, a comfortable sofa, wash toilet, desk and closet, and was so spacious that it could easily serve as a reception room for visits. Everything was lined with light-colored silk fabric, and in this luxurious chamber I would have gladly made the journey via the Siberian railroad to Vladivostok, which takes only eight days.

From now on, the unrivaled Russian hospitality took us completely into its sphere of influence. No sooner had we set off than we were asked to breakfast, which, like all Russian meals, began with *sakkuska*, a so-called snack in which unsalted caviar is eaten with spoons and all kinds of delicacies tempt the newcomer to eat his fill before sitting down to the actual breakfast. Here we drank our first schnapps to greet our new Russian friends, and then at breakfast we immediately switched to sparkling wine, a drink that plays a similar role on the Russian table as Moselle wine does here, the liter at fifty pfennigs. The bottle of sparkling wine remained our inseparable comrade wherever we came near a laid table until the moment when we crossed the border again on the way back and it was immediately replaced by the Seidel "Genuine Munich." We spent the whole day eating breakfast, dinner and soup, and after the first twelve hours we had already become so accustomed to caviar that we could hardly understand how it was possible for a decent person to live for days, even weeks, without it. How wonderfully one could have slept in the silken bed, softly cradled by the gentle shaking of the broad, slow train, if only one had not eaten so endlessly. I lay awake for a long time, looking at the fireworks of spraying sparks passing outside my windows. At last I closed the curtains and extinguished the electric light, then fell into a semi-slumber in which all the pies, hazel chickens, quail and smoked fish I had eaten appeared to me as a vision, while pot-bellied bottles of champagne with a wreath of caviar grains in their hair gazed around me, to disappear at last into the darkness of deep sleep.

Thus we drove kilometer after kilometer through holy Russia, through barren, snow-covered areas, through morasses and scrub, through winter and loneliness, into the infinite giant empire, whose immense space gives us narrowly accustomed Western Europeans the feeling as if we had left the planet and steered out into the boundlessness of the space of values. The next morning, the 16th, at 10 o'clock, we arrived in Petersburg. Our ambassador, Count Alvensleben, had boarded the train an hour earlier in Gatchina and brought the final provisions about the reception.

The Emperor could not appear at the station as he had intended because he was suffering from an ear infection that confined him to his room. All the Grand Dukes who were not ill with influenza were present at the reception. On the platform there was an honorary company of the Preobratschensk regiment, which corresponds to our 1st Regiment of Guards. Beautiful, giant-sized people with the open, good-natured Russian peasant faces. Everything now went according to the international pattern. Departure of the front, presentation of the entourage, etc. I have become an old acquaintance in these circles.

Then we drove to the Winter Palace, where we were all accommodated. Here the Crown Prince was received by the Emperor and Empress and escorted to his apartments. Then we were greeted by the majesties. In the antechamber the whole court was lined up. There was the Chief Steward, the old, fat Princess Galitzin, who, like the Jews in the synagogue, must always have the hat on her head, under whose large brim she blinks to herself with tired, drooping eyes, the Chief Court Marshal Prince Dolgoroucki, a brother of our companion, and a whole row of court ladies, all with the Empress's brilliant cipher on their armpits. In front of each of the doors are two Moors in fantastically colorful costumes, who also greeted me as an old acquaintance with white teeth grinning. A faint smell of incense floats through all the rooms, in one corner of each room hangs the image of the saint to whom the special supervision of this compound is entrusted, and the light of the electric lamps, which burn all day in the dull Petersburg atmosphere, glitters in the crystals of the chandeliers and casts brilliant reflections on the ornate, mirror-smooth parquet floor.

Their Majesties greeted us in the friendliest manner. The Emperor looked miserable, he had had an ulcer in his ear, which had recently opened and had caused him much pain. The Empress looked blooming. A few very lovely dimples had formed at the fine corners of her mouth, and her beautifully drawn eyebrows stood out splendidly on her white forehead. At last everything is over. The court is dismissed. With a deep sigh and a slight bow, the imposing Lord Chamberlain bids farewell to her ladies, who in turn glide out with a deep bow and a slight sigh.

We are shown to our rooms. I immediately realize the impossibility of ever finding my way back without a local guide. Fortunately, I have a German-speaking footman. Again, I live quite modestly. When you step through the door from the corridor, there is a bathroom on the right, my bedroom on the left. Straight ahead is my study with endless upholstered chairs, chaise longues, sofas, desk, etc. Next to this is my dining room, and next to this is my reception room. It takes me quite a while alone to find my way around my apartment.

We are free until the dinner at 7 o'clock. It is to be a large gala dinner. A. is already there with my things and unpacks. Then I get into the bathroom to wash off the travel dust. When I return, A. has disappeared and left me to my fate. He assumes with unshakable consistency that such trips are undertaken for his entertainment, and that I am a highly superfluous and incidental addition to it, from which it is best to refrain as much as possible. From his point of view, this is a very reasonable view, and I am already so used to it that I would not have been upset about it this time either, if only some Russian gentlemen had not just now come to visit me, and if only I could have found my pants. But they had disappeared just as without a trace as A.

In vain I searched all the cupboards without finding anything with which I could have covered my lower nakedness. Skirts, helmet, cap, everything was there, but not a single pair of pants! – Again and again the footman knocked on my door to tell me that he had led Count Lüttke, an officer I knew from Preobratschensk, into the reception salon. He, too, did not know where A. or my pants had gone. Only later did I discover them in a closet of the anteroom, where A., being a tidy man, had placed them, avoiding all the closets located in the bedroom itself. There they lay peacefully one beside the other, like kippers in the smoke.

As I gave up hope of ever finding them, I briefly considered whether I should put on the tunic without leggings, or whether I should draw the consequences of my situation to the utmost, decided on the latter, and received my visits in shirt and underpants! Only as the Prince Orloff had himself announced to me, who came on behalf of the Emperor to bring me a medal, the courage of my nakedness sank and I negotiated with him through the door gap without seeing him, so that I could introduce myself to him only in the evening. Through that crack in the door I received a red *saffiano* box in which lay a flashing diamond star. The hand which presented it to me was large and fat, from which I concluded that the prince belonging to it was large and well-fed. As I could see in the evening, I was not mistaken, he was big and fat.

I finally lay down to bed and waited for A. He appeared after a few hours and declared that he had eaten lunch. I did not dare to find anything improper in this natural process and sought to regain his friendship. The gala table was magnificent. All the grand dukes and grand duchesses had appeared, all the dignitaries of the empire were on hand. I sat in the center of the table, on my right the Grand Duchess Marie Georgievna, daughter of the King of Greece, on her right the Emperor. To my left, the Empress-Mother's Chief Steward, muttering an unintelligible French to herself. Opposite me, the two Empresses, who had the crown prince between them, sitting vis-a-vis the Emperor.

The Greek Grand Duchess spoke fluent German and was very lively, amiable and entertaining. The poor Crown Prince looked pale and preoccupied and ate almost nothing. Only after he had made his speech did he revive. The two Empresses shone in the most splendid brilliants. Both are very advantageous appearances. The Empress-mother is not exactly pretty, but she has a pair of wonderful eyes, whose brilliance the years have not dimmed, and over which one forgets the too large mouth. She has inherited from her father, the King of Denmark, the art of eternal youth; one would hardly give her forty years. Mentally important, clever and, when she wants to be, beguilingly amiable, she has a great influence on the Emperor. She is the first lady at all official occasions, preceding even the reigning Empress as long as the latter has no son. Until now, the Empress-mother is number one as the mother of the grand duke heir to the throne. The reigning Empress is made to grace a throne and wear the walnut-sized diamonds of the crown treasure on her white bosom in grand parade. Her dazzling appearance so suits this jewelry that one might think she was born with it.

After the table was lifted, ceremony was made. The Grand Duchess Vladimir, a princess of Mecklenburg by birth, who, like her husband, has always met me with the greatest kindness, took possession of me. She asked me to visit the Grand Duke, who was ill with influenza, one of the next days. Then the Empress talked with each of us. In the meantime, the Emperor introduced the main characters to the Crown Prince. There were quite interesting figures. Count Lambsdorff, a small, bald man, who always looks as if he were standing on his toes to appear taller, even his sparse hair brushed up behind his ears so that it sticks up in the air, and at the same time he makes a half-scowling, half-benevolent face and pushes his lower lip forward. Minister Witte, the all-powerful finance minister of the Reich, who managed the feat of introducing the gold currency in Russia without the country going bankrupt, a man of my size, with a clever little head and a dark full beard. Very modest, somewhat embarrassed, he prefers to huddle in hidden corners. The Minister of War, Kuropatkin, who keeps his gaze so firmly fixed on Asia that he can treat the little bit of Europe in his flank with benign indifference, – his antipode, the Chief of the General Staff, Sakharin, a short, fat man with cunning eyes, great friend of the French and eater of Germans, who would rather strike out against us today than tomorrow. Yes, if it were not for Kuropatkin with his Asia and if it were not for Witte with his plans for reform! But these two need us, because they need peace!

The little crown prince is trying valiantly to make conversation with all those introduced to him. He looks very nice in his dressy Russian uniform, his slim, elegant figure and his open, friendly face are generally pleasing. At 1 p.m., the gentlemen withdraw, and we go up the endless stairs and corridors – guided, of course, by people who know the place – to drink another glass of beer in one of my lounges. Having just reached the top, I am then called down to the Crown Prince, who probably feels the need to talk about his impressions and with whom I sit until 1 o'clock. When I return to my room, everyone is gone, leaving me only a thick smoke of tobacco and a battery of empty bottles!

This was our first day in Petersburg. But if I wanted to continue in the same style to describe the following eight days to you, this letter would become a book, and I fear that you would fall asleep over it. So I have to proceed a little more cursorily.

The second day after our arrival was the feast of the consecration of water. This festival, celebrated throughout Russia, is always celebrated in the most brilliant manner. It is dreaded by all concerned, for in general January 18 is considered the coldest day of the cold Russian winter, and it is a doubtful pleasure to stand outdoors for half an hour with one's head uncovered on a day twenty degrees *Reaumur** below zero. In honor of this celebration we had all equipped ourselves with furs and felt boots. We were not to use them. All the time of our stay in Petersburg the thermometer did not fall below eight degrees. It was warmer than it was in Germany at the same time, and there was little snow, so that large loads of snow were brought into the city every day from outside, where the snow was spread on the streets as sand is spread here to improve the sledding track. Even on the day of the festival there was only seven degrees of cold, but the air is still cutting and every breeze seems to bring doubled cold. The Neva, that mighty, proud stream that cuts through the city in a width of two kilometers, lay tamed by ice.

Electric railroads, roads for sleighs and wagon traffic pass over the ice cover, gas pipes are laid across the ice, and in the evening all the streets are lit up, under which the black Neva water gurgles. The Feast of the Dedication of the Water is the commemoration of Christ's baptism in the Jordan River. On the bank of the stream, a pavilion is built for the clergy and the court, from which a staircase leads down to the ice, in which a hole is made. Into this hole, with singing and blessing, the cross is plunged, and with it the water is consecrated.

At 11 o'clock the ceremony began in the palace. There, in the endless halls, which were lined up in a long line, stood deputations from all the Petersburg regiments. Always sixty men from each regiment in parade costume. A beautiful sight. All selected people. There were, for example, the *Gardes a cheval*, all people my size, all with black hair and short black full beards, which looked splendid with the white tunics. Next to them the *Chevalier garde*, all blond people, the Paulovsk regiment, where only people with blunt noses are recruited, in memory of Emperor Paul's blunt nose, who founded the regiment. There are the Cossacks of the body convoy, in their scarlet skirts falling down to the feet with silver-studded military hanger, the black Kirghiz cap crooked on the right ear, while around the left one there is a big curl of the thick curly hair. The Don Cossacks in sky-blue skirts, the grenadiers on

---

* A temperature scale in which water boils at 80 degrees and freezes at 0 degrees.

horseback with long tails on their old-fashioned bear caps, the naval guards, to which only the choicest people come who serve there for seven years – who knows the troops, names the names! – A flower selection of the guard, as no nation on earth can provide more beautiful. In Russia, only about one third of the crew is recruited each year; one can imagine the choice one has there, and only the very best come to the Guard.

Through these troops, who form a line, the court strides in a long, solemn procession into the chapel of the Winter Palace. The Empresses in the jewelry of their brilliants, all ladies in the red velvet, gold-embroidered court dress with long train, on the head the *Kokoshnik*, the old Russian, half-moon shaped headdress. In front of them the clergy in their silver-glittering vestments, the patriarch with the bishop's cap, on which a fortune of stones sparkles, golden monstrances, incense burners, embroidered flags, an overwhelming picture of the utmost pomp and the greatest splendor imaginable. With the proceeds of the stones that pass before our eyes here, one could buy a kingdom. And in front of all this pomp, in which the highest that the Russian giant empire is able to offer in worldly and spiritual power, in earthly and heavenly splendor is united, the Russian peasant son in his parade uniform stands with presented rifle and stares with widened eyes at all the gleam. Is it any wonder that he thinks he sees God himself and his saints passing by, is it any wonder that in his loyal peasant sense the concepts of divinity and monarchy merge and that he sinks to his knees before his Tsar Father, who is not only his worldly ruler but also the bearer of the highest spiritual power!

Here lies the giant power of the Russian monarchy. The two pillars on which the whole Russian polity rests: Church and Emperorship unite in the person of the Tsar. One is inseparable from the other and they dominate everything that is sacred and mystical in the soul of the Russian peasant. And how is it with us, where two different denominations fight each other and where the title of *Summus Episcopus** is all that is left to the holder of the throne, a title that hardly anyone knows or understands!

---

* "The High Bishop."

Now the high mass begins in the chapel. This chapel is at least as large as the garrison church in Potsdam. The singing of the imperial choir resounds with indescribable beauty from its high vault. This famous choir, probably the most beautiful *a cappella* choir in the world, consists of eighty boys and as many men. As if on the wings of angels, the silver-clear boys' voices float above the organ-like basses. To hear such basses, one must come to Russia, one can hardly believe that they come from a human breast, and yet, there is no instrument that could sound so soft. The whole choir is dressed in scarlet, in front the children stand with devout faces, like mystical rapture it sounds from the singing. Gradually the church fills with incense. What is being performed here is no longer a worship service in our sober terms, it is a show, but worship, and of the most sublime kind, is the singing. And yet, as I looked at the behavior of the clergy, how they come and go, decorate the patriarch, surround the sacred instruments with mysterious ceremonies, I became aware of how in all this lies only the endeavor of man to form what is most sacred to him in a way of external celebration, into which he wants to put everything that is given to him in the way of beauty and celebration. All splendor and magnificence is to be laid down before the altar of the Most High in the thought that the most glorious thing we possess is only just good enough to worship the Divine. This thought may be earthly enough, but it is comprehensible to the great mass of people who have not yet learned to worship God in spirit and in truth.

Such a Russian high mass lasts a good hour and a half, and all participants have to stand during the entire time if they don't kneel down for a change. This is an exhausting thing and, when it is over, most of the devotees are lame as crosses. After the celebration was over, the solemn procession went back again and now the celebration began outside at the Newaufer. The Emperor did not go out because of his ear ailment and so the Crown Prince and with him we stayed inside. We watched the ceremony from a window of the palace and felt heartfelt sympathy for the poor people who stood around the hole in the ice of the Neva with their heads exposed. After this too was over, the Emperor had all the flags of the Guard Corps marched past him in a hall. All of them came one after the other, each led by an officer. The music played a parade march. It was a most peculiar parade. Then breakfast was served. About two thousand people at small tables. All placed. The Russian court marshal's office is great in such arrangements.

After breakfast, the crown prince handed over to the Emperor a model ship we had brought with us. He already complained to me about exhaustion and fatigue. In the afternoon, he had really gone to bed and was ill. Influenza, as the doctors said. I think it was just overexertion, because after two days he was quite lively again.

This illness, of course, put a crimp in our program, but it only served the purpose of the trip to bring about a personal rapprochement. The Emperor and Empress were touching in their care for the sick man. They sat for hours at his bedside, brought him small gifts, ate in his room, and, I believe, became really fond of him. Likewise, a very pretty relationship was established between him and the heir to the throne, who is a very sympathetic, open and kind person.

The next day, in accordance with the Grand Duchess's wish, I went to see Grand Prince Vladimir. When I arrived, I was told that he was sleeping, but the Grand Duchess asked me to come up to her. I then sat with her for about an hour. She would not let me leave, claiming that the Grand Duchess would be angry if I were gone, that he had not been awakened. Then the Empress-Mother was announced and came into the room before I could say goodbye. She immediately told me: "Your crown prince is quite a charming young man. He sent me a very nice bouquet. Very attentive, etc. I was pleased that he had put himself in such a good light with the most important lady of the court.

In the afternoon I had to come back and was immediately shown in to the Grand Duke. He was lying in bed and looked quite miserable. It was painful to me to see this man, whom I still knew in the fullness of his strength and manly beauty, so broken and aged. I fear he will not live long and we will lose a good friend in him. The Grand Duchess was sitting at his bedside with a handiwork. He greeted me very kindly and extended his feverish hand to me. Then I had to sit down and tell how Petersburg pleased the Crown Prince. It took me quite a while to collect myself, always searching that sick face, over whose sunken cheeks the lamp covered with a green shade cast uncertain lights. After sitting and talking for about half an hour, I was released.

In the evening of the same day we all dined at the famous Cubat restaurant, which to my knowledge marches at the head of all the most outrageous prices in the world. Then we went to the German Theater, where a Viennese farce was performed, and then late at night we took a sleigh ride in troikas to the islands, where we hurtled down a Russian slide in a sleigh that made you lose your hearing and sight. Then we went to the Aquarium, a large entertainment center outside the city, where a delicious meal was prepared for us in a reserved room, while a choir in Russian national costume played music for us. We arrived home at 4 o'clock in the morning.

The prettiest part is the troika rides. A big sleigh with wide sweeping snow wings. You sit up to your ears in fur, warm and cozy, like yolks in an egg. The coachman is standing in front of the seat, wearing the Russian coachman's costume, the long fur with the colorful embroidered belt and the fur beret. Of the three horses richly harnessed with silver harnesses, the middle one walks under the high stirrup with bells hanging from it. The two side horses, which walk without drawbars, are tied sharply to the right and left, respectively, so that they gallop with their necks bent all the way to the side, while the middle horse may only trot. The best hard trotters are taken to him. I was told that the side horses do not last more than two to three years. So the ride goes forward at a furious pace. The loud shouting of the coachman, who soon speaks to the horses, soon calls other sleds to make way for him, resounds with the bells, and everything reverently swerves to make way for the troika, in which only a *barim*, a "gentleman," can ride. Such a carriage, with night-dark horses, is really a wonderful sight, however, it can drive only on the wide Russian roads, with us it would block almost the whole road. One sits splendidly in the deep, comfortable sleigh, the cold air blows around one's face, and whole clumps of snow, hurled by the hooves of the galloping horses, whiz past, while a fine dusting of snow dusts one from top to bottom.

I cannot tell you everything we experienced and saw, I would have to sit at my desk for days. We went to the Hermitage, that unique museum with its exquisite art treasures, we visited the

Cathedrals of St. Nicholas and Kazan, we went to an industrial exhibition, we dined at the Embassy, we drove and walked on the ice of the Neva, we visited the barracks of the Preobratschensk Regiment and had breakfast with the officers in their beautiful mess hall, we were with the *Gardes a cheval*, who showed us a squadron drill in their large, heated ring or as we say riding arena, we dined once with them and had breakfast once there, enough, we always stood a few inches high under champagne and I had to make speeches to the Russian comrades. So the days flew by.

On the 23rd there was a big ball at the Grand Prince Michael's. The Crown Prince was healthy again and was very much looking forward to dancing. The cream of Petersburg society was united in the large hall, it was teeming with princesses, countesses, etc. As the *cotillion* was being danced, the reigning Empress had me called and I had to sit next to her. So we danced a seated *cotillion* together, to the right and left of us an empty space of ten steps, filled only with awe, and the two of us in the middle of it. We talked very well and I also got to know her as a human being for once and found opportunity to admire her natural kindness and simple straight sense. I gave her all the bouquets, bows, baskets and other things that the tours brought and she happily accepted it all, to bring, as she said, to her children. Then came the bows for the ladies, and now I got one from her. I told her, "Your Majesty, this is the first time in my life that I have received a cotillion ribbon from a reigning Empress." The *cotillion* lasted almost an hour and our conversation did not break off for a moment. But she did not want to dance, although the old Grand Duke Michael came to tell her that she would like to dance with me. He said, pointing at me, "*Je suis sur, que Monsieur est un bon marcheur!*"* – but she didn't want to. I preferred it that way, too. Then came the souper, at which I was seated next to the Empress-mother, so that I spent that evening consorting almost exclusively with Empresses.

The next morning we said goodbye to the Majesties and drove to Novgorod to the Vyborg Regiment. The Crown Prince was greeted with endless cheers by the densely packed population.

---

* "I am confident that the gentleman is a good dancer!"

From there back in the same comfortable court train to Eydtkuhnen, where we said goodbye to our Russian friends. On the 26th, at 6 o'clock in the morning, we were in Berlin.

Now just a short note about how to shoot bears. I have only the unique experience, which I take as a basis. So you get up at 8 o'clock in the morning. This is very early for Russian conditions. Then you go to the station in a light hunting costume, where a special train is waiting. In the train there is already a breakfast with tea, coffee, cold cuts and champagne, of course caviar. The train starts moving and you travel for two hours, which is very long, but the bear has the whim to hibernate so far from Petersburg. Just before arriving, one puts on the warm clothes kept ready. A fur, a fur hat and white, soft felt boots, into which one merely enters with stockings.

Then the train stops, you get off and sit down in a waiting sleigh, which is completely lined with fur. There is a sleigh for each of us. The chief hunter Prince Galitzin takes the tete, and we now have ten minutes to ride on a smooth track. In the forest all branches that could become uncomfortable are cut out. We come to a free place where the snow has been carefully trampled down so that we don't get our feet wet when we get out, and we get out. The drivers are already gathered there, about a hundred men, who greet us with their caps off. About twenty men wear red smocks, caps and gloves. These are the special drivers who are to "lift" the bear if it does not get up voluntarily. From this place, a neatly trampled path leads to the interior of the thicket. In single file we proceed. Now we are not allowed to speak loudly. Everything moves forward in silence, hunters and drivers. After two minutes we are at the numbered stands. I get the one intended for the crown prince. A strong breastplate woven from fir branches, the floor covered with small fir twigs. An imperial body hunter places a double rifle next to me, smooth barrels and round ball. He places my rifle sideways as a reserve. He himself is also armed with a double rifle and a spear as thick as an arm. A beater with a mastiff as high as a table stays behind us, it is trained to immediately grab an attacking bear by the throat. So one feels reasonably safe. After the hunters are positioned, the "ring" is already formed by the drivers. They surround the bear's camp in a semicircle of about three hundred paces in diameter.

A bugle call and the spectacle starts. Everyone shoots guns, screams, squeals, shrieks, lets loose cannon blasts. It lasts ten minutes, no bear comes. Horn signal: the bear must be lifted. The red beaters proceed with dogs. They bark at the bear in its den, the beaters advance and push into the camp with long poles. Sudden explosion, snow, pieces of ice, twigs and leaves fly around, the bear is up and has blown up its den, it is "lifted." Horn signal announces this to the hunters. Another ten minutes. The dogs bark after the bear, which slowly moves in the circle of the hunters, looking for a way out. Suddenly he comes straight pointedly toward me. He wades slowly through the knee-deep snow. Forty steps in front of me he stops and backs up.

I can't get my head free, which is covered by a tree, but I hold onto the shoulder and draw fire. The bear collapses, makes a jump to the side, I get the leaf free and give him the second bullet there. He falls, tries to get up again, another rifle is already shoved into my hand and I fire two more bullets at the poor *Petz*, who is now dead as a doornail. The hunt is called off, the bear is dragged out. It is a beautiful specimen, almost black, a male. Now back to the train. Breakfast is already waiting in the train, starting with caviar and champagne. Then back in the sled and to the second bear, which, however, is sixteen kilometers away. Here exactly the same. I ceded my place to Pritzelwitz, and he shoots the bear. This time it was a female bear with two cubs, barely eight days old, who bit the dogs to death. Then back on the train, where tea and coffee are served. At 6 o'clock we are back in Petersburg and at 7 o'clock we are sitting at the diner.

Good health, you will say. And I tell you: Enjoy it, namely the reading of this work.

Berlin, 31 March 1903.

Believe me that nothing is further from my mind than to want to take away your faith or even to touch it. Only I would like to admonish you to be careful, because your good heart is abused only too easily and you see the people in the transfiguration of common circle of vision, not objectively, as they really are. I would like to share with you what is really beautiful and comforting in this faith, I believe that we will always find each other in the striving for the ideal, only in these ugly externalities I cannot go along. You idealize them for yourself, I always see the naked and often repulsive reality, and am not able to classify them in the ideas I have of the spirit and spiritual being. They are unclear, these ideas, but I must try to underlay them with a certain clarity, something that lies above our earthly existence and does not dive into the murky depths of it. Whoever owns a precious stone should not put it to his chest and go to the market with it, otherwise dirty hands will grab it and it can easily fall into the excrement and be trodden under the feet.

Copenhagen, 2 April 1903.

Now I'm sitting here in old Copenhagen, in the castle I used to pass so often in the old days, looking out of my window at the castle square with its old equestrian figure! – It is quite strange. Our trip was excellent. We boarded the ship in Kiel at 7 o'clock this morning, and the weather was cold and unfriendly. The more we approached the Danish coast, however, the brighter it became, and as we approached the forts, which greeted us with cannon thunder, it had become quite clear and the sun shone kindly. Many thousands of people stood crowded on the shore as we passed Tre Kroner and dropped anchor. The king with all the princes came aboard, where we stood assembled in parade costume. The Emperor rode with the King in a glass state coach, escorted by a squadron of hussars. Troops were lined up as a trellis all along the way, and an innumerable crowd thronged the streets.

Copenhagen, 6 April 1903.

We have been on the road all day and have seen a lot. The mood is good, the Emperor has gained a lot by his affability, and his speech has made an excellent impression.

Kiel, April 6, 1903.

The time in Copenhagen was very nice and successful in every respect. The relationship between the two monarchs was excellent and very cordial. The mood was excellent and also in the audience became warmer day by day, at the departure the Emperor even got a very nice cheer. The Emperor was constantly in a very good mood and always very friendly towards me. I had breakfast every morning with him and the two wing adjutants on duty. The Danish gentlemen were touchingly kind.

For the first time on the occasion of this visit, although I have been to Copenhagen so often, I got to see Rosenborg and Frederiksborg, both highly interesting castles with very valuable contents. We also went to Professor Finsen's sanatorium, which was interesting but ghastly to look at. Never in my life have I seen so many people without noses.

Berlin, 10 April 1903.

Today E. and I were in the Kaiser Friedrich Church, where we heard a very beautiful sermon. Rarely has a sermon gone to my heart and the sublimity of the pure Christian faith in its indefinable violence come to my inner consciousness. How enviable are the people who, out of full inner conviction, have this peace-bringing faith in salvation, which must fully satisfy the deep inner need of the struggling and searching soul of man, if it really rises to the whole height of unshakable certainty. You know that this benefit is not given to me and that I have struggled and still struggle for it in vain. If I could eliminate my so-called reason, I might succeed in attaining the peace that is higher than all reason. But the dogma of salvation stands before me incomprehensible and inconceivable. I cannot understand why it was necessary for a God who is supposed to be love to require a bloody sacrifice of the innocent in order to reconcile with the guilty, and how it should be possible that my guilt should be forgiven because another has suffered. I cannot get out of this conflict, and since I thus cannot comprehend redemption and therefore cannot claim it for myself, I also cannot come to the rocky bottom of faith and wade steadily on in the quicksand of brooding doubts. But I hope that God will help me, and if not in this life, then in another, give me a ray of light that I can follow.

At 2 o'clock we had your mother at our table. E. had set up a small birthday table for her – a picture she had provided, of the blind walking through blooming poppies, was like a parable of my soul, she too goes her way blind and groping, darkness covers her eyes, and yet she knows that the sun is shining and that the poppies are blooming in red splendor, the poppies, the symbol of sleep – that sleep which will also open the eyes of the blind.

Berlin, 15 April 1903.

Certainly we should strive for ever greater spiritualization, but in my opinion not by simply negating and despising the material, but by letting the ideal moments emerge from it ever more purely, by transfiguring it and illuminating it with the spiritual, as there is: love, care for one's neighbor, tenderness of feeling, forbearance with the faults of others. In this way we will create a spiritual world for ourselves in the material dress, we will not despise the earthly but ennoble it, we will not want to forcibly unhinge the world in which we live, but recognize our material existence as what it should be, a passage to a better existence. If we want to break this step out of the ladder of world development, our foot will step into the void and we will fall, because we do not have wings yet. I mean, we should stand firmly and securely on this step, looking upward, aware that there are more steps to come, but also clearly aware that we can only move on to the next one when we have achieved balance on the present one.

Berlin, 16 April 1903.

I read the last days a quite interesting book of Chamberlain, it is called "*Dilettantism – Babel and Bible – Rome,*" let it come to you. Among other things, I found in it, as evidence of the defective translation of the Bible by Luther, and thus the conclusions that can be made to literalism, the proof that the first verse of Genesis, which according to the Lutheran translation reads: "In the beginning God created the heavens and the earth" – period –, the former only the prefix to the then following suffix: "and the earth was desolate and empty" – that therefore there must be no period; secondly, that literally translated from the Hebrew it should read: "When the demons began to separate the air and the solid land, the earth was still empty and uninhabited." Indeed, it says *"elohim"* in the text, which is plural and means "the demons."* In the singular it should be *"el"*, which means God. So the very first verse is falsified in favor of monotheism, etc. Whether Chamberlain is right, I cannot judge of course, but I would like to believe it.

Berlin, 23 April 1903.

I was at the Little Theater yesterday, where I saw "Pelleas and Melisande" by Maeterlingk, an excellent performance of this strange fairy-tale play, which is not very dramatic, but very poetic. I knew it from reading it, had once intended to translate it myself, but never got around to it.

Berlin, 25 April 1903.

In the evening I went to the "Nachtasyl." It's a terrible play! Nothing like misery and squalor, a photograph of the swampy human existence. At the same time it is unsatisfactory, without dramatic climax and without conclusion, purposeless like the misery of life, and bleak, because not a single person works his way out of the misery, but all perish in it or remain hopelessly stuck in it. The few who want to make a feeble attempt at their own salvation are ensnared anew in guilt, not a single ray of light in all

---

* Publisher's note: This is incorrect. *"Elohim"* refers to gods or deities, not demons. The Hebrew word for demons is *"Shedim."*

the suffocating darkness, life grinds indifferently and heavily like millstones these wretched people who with all their humanity cannot get beyond the dull question: What am I in the world for? The play left me with a deep and ugly impression, and I cannot acknowledge the justification of this view of life. If all that is said is: "Why work?" It has no purpose at all, is completely pointless, then this is pessimism in its ugliest form. If there were even one character in the play who made himself free through work, it would be something else. The old goofy pilgrim is not a point of light either; his efforts may comfort a dying woman, but they drive a living man to his death, and his theory that people are only there for the most capable is worthless, since not a single one can be found who now wants to become this most capable by his own efforts.

Berlin, 27 April 1903.

That the sight of such a devastation has a nauseating effect on you, I can explain well. It is the senselessness that you feel as such, the destruction as such, without conceivable reason; one is used to connect cause and effect, if one cannot construct this logical conclusion, the firmness of the thought connection is missing, the concepts falter, one becomes mentally seasick.

Berlin, 27 April 1903.

Tomorrow is the day we are all looking forward to with apprehension, the Emperor's inspection of the battalions of the 1st Guards Regiment. No one looks forward to this day as it used to be when the old gentleman came to see his regiment. Now, at best, there is a dull resignation as if facing fate, and when it is happily over, without a break in the wind, everyone breathes a sigh of relief. Where has the joyfulness gone with which everyone used to do his duty!

Berlin, 30 April 1903.

You wonder about H.'s appointment as field marshal, but he was already colonel general, which is about the same thing. He took part in all three last wars and always distinguished himself. You probably mean that he is not appointed to it following a war, that is correct. As long as Uncle Helmuth was the only field marshal, people had a different idea of this title, but since we no longer have any wars, we have to make peace marshals – if they are considered necessary at all.

Berlin, 4 May 1903.

How long will it take until one stands before the answer of all the unsolved questions, with which one has toiled here in the life so constantly? In the meantime it is nice when a new generation sprouts and grows around the old trunk with new views, new sufferings and joys and new unresolved questions!

Berlin, 6 May 1903.

All the trees except the old oaks are green, the beeches are magnificent in their fresh green foliage. I cannot see such a spring-fresh beech without thinking of my childhood days, of the beech forests in Ranzau, which are unforgettable to me. I see myself as a boy roaming through the forest, observing the animals and listening to the songs of the birds, whose voices I all knew, and I have the sensation as if I could still be as vividly interested in the moss-covered nest of a chaffinch today as I was half a century ago.

Berlin, 14 May 1903.

In military circles, people are racking their brains over who will get the VI Corps. First and foremost, Duke Albrecht of Württemberg is mentioned. Prince Frederick Leopold is also being strongly considered. I think it would be best for Breslau if there were no prince for once, so that people could calm down again and the race for princely favor would stop.

Berlin, 31 May 1903.

I had church consecration this morning, that is, a church dedication, together with M., who represented the Empress. We heard two sermons, the first by F., very interesting as always, more philosophical than dogmatic. The man always gives me the impression that he wants to persuade himself that everything he says is true and that he himself believes in it. But he is witty and captivating, though not to the heart, but addressing himself more to the mind. Then came the local pastor with an endless speech devoid of content, much words and little sense. He tried to stir the hearts of his listeners more by emphasis than by thought!

Norway, Molde, 21 July 1903.

Today at the table the Emperor declared me a pagan, because I claimed that three disciples went to Emmaus, while there should have been only two! I told him, I do not believe that I go to hell because of the one disciple, besides, one cannot know whether not another went along! – The Emperor is always uniformly nice and friendly with me, and here on the ship it is said that I am the only one to whom he has not become rough.

Norway, Florö Island, 4 August 1903.

It occurs to me that today the new Pope has been elected,* as was to be expected, an outsider, a compromise Pope. The cardinals have not been able to agree on the prominent personalities standing

---

* Pius X.

for election, and finally choose the one who is least inconvenient to them all. What monstrosities arise when one thinks about this matter. Now the man elected for such reasons is the infallible one! – The sovereign ruler of the salvation of millions of people to whom he can open the door of paradise or slam it in their faces. It is quite incomprehensible how a thinking man can believe that God has ordered his representation on earth in this way. And what power this belief embodies, which is based on the broad basis of the inability to think of the great mass of people!

Norway, Odde, 8 August 1903.

We live on so calmly as if there were no death, and do not know how near ours is – . How tender and transient a human life is, if one measures it by the many-thousand-year duration of these granite mountains. And yet they too will pass away one day, the difference lies only in the span of time, and what is time if it is measured by eternity!

That is the kind of life I would like to have, to end the day, which has had its burden, with a lecture of deep content, and then perhaps a discussion to clarify opinions, in which everyone descends once into his own world of thought and searches for the pearl of truth.

CABINET ORDER.

I hereby order you to the service of the Chief of the Army General Staff until further notice.
Berlin, 1 January 1904.

Wilhelm R.

To My Adjutant General, Lieutenant General v. Moltke, Commander of the 1st Guards Division.

CABINET ORDER.

I hereby appoint you, leaving you in the capacity of My Adjutant

General and transferring you to the General Staff of the Army, Quartermaster General.
Berlin, 16 February 1904.

Wilhelm R.

To My Adjutant General, Lieutenant General v. Moltke, Commander of the 1st Guards Division and Commanding General of the Army.

Berlin, 5 March 1904.

How lovely it would be if we could all have been together. Yes, if one were free! It is not only my uncertain position and future that weighs on me, I feel like a pressure the whole untruthfulness and aloofness of our patriotic conditions. The German people as a whole is a miserable society. They are all church-tower politicians, without a trace of generosity, petty, malicious, full of envy and resentment, spiteful and short-sighted to the point of pity. Everywhere they tear down, throw dirt, slander and lie, and all this under the cloak of virtuous indignation. Hypocrisy everywhere you look, narrow-minded egoism and crass materialism. No ideals are valid anymore, everything is an outward appearance. What was still enduring is being torn down, everyone wants to elevate himself, and when the great heap of rubble is finished, the judgment will come upon us.

Does it not sound like a statement from the fool's house when it is said in the Reichstag that we must not build any more ships now, but must first wait for the experience of the naval war in East Asia? And this is said by men who consider themselves wise. They want to wait and see which lid will fit best on the well into which the child will fall. No one has any idea of what storm is gathering over us, instead of preparing for heavy things with holy seriousness, the nation is hacking each other to pieces. How long will it be before the pillars crack in the proud imperial edifice, built with blood and iron and now being undermined in petty bickering.

Berlin, 6 March 1904.

Waldersee's death came as a surprise. I have lost no friend or patron in him, but I do regret his departure. After all, he was one of the "elder statesmen" of the army.

The General Staff is of the opinion that Count Schlieffen will now become Army Inspector in place of Waldersee and that a successor for him will be appointed soon. I hope that at least His Majesty will talk to me beforehand and not simply send me another blue letter. I had hoped that the decision would be delayed until I was ready for the corps, but God knows how many years could pass since there is no more advancement and the higher positions are fixed as if rammed into place.

I am now reading a very interesting book by Dr. Steiner about Nietzsche, who was completely incomprehensible to me until now. In this book his development and his train of thought is so clearly and comprehensibly set forth that it is a real pleasure. As Schopenhauer traces all human action and thought back to the transcendental will to life, so Nietzsche asserts that the basic motive of all action is the real will to power. The weak, afraid to follow this will to power, construct for themselves an alien (divine) will to which they submit. Hence the concepts of good and evil, while in reality it is not proven at all what is actually good and evil. Beyond good and evil. You must also read the book once. You get an idea of what the man actually wants to say.

Berlin, 8 March 1904.

Yesterday evening I read another book by Steiner about Haeckel, which, like all his writings, interested me very much. In it, he completely confesses to Haeckel's monistic natural philosophy (not to be confused with monotheistic), and it is quite incomprehensible to me how he made the leap from it to theosophy. I am very eager to see him again some day to ask him about it. After this work of his, one can confidently place him in the middle of the phalanx of the materialists, and yet it is one of his more recent writings. But he is always clear and captivating. No philosophizing writer has ever been as comprehensible to me as he is.

Saarunion, 16 June 1904.

We rode off at 6 a.m. today and arrived here after 12 noon. Today we crossed the entire northern foothills of the Vosges from Zabern to Saarunion on the banks of the Saar. Here is already Lorraine, and a characteristic difference makes itself felt. The houses are built differently, all of them have the dung heap towards the road. The French inscriptions multiply. In the middle of them, the most stately building is always the "Imperial Post Office." The terrain becomes less mountainous here, wide, flat ridges have replaced the wooded often quite steep hilltops of the mountains. Tomorrow we will return to it once again by moving our quarters to the small mountain fortress of Bitsch, which resisted us in the war of 1870/71 until peace was concluded. This brings us to the area that the 3rd Army, to which I belonged, passed through after the Battle of Wörth. I often have to think of this time, which is now so far behind me. At that time a young ensign, today when I come back to this area for the first time, an old, bald general. *Sic transit gloria mundi!**

You can imagine how these rides interest me. I get along very well with Schlieffen. He is polite and sometimes even kind to me. Sometimes he even tells me something. I sincerely admire his sprightliness. Not many at his age would do these rides anymore, and at the same time he works diligently in the quarters. The officers are given a good workout, have to do reconnaissance and reconnaissance, and have a lot of riding and writing to do.

St. Avold, 18 June 1904.

I live in the "Hotel to the Post Office" in the room where the old

---

* "Thus passes the glory of the world!"

Kaiser Wilhelm lived in 1870 from 11 to 13 August. Uncle Helmuth also lived here. Today is Sunday, and the horses have a day of rest, which will be very pleasant for them. From 4 o'clock the war game continued in the room until 7 o'clock, when we ate. Count Schlieffen asks my opinion from time to time, and it almost never coincides with his. One can think of no greater contradictions than our views on both sides. I, however, state mine plainly, and he accepts my statements with decency and dignity.

Berlin, 29 June 1904.

I was very interested in the fourteen-day ride through the Reichslande. Alsace and the Vosges are a magnificent country. In Lorraine the population is degenerating into filth and indolence. I was saddened to see that thirty-three years of membership in the German Reich had not had the slightest effect, and that the district councils or, as they are called there, district directors, should be sent to the devil. Nothing at all has been done, not even a proper administrative authority has been set up, and everything goes on in the grossest slovenliness, as it may. One has no idea of the dissoluteness of the field occupation, mostly one does not know whether people grow wheat or weeds, although it is a wonderful, fertile soil, on which everything grows by itself, the vine and the nut tree thrive. Half of the villages consist of dung heaps, all of which are situated in front of the ragged houses facing the street, with wells in between them. Typhus is rampant as a result. It is a crying shame for the beautiful country. The people have very beautiful cattle, similar to the Simmentals, only a little smaller, and all they get is rancid butter. Cabbage grows in the gardens like in the Osdorf sewage fields, full cherry trees and apricots everywhere, but the inns are full of dirt, all the rooms with hanging wallpaper, the food is terrible except for the good fresh potatoes. It is a pity to see how this blessed land becomes desolate and ruined without anything being done.

CABINET ORDER.

I have determined that you will be used as a referee in the maneuvers of the Guard and IX Army Corps that will take place before me this year. I hereby inform you that you will be used as referees in the maneuvers of the Guard and IX Army Corps that will take place before me this year. At the same time, I am enclosing a list of the other referees appointed by me.
Kiel, on board M. J. "Hohenzollern," 30 June 1904.
Wilhelm R.
To My Adjutant General, Lieutenant General v. Moltke, Quartermaster General.

Norway, Bergen, 10 July 1904.

I am now reading a book by the philosopher Hartmann: "Philosophy of Religion." He tries to prove that religion must develop just like the world view if it does not want to become backward and die off.

Norway, Bergen, 12 July 1904.

Yesterday, after dinner, the Emperor read a beautifully written article from an English magazine, which he immediately translated into German, about radium and its strange properties. The following image was used to illustrate the atom, the smallest part of a body that can no longer be disassembled. Imagine a drop of water enlarged to the size of the earth, then an atom would be about the size of a walnut. In this atom about hundred fifty thousand so-called electrons are contained. If one imagines now this atom in the size of the Peters church, then each electron would have the size of a point in a print. These one hundred and fifty thousand electrons are separated by spaces which relate to their size like the distances of the planets from the sun and all these electrons move around the central point of the atom with furious speed. The greatest speed of a body known so far is that of the star Arcturus, which travels a hundred miles a second. The speed of motion of electrons is about three times that. They are incessantly thrown out by the radium and penetrate unhindered through a five-inch armor plate.

Regarding the strange phenomenon that the element radium transforms itself into the element helium, a phenomenon which science considered impossible up to now, it was said that in this lies a salvation of honor for the old alchemists who wanted to achieve the same and about whom so much was mocked. In the atom, therefore, the appearance of the solar and planetary system is repeated in the smallest in the large. Everything is movement, all matter is movement and, in the last analysis, electric force, thus matter equals force. Now one only has to conclude: Force is spirit, then one has the spiritualistic world view.

Interesting was also the conclusion drawn that the whole matter is in evolution, which must lead constantly in unmeasured time courses to a refinement, i.e. spiritualization. Strange conclusions, to which a purely materialistic view comes, and all this has caused a grain of radium, which is not bigger than the head of a pin. The old L., as a representative of the old science, shook his gray head incredulously and denied everything at first. He belongs to the direction of the science which thinks to have fathomed everything and in whose sharply circumscribed area there is no room for something new.

Norway, Molde, 17 July 1904.

I am now reading "The History of the French Revolution" by Carlyle. The book is wittily written, if somewhat mannered. Besides this I am occupied with Steiner's "Theosophy." Yesterday, by chance, the conversation came to the Theosophical conception of the world. We sat together, the five or six of us, and since I was the only one who knew something of these things, I had to lead the discussion. First some laughed, then they became more and more serious and finally they listened to me like the pastor in the church. It is strange how this subject interests all the people, even if they pretend to be high above it.

There is a prince on board here, whose brother is a zealous spiritualist, and in the end almost everyone had experienced one thing or another, had witnessed something himself or in his immediate environment. However, hardly anyone had tried to account for it or to think about the events. People are so lazy to think and put aside what could give them a headache and does not fit into the usual scheme of life.

Norway, Trondheim, 23 July 1904.

The Emperor harangued me on the way because of the maneuvers, etc., I had to stand by Count Schlieffen. I see more and more how difficult the legacy will be that his successor will have to assume. That this is the case is certainly largely Schlieffen's fault.

Until it comes to the point that people are so spiritualized that they can control the forces of nature, it still has good ways to go. Many thousands of years will be necessary. You live in your own world, among books and people of the same mind, you lose sight of the great mass of mankind, you have no real idea of its enormous backwardness and you think you see light where there is nothing but darkness as thick as a fist. Your light burns within you, in the heavy burdening mass it is dark and will still remain dark in unthinkable times. However, all beginnings are small. Even the highest human spirit had to develop from the egg of the mother and slowly mature, and it is certain that the truth will triumph, even if after long and difficult struggles. I was so happy that you wrote to me philosophically again.

Norway, Trondheim, 25 July 1904.

Our main traffic is Americans. All the financial giants of the New World are lying in wait for the Emperor here and know very well that he is coming on board with them. And the Most High Lord really believes that with this concession against a few American money lords he can exert an influence on the mutual political relationship of the two states, believes that when he comes aboard a Mr. Vanderbild, Drexel or Goelette, if he receives and entertains these people with selected courtesy on the "Hohenzollern," he can arbitrate the conflicting economic interests of a hundred million people who are all in a struggle for existence, who all want to live and become rich, each at the expense of the other, who struggle for their existence in agriculture, trade, industry, who are hungry and thirsty and who do not give a damn about anything but the most favorable living conditions.

Yesterday's sermon, which was better than its bland predecessors, had as its theme: If life has been delicious, it has been toil and labor. How true that is we all feel in our imposed idleness. All but one, unfortunately.

I have now finished Carlyle's "History of the French Revolution," three volumes. It is written wittily and dramatically, from the point of view of the philosopher who searches for the driving motives in the colorful confusion of phenomena and finds them deep beneath the foaming, bloody surface in the hearts of men. That is the bad thing about most monarchs and the ruling classes, that they forget how in the breast of each, even the least of their subjects, beats a heart full of desire for happiness and joy of existence, that they are all human beings with human feeling and the will to live. Here we are, eating and drinking, as if there were nothing else to do in the world, and up there in Silesia the land is dying of thirst, even the earth is refusing the only thing it is used to giving for free, water, the economically weak have to sell their cattle, perhaps lose house and farm, how many destroyed livelihoods, how many embittered hearts, sorrow and misery, whose cry of distress, of course, does not penetrate into the elegant American deck salons where we drink tea and smoke cigarettes. In such surroundings it is good to read a book like Carlyle's!

Norway, Molde, 31 July 1904.

All our services begin with a woe cry from the old Jehovah, woe to you that you do this, woe to you that you do that! – Then the Gospel is read, but not explained, but again an Old Testament saying is added to the sermon. Today we heard the Gospel of the unjust steward, one of the most confused parables from the whole Bible, which is obviously completely misunderstood or mutilated by the copyists of the old manuscripts, wisely leaving the thoughts about it to the listeners' own acumen.

A few days ago I read a book that you absolutely must read, it will interest you very much, it is called: "The Sources of the Life of Jesus" by Professor Dr. Paul Wernle, Basel. It is the best thing I have read so far about the origin of the Gospels and seems almost convincing by its clarity of thought and logical conclusions. For me it was interesting to find confirmed the view I had gained by reading the Gospels, that the Gospel of Mark is the most original in its naive presentation.

Another writing in the same genre I have also read: "What do we know of Jesus?" by Bossuet. But it is not on the same level as the first one, it is more a polemic against a writing of Kalthoff, who wants to see in the history of Jesus nothing more than a posthumous dressing of the history of the Christian church in the garment of the person of Christ. Kalthoff thus wants to eliminate the historical Christ altogether, which in my opinion is absolutely wrong.

Norway, Bergen, 5 August 1904.

The poor Russians, they are doing too badly. Manchuria is as good as lost to them, and I fear that a catastrophe is yet to come and that Kuropatkin will have to surrender, if not with his entire army, then at least with considerable parts of it. He is already almost completely surrounded by the Japanese, and I consider it very unlikely that he will be able to march on Mukden and on to Charbin.

Berlin, 1 September 1904.

"Clever Hans" is beginning to play a role similar to that of the Red Party. The dispute of opinions has flared up fiercely, but it seems to me that the party that only wants to see dressage is gradually winning out. It is regrettable that this matter is also treated and judged with a passionate fanaticism pro and contra. Fanaticism always clouds view and judgment and if one cannot even remain objective and dispassionate towards a horse, how should one then be towards a man.

It is completely incomprehensible to me why people get so worked up over a problem that is neither new nor of earth-shattering importance. One has already told quite different things about dogs, parrots and starlings and already in Brehms Tierleben one can read many features of these animals which unmistakably point to a certain degree of intelligence, and who would want to deny that a dog which socializes a lot with people understands human language to a certain degree? This is actually quite self-evident.

Berlin, 4 September 1904.

I still hoped that Kuropatkin would prevail in this main battle. Now, for the time being, it will be all over with him and the Russians will have to start a whole new campaign on a new basis if they do not want to take upon themselves a humiliating peace and thereby harm their prestige before Europe and Asia in a disastrous way.

Berlin, 5 September 1904.

I read long yesterday in Chamberlain's "Fundamentals" and found that I can understand and judge many discussions much better now than before. One sentence struck me as very apt. He speaks of the duality of phenomena, roughly as one might say, of the material and spiritual worlds, and says that one can best define these two sides of existence as those phenomena which are mechanically explicable and those which are not. I think this is very well expressed. "The Four Religions" by A. Besant I have read with great interest. I am surprised that she limits herself to these four, Hinduism, Zoroastrianism, Buddhism and Christianity, and does not mention the religion which, next to Buddhism, probably has the most adherents on earth, the Mohammedan religion. Much of her remarks about Christianity coincide with those of Chamberlain. When one reads these things, it becomes more and more inexplicable to one how it was possible that the distorted image of religion which mankind has made of the teachings of Christ could be sufficient for itself for so long. A proof of how thoughtlessly the masses cling to the outer form and how powerful the spiritual life of this teaching must be, if it is not completely suffocated in it.

Berlin, 6 September 1904.

The poor —— I have no doubt that he is a truth-loving man, and according to his statements most of what he is accused of is simply a lie. Woe to the man on whose trail the bloodhounds of an unscrupulous press are rushed, they rush him to death, and the more decent he is, the more defenseless he is. He had the misfortune to cause inconvenience, and thus the ground was pulled from under his feet on which he thought he was standing so firmly. A speaking portent for all those who think they have a firm backing. It's good to always keep in mind that nowadays there is only one standard by which one is measured, whether one is comfortable or uncomfortable. What one does otherwise is less important.

Berlin, 18 December 1904.

I am now reading a book by General Bonval: "*Le Manœuvre de Saint Privat,*" from which I am extracting and translating into German some passages that provide quite instructive insights into the way one of the most outstanding French military writers imagines a future war between Germany and France.

Berlin, 20 December 1904.

That E. does not particularly like the old lactating Madonnas, I can imagine. For the most part, they are not beautiful, but only interesting as a testimony to how art gradually developed at the hand of religious feeling, until it finally outgrew this teacher, became independent and directed its increasingly firm steps into the large area of nature, as a child does when it has learned to walk alone and now runs into the garden to pick flowers.

In this first time of the awakening of the art an urge was active in it, the deepest feeling of which the people were capable at that time, the religious, this moved them most profoundly and they felt the urge to give it visible expression. Therefore, all ancient painters stuck to religious themes, and thus Madonna painting became the mother of today's painting, as Christian architecture is the mother of today's architecture. As these old painters painted, one had no knowledge of the long lost masterpieces of Greek art, the need for artistic expression awakening in the Central European peoples had to grope its own way and only in the slow development overcome many crudities and childishness.

Hanover, 8 January 1905.

I went to see His Majesty last night. I had a conversation with him lasting three quarters of an hour and told him everything that was on my mind. I don't think anyone has ever spoken to him like that before. I will write to you about it in detail when I find peace.

Berlin, 25 January 1905.

At a dinner in Rome, at Rotenhahn's, I made the acquaintance of a priest, whose name has unfortunately slipped my mind, who has become known through his work on the catacombs of Rome. He is an authority in this field and has been supported financially by the Emperor, a very interesting man, German, that would be such a man for you.

Things look bad for our neighbors, the Russians. You have probably read that there were workers' revolts in Petersburg, which were put down by force of arms and in which much blood flowed. As long as the military remains loyal, they will be able to deal with it in Russia, but the "ideas" are spreading and taking hold of broader and broader layers of the population, and you can't deal with them with soldiers. I fear that the era of assassinations will begin again. Kuropatkin is still immovable in the face of the Japanese. Such a crazy way of warfare has not existed as long as the world has been standing.

Berlin, 26 January 1905.

I think it would be interesting to read some Roman history that you could relive right there on the spot. But probably more interesting than a novel of any kind. If you could get hold of Mommsen's "Roman History" for example, maybe someone from the embassy has it.

Berlin, 29 January 1905.

About four weeks ago, I rode together with the Reich Chancellor one morning in the Tiergarten. The conversation turned to the political situation, which was very tense at the time. He asked me, as we parted, whether I would not soon replace Count Schlieffen, with whom he apparently disagreed, to which I told him I hoped that this cup would pass me by. A few days later —— came to me to tell me the following: In a conversation with His Majesty, the Reich Chancellor had told him that I would not be inclined to accept the position of Chief of the General Staff. His Majesty was extremely astonished and disturbed by this, and he is now sending ... to tell me that he has unconditional confidence in me. He was sorry that, if I did not want to accept, I had not told him this myself, and that he had only found out through the Reich Chancellor. I now had a longer discussion with —— in which I developed for him my reasons which made it difficult for me to accept this position. He also agreed with me and asked me whether he should tell His Majesty this, to which I replied that it would be most agreeable to me if I could express myself to His Majesty myself and that I would be grateful to His Majesty if he would receive me and listen to me.

Two days later I received an invitation to dinner at the castle and at the same time the message that I would like to come half an hour earlier and have myself reported to His Majesty. You can imagine that I went to the castle with my own feelings. I was determined to tell His Majesty everything straight out and did not know how the matter would go. But I told myself that it did not depend on the person, that I was obliged to sacrifice myself to the cause if necessary, and that I could only really benefit His Majesty if I told him once what was being talked and secretly rumored everywhere in the officer circles without anyone ever having found the courage to tell His Majesty. I was led by the wing adjutant into His Majesty's study, I stood, for how long I do not know, and waited! – At last the Emperor came in and greeted me very kindly. He leaned against the work table as if to say: "Now let me hear what you have to say!"

I began by telling him that my statement to the Imperial Chancellor had been a purely private one and that it had not occurred to me that he would bring it back to His Majesty. I did not get any further, because the Emperor interrupted me with great liveliness and told me: "Now I will tell you how this is connected. The other evening, when the Imperial Chancellor was with me, we spoke of the difficult political situation we were in *vis-a-vis* England, and that we had to be prepared to be attacked from there one fine day. It is clear that this war cannot be localized, but that it will lead to further European entanglements. Then the Reich Chancellor said that he thought Count Schlieffen was getting quite old, to which I replied that if he was no longer able, then Moltke would be there. To which he replied: 'Your Majesty, he will not accept the position.'

"You can imagine that I was completely taken aback by this statement. I ordered you to the General Staff a year ago to get your bearings, and of course I had certainly counted on you being there to step in if Count Schlieffen had to resign for some reason. He is old and something can happen to him, he can fall ill or something like that, and then someone has to be there who can replace him. Now General v. der Goltz has been suggested to me, whom I do not want, and then General v. Beseler, whom I do not know. I know you and I have confidence in you. I know well that you are too modest to believe that you could do justice to the position. Count Schlieffen, whom I asked, tells me that he has been watching you for a year now and that he could not suggest a better successor than you in the first place. Your late uncle once said that in the choice for this position it is much less important that the person concerned is brilliant than that he can be relied upon under all circumstances, that character is the main thing, and it is this that is put to the test in war. I can only tell you that I have complete confidence in you. You are a well-known personality in the army, everyone appreciates you and will trust you as I do. When I came to the throne as a young man, I also said to myself, the task is beyond your strength. I was completely on my own, no one could help me, and when I had to accomplish the hardest thing right away, the farewell to the old Chancellor of the Reich, I told myself that I had to do it, and I did what I had to do. It will be the same for you. When you approach the task, you will find the strength within yourself."

This was briefly the content of what His Majesty said. He spoke at great length in his vivacity and elaborated on everything much more than I have reproduced here. I saw it coming that he would not give me an opportunity to say what I had to say, but I was determined not to leave until I had done so. So I listened reverently until he had finished speaking. Then I said: "Your Majesty will allow me to express my heartfelt thanks for the honorable expression of confidence which Your Majesty has shown in me, but I feel all the more obliged to express myself to Your Majesty quite frankly and honestly. It is not only important that Your Majesty has confidence in me, but also whether I deserve this confidence or not. Your Majesty will only be able to judge this when Your Majesty is fully acquainted with my views, and I therefore most humbly request permission to express my concerns to Your Majesty as openly as I do to my own conscience. Should I thereby say something that may not please Your Majesty, this will in any case have the consequence that Your Majesty will be able to judge me completely and fully and assess me accordingly.

"Your Majesty has envisaged me as a possible future Chief of the General Staff. How I would prove myself as such in the event of a campaign, I do not know. I judge myself very critically. In my opinion, it is very difficult, if not impossible, to form a picture of how a modern European war will develop.

"We now have over thirty years of peace behind us and I believe that we have become very peace-minded in our views. How and whether it will be possible at all to lead the mass armies we are going to raise in a unified way, I think no one can know beforehand. Our adversary has also become a different one; we will no longer have to deal with an enemy army that we can confront with superiority, as in the past, but with a nation in arms. It will be a people's war, which will not be settled with a decisive battle, but which will be a long, arduous struggle with a country which will not give itself up until all its people's strength has been broken, and which will also exhaust our people to the utmost, even if we should be victorious. When I see how the strategic war games, which are submitted to Your Majesty year after year, regularly end with the capture of enemy armies of five to six hundred thousand men, and that after the course of a few days of operations, I cannot help feeling that they in no way do justice to the circumstances of the war. I cannot make such war games. Your Majesty knows that the armies you lead regularly encircle the enemy and thus supposedly end the war in one fell swoop. In my opinion, these results can only be achieved by doing violence to the circumstances in a way that in no way corresponds to the principle that the war game should be a study for the real war and that it must take into account, as far as possible, all the frictions and obstacles that occur in war. This kind of war game, in which the adversary is, as it were, delivered up from the outset with his hands tied, must give rise to quite false ideas, which must become pernicious when war really comes. But in my opinion this is not yet the worst. I consider it even more alarming that by the violence done to the war game, the whole large circle of officers involved in it is deprived of interest in the matter. Everyone has the feeling that it does not matter what you do, a higher fate is directing the matter and will lead it to the desired end one way or another. Your Majesty will have noticed that it is becoming increasingly difficult to find officers who want to lead against Your Majesty. That's because everyone says to themselves, I'm only going to be slaughtered.

"But what I deplore most of all and what I have to tell Your Majesty is that the officers' trust in their Supreme Warlord is being shaken to the core. The officers say to themselves that the Emperor is much too clever not to notice how everything is being arranged here so that he should win, so he must want it that way after all."

Here the Emperor interrupted me and assured me that he had had no idea that both sides had not fought with equal weapons. He had been completely bona fide. I should tell Schlieffen that he would not treat him better than his opponent in the next war game.

I answered him: "Count Schlieffen says that when the Emperor plays, he must win; as Emperor, he cannot be beaten by one of his generals. That is also quite correct. Therefore, Your Majesty must not lead at all. Let Your Majesty present a war game in which Your Majesty is in charge and thus stands above the parties instead of being a party himself."

The Emperor agreed with me on this. I then told him that, "if Your Majesty wanted to inquire with the gentlemen, I believe they would all confirm what I have said here, that is, if they have the courage to tell Your Majesty the truth."

And the same thing I said about the war game applies to maneuvers. The value of the great maneuvers as preparation for war lies in the exercise of the higher leaders against an enemy who has his own resolve. The troops as such learn less in the large maneuvers than in the detachment exercises, where one can pay attention to all details. If the decisions of the commanding generals are always influenced by the intervention of His Majesty, they are deprived of the desire to take the initiative, they are made unenthusiastic and uncertain.

Here the Emperor interrupted me again and said that he had always left the commanding generals the freedom of decision. I replied: In the last Imperial Maneuver I was used as an arbitrator and was therefore not present myself, but I have been told that on one day His Majesty gave the commanding general of the . Army Corps the order for his corps, contrary to his intentions. His Majesty had to admit that. He said: Oh yes, that was how he wanted to go back with his corps, so that there would have been no fighting at all that day.

Me: "Your Majesty could have simply told him that I wanted to see a battle tomorrow and then left it up to him to decide how it was to be carried out, or Your Majesty could have given him some kind of supposition that would have made him stop. Thus the whole army knows that Your Majesty has simply dictated to a commanding general the orders for his corps, and this does not help to raise the general's prestige towards his corps and must have a depressing effect on him. A Commanding General may have only one opportunity to lead his corps against an enemy during the entire time he is in his position, during the Imperial Maneuvers, and that is usually only three days. If Your Majesty himself leads a corps in maneuvers, he loses one of the three days of practice. In wartime, Your Majesty does not lead a corps."

His Majesty: "No, that is correct."

Me: "Then the Commanding General should do it, and he must take advantage of every hour in which he can practice."

His Majesty: "I lead to show the Commanding Generals how I wish it to be done."

Me: "Your Majesty can express that at the briefing. In my opinion, the maneuvers can only be warlike and thereby beneficial if they take place without violent intervention from above. If mistakes are made, there is no harm in that, for one never learns more than from one's mistakes. But if Your Majesty leads, everyone knows that Your Majesty must win, and the entire opposing party feels from the outset that he is a battle victim and becomes discontented. The maneuvers are discussed in the whole army, the whole officer corps judges them and the criticism becomes sharper and sharper.

"And then there is one more thing. The troops do not get to see Your Majesty, which is of the greatest importance, because the soldier who has seen Your Majesty in maneuvers does not forget it all his life. Your Majesty will be gracious if I have spoken more freely than Your Majesty is accustomed to hearing. I would not have dared to do so if it were not for what is most important to me, Your Majesty and the good of the army."

The Emperor now said to me: "Why did you not tell me all this long ago?"

Me: "I did not feel justified in imposing my view on Your

Majesty. Surely not everyone can come to Your Majesty and say: I don't think this is right, what you are doing, and that is not right."

His Majesty: "But you are Adjutant General, and you know that you can always visit."

Me: "If Your Majesty asks me for my opinion, I will always express it frankly."

The Emperor then shook my hand and said, "Thank you." – I then said to him: "If Your Majesty really wants to try it with me, then give me the opportunity to test myself once. Let me try out the imperial maneuvers this year. If it goes well, Your Majesty can keep me, but if it turns out that it doesn't work or the difficulties are too great, then Your Majesty can simply put me aside and take someone else. Here there is really nothing to do with a person, it is only a matter of serving the cause."

The Emperor agreed completely and said: "I will tell Count Schlieffen."

Me: "If Your Majesty will allow me, I will report this to Count Schlieffen myself and ask for his consent."

Then His Majesty shook my hand again and went ahead to the reception room, where the Empress and the table party had been waiting for a long time. The Emperor was very silent and thoughtful the whole evening. I actually felt terribly sorry for him, but God knows, I couldn't help it.

I was very curious to see how he would be against me when I saw him again, after a time had passed and the first surprise had been overcome. But even then he was uniformly friendly. How all this will now continue to work, I do not know. Perhaps it will last, perhaps time will blur it again.

When I reported this to Count Schlieffen about the maneuvers, he made a very puzzled face. It was obviously extremely unpleasant for him, and he tried to evade it, saying, as I asked him directly: "Will Your Excellency agree if I start the maneuvers this year? – We can still talk about that. If he does not agree, I will take up the fight. I have Your Majesty's assurance, and I won't let him take it away from me."

So, now you know. Please, let me know right away that this letter has come into your hands, because I don't want anyone else to know about it, and I am actually anxious to put it in the mail.

Keep it in such a way that it does not fall into the wrong hands.

Berlin, 1 February 1905.

The conditions in Russia are very alarming. Until now, there have only been workers' unrest, which has been suppressed with slight effort by the military, with quite a lot of blood being shed. But these were probably only the *ballons d'essay*.* There is ferment everywhere, especially in the circles of the intelligentsia. If the Tsar is not reasonable and gives his people more freedom, things will get bad. Russia is probably not yet ready for a constitution and universal suffrage. But he must give a habeas corpus act, that is, a protection against arbitrariness and violence, and a representation of the estates. With that, everyone would be satisfied, and he would be the father of the fatherland. If he does not do this, but insists on the standpoint of brute force, he will provoke it against himself and sooner or later fall a victim to fanaticism. The troops have so far proved reliable everywhere; the rumors of mutiny are English inventions. Russia will willingly endure the very harshest laws, but they must be laws and not arbitrary ones in which no man is safe. May God give the poor Tsar wise counselors.

Colonel Shebekov told me the other day that he had been asked several times whether there was any prospect of my being sent there! What do you think of that?

The war is also in a bad way for the Russians. Kuropatkin made another unsuccessful attempt to advance, got punched in the nose and crawled behind the Hunho again. It is pure misery. By the way, I believe that we owe it indirectly to the great weakness of Russia if England is now so peaceable against us. I think that France has made representations to England to keep the peace. The French know very well that they will have to deal with us if war should start between England and Germany, and since their good friend Russia is quite powerless at present, they would have to take us on alone, and they have a hell of a lot of respect for that. If it

---

* "Trial balloons."

were not so, I could not explain the English calls for peace. But enough of politics. A nasty song, fie, a political song, says the student in Auerbach's cellar.

Berlin, 4 February 1905.

The Tsar seems to really intend to introduce a somewhat more liberal regime, which would be a blessing for him and the country. For the time being, he is receiving workers' deputations, which does not mean much. In Manchuria, after the recent miserable attempt at a Russian offensive, things have gone quiet again. Warfare there is equally miserable from both sides.

Here at home, the coal workers' strike in the Ruhr region, which has been going on for weeks now, continues to have a disruptive effect. The coal shortage becomes urgent. Many factories have to stop work, English and Belgian coal is imported en masse, but does not cover the demand. Once again, one can see how artificially our modern cultural life is constructed; when one factor fails, everything comes to a standstill. By the way, peace and order are not disturbed anywhere, and the striking workers have plenty to live on from the aid that flows to them from all sides. Even our good clergy is collecting for them. The people are quite foolish, their politics do not reach further than the tips of their noses; here, too, everything is governed by slogans.

Berlin, 6 February 1905.

I now have a very interesting book "Paul, the Beginnings of Christianity and Dogma" by Professor Weinel. It smells a little bit of orthodoxy, even if the professor would be indignant about it if he were told that, because he is known as the most free-minded of all free-minded theologians, but no man can get out of his skin, even if he thinks so, And even if he thinks that he has completely shed the Christian dogmatic skin that he was probably taught in his youth, there is still a little bit left here and there, so fine that you cannot see it, only feel it if you trace the structure of his work with the finger of the spirit.

Berlin, 7 February 1905.

That this people (the Italians), who once ruled the world, has become so degenerate that they have become thieves and rags, that is sad enough, but it is probably in the course of the world. They are on the dying branch, we Teutons are still younger, but will probably go the same way in time to make room for younger ones. In the relationship it is with the nations like with the individual human being.

Berlin, 9 February 1905.

Yesterday's court ball did not captivate me further. It always makes a very strange impression on me when I see the court moving into the White Hall; the Emperor always brings such a piece of the Middle Ages behind him. S. in wig, as well as the old "Sweet," the officer of the Empress's bodyguard as well; it is as if the dead are resurrected with braid and powder.

Berlin, 12 February 1905.

I am enclosing a few words that I have extracted from the Weineian work on Paul. It is only brief and pressed. The development struck me because it corresponds exactly to my view of the sacrificial death of Christ. I certainly agree with it. Hopefully you can read it and will be interested.

Paul : Two ways mankind tries to get to their God: revelation, sacrament – prayer and sacrifice. In Paul since Damascus, Christ has come alive, has revealed himself to him. Now I live, but not I, but Christ lives in me. Now his God speaks to him no longer from the papers of the laws, but from the flame of fire that blazes in his heart. He thus has living religion, he has it as a personal experience.

Berlin, 14 February 1905.

The funeral of the old Menzel* was held with great pomp in the rotunda of the Old Museum. In front of the portal the body company of the 1st Guard Regiment with grenadier caps, on the outside steps the Castle Guard Company and the art student associations in dress with their flags, a colorful picture. Inside, a crowded assembly of all classes and professions, even Singer was there as a Reichstag deputation! On the balustrade above Joachim with his quartet and the choir of singers of the college. Next to the small coffin, which looked like a child's coffin, Dryander. After the Emperor, Empress and all the princes had arrived, a very beautiful cantata by Beethoven was sung, then Dryander gave a simple and therefore effective speech, followed by a quartet, a movement by Haydn and then the blessing, after which again choral singing. Then the coffin was carried out by six non-commissioned officers of the 1st Guards Regiment and placed on the hearse, which was harnessed to six stable horses and escorted by imperial coachmen. At the *tete* of the procession the Leib-Kompagnie, then the *chargés* of the student fraternities with their colorful costumes and feathered hats. Behind the coffin the Emperor with the whole generality, and then an endless retinue of black top hats. In front of the castle, the Emperor turned to the left, the company to the right, and let the procession pass by. No artist has ever been honored in such a way, and the little Excellency will have taken pleasure in it, if he was able to see his own funeral!

Berlin, 20 February 1905.

The spiritual era you are hoping for, I believe, will not come soon. I am afraid that humanity will have to go through a lot of blood and misery before it reaches that point. We will probably not see the dawn of the Millennial Kingdom, which mankind has been hoping for since the time of Christ. The new terrible act of blood in Russia is also like a blood-red torch shining into a dark future. The poor

---

* Adolph Friedrich Erdmann von Menzel (1815 - 1905), a renowned Realist artist.

Tsar, who himself can be the new victim at any moment! And at the same time he has no energy to take new paths and save himself and his people! I believe that Russia and Japan will soon make peace. The war is hopeless for the former.

Berlin, 4 March 1905.

I am glad that you have made the acquaintance of the catacomb priest and that he will show you something. He is an authority in this field and will certainly be able to tell you interesting things. Perhaps at Rotenhahn you will meet the Cardinal Secretary of State, Merry del Val, who has interested me very much. He is the man at the syringe who has all the far-flung threads of Vatican diplomacy in his hands.

Berlin, 7 March 1905.

Today I fought through a first squabble with Count Schlieffen. I wrote to you that the Emperor had allowed me to start the maneuvers this year. I reported this to Count Schlieffen, whereupon he told me that he still wanted to think it over. Since then I have asked him twice again whether he has now thought it over, to which he always replied in the negative, saying that it was still a long time away, etc., and always making excuses. A few days ago, without my knowing anything beforehand, he presented to the Emperor a maneuver plan he had made. As —— told me, the Kaiser had said: "I think Moltke is making the plan?" To which Count Schlieffen mumbled something incomprehensible. I then went to H. and asked him to inform His Majesty of the facts, so that he would not think that I wanted to shirk or something like that. Today the Emperor sent H. to Count Schlieffen with the order that I had to work on the maneuvers. The latter came in to me rather depressed and told me that he had received the order to leave the arrangement of the maneuvers to me. Then he made all kinds of excuses, that he had not understood me correctly, etc.

I only told him that I had reported everything clearly to him at that time. It was obviously very unpleasant for him, but I could not change it, and after the events there was nothing left for me to do but to bring about a decision by His Majesty. He could have spared himself this if he had been more loyal to me. If he wants to take it by hook or by crook, that's fine with me; in any case, he has misjudged me if he thinks he can simply push me aside. In this case, I have now won, which he could have arranged differently and without all inconvenience if he had taken the stand of helping a man whom he himself has designated as his successor instead of, as it were, humping him. By the way, I am not indulgent, and it will not be up to me if my relationship with him should be disturbed. Of course, you must keep this to yourself. I know that you do anyway, and I am only saying it for me, not for you.

Berlin, 11 March 1905.

I met Frau v. B., whose husband, as you know, is with Prince Frederick Leopold in Manchuria with the Japanese, where he must have witnessed the great victory that the Japanese have won over the Russians. With the latter it is now probably definitely over. It seems as if the army is completely beaten and scattered and probably for the most part in captivity. A terrible embarrassment for the Russians, who were stronger than the Japanese by about a hundred thousand men. In my opinion, they now have no choice but to make *coute que coute** peace.

The consequences of this war will be felt very soon in the East and will consist in an unrestricted domination of the Japanese. I only hope that we do not clash with them over Kiautschou, for we would be even more powerless against them than the Russians, and if they wish they can throw us out of China at any moment, to which our friends the English would willingly offer their hand. For these reasons I regret the utter failure of the Russians, much as they should otherwise be given a good thrashing. The conditions in this country are too rotten after all.

---

* "At all costs."

Berlin, 12 March 1905.

When I see this peace picture, I always think of the poor Russians in Manchuria, scattered, beaten and persecuted, wandering through the desolate mountains or lying mutilated in their blood. The defeat must have been appalling. I do not believe that the army as such still exists at all. The Tsar should only make peace as soon as possible; he no longer has any chance of success, that's for sure.

Berlin, 13 March 1905.

The Russians seem to want to continue the war after all, despite all the defeats. But I think they are almost incapable of doing so. They cannot pull many more troops out of the country where they need them in order to put down the unrest everywhere, and I am convinced that with the spring the unrest will begin even among the peasants, who will follow the example of the cities. In the last defeat at Mukden they lost the third part of their army in dead, wounded and prisoners, about 150,000 men and 60 guns.

Berlin, 21 March 1905.

I now have a different quartermaster position in the General Staff than before. I wanted to swap and asked Count Schlieffen for it, who immediately approved it. Now I have the departments dealing with Russia, Japan, France, England, Austria, Italy, Switzerland, Turkey, etc., which is infinitely more interesting than my previous position. So I get all the first-hand reports and the news from all over the world.

What is to become of the Russian campaign is quite unclear to me. It really seems that the Russians want to continue the war. They have enough people, but they are running out of money, which is not so easy to come by. According to a rough estimate, they should be out of money in a month or two. For the time being, the entire army is in continuous retreat, and the Japs are always firmly behind. This time, however, they have not succeeded in destroying the Russians, or even in capturing larger parts of them.

Berlin, 31 March 1905.

I always have a feeling of shame as a European when I meet with these little yellow people who, since their successes in the war, look down on all of us with sovereign contempt. It seems, by the way, that the Russians now want to make peace; it is said that the Tsar has fallen over, after having just become extremely belligerent and determined to the utmost. That Japan will be inclined to make peace on favorable terms I readily believe; she can hardly achieve more than she has already achieved, and will probably be quite finished with her funds.

I am eager to see how the Emperor's visit to Tangier will go and what results it will produce between Germany and France. The mood in France is rather irritable; if Russia were not so miserable on the ground, she would surely seize the opportunity as a *casus belli*. It is, of course, a bit risky to tie up with us now, but since France is the land of whims and passions, one can never know how things will turn out there.

Berlin, April 12, 1905.

I am curious to see how the Morocco affair between France and us will develop. I don't think it will degenerate into saber-rattling, even if there is some snorting from both sides. I am just as curious about the outcome of the Russian Argonaut campaign; I have lost all confidence in a happy outcome for the Russians. The conditions there, when one learns more about them, are even more rotten than I would have believed. I prefer our conditions, as much as there is to criticize about them.

S.M. Yacht "Hohenzollern," 10 July 1905.

I have just presented to the Emperor my maneuver plan for the

Imperial Maneuver, with which he was in complete agreement and which he found very attractive and interesting. I am very glad that everything has been well initiated, and I have the audacious hope that I will succeed in making a warlike maneuver without violent interventions and without unnatural cavalry battles, etc. If I succeed in this, I will not have lived in vain. By the way, I would not hesitate for a moment to sacrifice myself for the sake of the cause if it should become necessary. But I hope that everything will go well. The Emperor apparently wanted to accommodate me in everything and was extremely gracious and pleased. This relieves me of an anxiety that was rather heavy on me, and I have hope and confidence. I know that if I succeed in keeping the Emperor from unmilitary unnaturalness, I will be doing a great service to the army, and not only to it, but also to His Majesty himself. This is a goal worth striving for, and next to the achievement of which the person of the individual cannot be of any importance.

Sweden, Hernösand, 18 July 1905.

The Norwegian crisis seems to be resolving itself into Prince Charles of Denmark running as a pretender, since the King of Sweden does not want to grant a prince. This would make English influence dominant in Norway, since the prince is a son-in-law of King Edward. Whether the Norwegians want him I do not know, but I believe that the ambition of this people is to have their own king. A reunion with Sweden seems to me quite out of the question. This matter, too, is part of the great uncertainty and insecurity that is rising all around. Who could see into the future, and yet, one would perhaps understand it just as little as one understands the present, which also usually only becomes clear when it has become the past.

S.M. Yacht "Hohenzollern," 21 July 1905.

The Emperor absolutely wants to make me chief of the general staff right after the maneuver. I advised him to wait for the result of the maneuver first to see if it would work with both of us at all. I will probably not escape my fate. Today, the Kaiser wanted me to give the speech at the unveiling of Uncle Helmuth's monument this fall, but I told him that he could not do that to old Schlieffen, and he then agreed to let him stay in his position for so long. I only have to do that he does not send him away head over heels, which would be very wrong against the deserving general.

Sweden, Wisby, 26 July 1905.

We arrived here at 7 o'clock, directly from Björkö in the Gulf of Finland, where we had the rendezvous with the Emperor of Russia. As we departed from Hernösand, we knew nothing other than that we were to head for Gotland. However, when we woke up in the morning, we were on the open sea and soon realized that we were not on the way to Gotland, since we were heading east. But about the destination of our journey deepest silence was observed. Hour after hour passed, and still we were heading east at eighteen knots. Then it gradually became clear to us that we had to sail into the Gulf of Finland, otherwise we would have reached a coast long ago. Our tension grew constantly during the day. All possible conclusions were made, but we did not get any clarification. It became afternoon, still no land in sight, and always the course to the east.

Suddenly a ship came into sight, a warship, saluting, flying the Russian flag. Now our suspicions became certainties, but where we were headed none of us suspected. The Emperor was impenetrably mysterious. The naval officers had strict orders not to give any information.

At 6 o'clock, as we all sat in the salon guessing back and forth whether Reval, whether Riga, whether Kronstadt, the Emperor came in and said: "Now, my children, get your parade suit in order, in two hours you will stand before the Emperor of Russia." – No one said a word, we were as if struck, dead silence in the whole room. None of us suspected the motives of this sudden and so mysteriously initiated visit, but we all felt the tremendous political importance of the coming hours, the consequences of which no one could calculate.

At 9 o'clock we entered a bay, flat lonely shores, covered with sparse fir trees, rocky heights behind, no human habitation as far as the eye could see, no living being, gray sky, gray water and an infinite loneliness. Ahead of us in the descending darkness a mighty dark ship, the "Polar Star" with the Tsar on board. We dropped anchor a short distance from him, the boats were launched, and the Emperor sailed over. Soon after, an order was sent for all of us to come across. A few minutes later we were standing on the deck of the "Polar Star" and were introduced to the Tsar by the Emperor. He looked serious, but not broken, as he has so often been portrayed. Addressing all of us in German, he said to me: "It is a great pleasure to see you again."

As soon as the performance was over, we went back to the "Hohenzollern", where the two monarchs with the Russian entourage arrived shortly afterwards. Then we dined on the "Hohenzollern." I was quite amazed by the Tsar. The longer we sat at the table, the more he thawed out; at last he was quite cheerful, laughed and talked animatedly; one could clearly tell that he felt at ease in surroundings in which he was safe. He as well as all the gentlemen of his entourage were of exquisite amiability, all of them spoke German at once, they were not recognizable at all. After dinner the Tsar talked for a long time with each of us. He spoke fluent German, when and how he learned it is a mystery to me. It was 3 o'clock in the morning when he returned to the "Polar Star" with his entourage. As we awoke the next morning, six to eight Russian torpedo boats had gathered around us, patrolling constantly.

The Emperor went alone to the "Polar Star" at 9 o'clock for breakfast, at 11 o'clock with the Tsar to the cruiser "Berlin", our escort ship, and at 1 o'clock we were all ordered to the "Polar Star" for breakfast. We were again received with excellent kindness – the Tsar's brother, Grand Duke Michael, had accompanied him, otherwise with him were the Court Marshal Count Benckendorff, the General Frederiks, the old personal physician Dr. Hirsch, a splendid old gentleman, German-Russian, seventy-seven years old, but quite spry, the Navy Minister Birilew, the Governor General of

Finland, Prince Obolenski, and some wing adjutants from the Navy.

At breakfast I sat next to Dr. Hirsch, who spoke very frankly. He said that it had been a great joy for the Tsar to see that in his misfortune someone still cared for him, and one could not be grateful enough to our Emperor for this proof of friendship. The Tsar had endured all misfortunes steadfastly and calmly, his health was good and his nerves were perfectly in order. With great contempt the old gentleman spoke of his monarch's surroundings. "You can imagine," he said, "that it must be a real rest for the Tsar to feel himself in a circle of decent people. Just look at his surroundings, no intelligence, all below mediocrity, no heart and feeling." – In the intercourse between the two Emperors there was a great cordiality; our Emperor told us afterwards that the Tsar, as they were alone, repeatedly fell around his neck and embraced and kissed him.

Among all the Russian gentlemen there was an incredible lack of energy with regard to the war. No one got beyond the thought that it was necessary to wait and see what the Japanese would do further, no trace of offensive spirit. When asked whether the Russians, if the army were now completely re-established, as was claimed, would not attack and throw the Japanese, it was replied that this was not possible, for both armies held such firm positions that the part which would attack would infallibly be beaten off. What would happen if the Japanese did not attack either? Then the war would continue until Japan was exhausted.

On the whole, opinions about the internal political situation were very optimistic, Russia had repeatedly gone through such crises and had always overcome them happily, for example after the Crimean War. In 1858, the conditions were exactly as they are today. This is indeed confirmed by a letter of Bismarck, which he wrote at that time as an envoy from Petersburg to the minister Schleinitz, and which is reported in the last issue of the *"Preußische Jahrbücher."* One could believe that the letter was written today. Even then, Bismarck believed that the collapse of Russia was inevitable; he was mistaken. Today, however, the enlightenment is more advanced and the international revolutionary propaganda is organized, the bombs play their role and wider layers of the people are imbued with ideas of freedom. The Tsar seems to be leaning towards peace. God grant that it may soon come about and that we may return to calmer times, so that at last the threatening torch of a general European war of murder may disappear from the horizon.

I can imagine how the newspapers will drag this latest imperial surprise back and forth. Stuff enough for several months to the most dissolute combinations! The idea of purely human feeling, the desire to give a humiliated and unhappy monarch a proof of participation, to encourage him, perhaps to persuade him to peace, to show him how necessary it is for Russia to give justice and righteousness to the people, will probably not occur to any of the newspaper writers and article smiths.

I will never forget that evening and the following day. The whole thing was too strange, almost like a fairy tale. The momentous meeting, the transformed mood of the formerly so haughty Russians, the gray loneliness, the remote bay, a flicker of gratitude in the ruler who year and day ago spoke the proud word: "One does not attack Russia, it is not a state to which one declares war, it is a continent" – and who now reaches with a searching hand for the firm staff of Germany, – all this made a deeply moving impression.

And then, in the afternoon of the second day, farewell, salute, embrace, thanks and thanks again that you came! – The ships steamed up slowly, sailed side by side for a while, the Emperors stood on deck, waved and saluted, the sounds of the Russian national anthem and the "Hail to thee in victory wreath" were mixed, the sailors shouted their hurrahs back and forth, then the "Polar Star" turned to the north, we to the west, once again signals were exchanged: "Happy voyage! – Then the mighty, dark Tsar ship gradually disappears from our sight and dives into the gray, misty distance as we head for the open sea. The performance is over, and before us, huge and dark as the Sphinx, stands the question: What will be the consequence of these hours?

How different this trip is from the trips in the Norwegian fjords. This time we are not looking for the silence of the glacier world and the bright nights. We are traveling around and turning the rope of politics, the end of which is lost in the darkness of the future and which will lead our fatherland with its sixty million people towards the unknown. God grant that it may be for his salvation.

Danzig, 30 July 1905.

Unfortunately, the disagreement between Germany and England is worsening in an ominous way. The visit of the Channel Fleet to the Baltic Sea, announced by England, cannot be taken otherwise than as a demonstration. How these matters are to run out and unravel I do not know. There is agitation on the part of England in the most incredible manner, the most atrocious lies are put into the world, and Germany is represented as the evil spirit of the whole world. The first shot exchanged between England and Germany will certainly be the signal for a general European massacre, the atrocities of which one can only think of with a shudder. And there is absolutely no real reason for it, no vital interest of either state is threatened or injured, and when it comes to blows, no one will know why it has come to this. The future is dark before us. May Germany have the strength to endure hard times.

S.M. Yacht "Hohenzollern," 3 August 1905.

As you know, I accompanied the Emperor to Bernstorff. The old king was as always of a touching kindness, he was fresh and lively, of undiminished elasticity and sprightliness. In addition to him, the Crown Prince, who sends you his best regards, was present with his wife and all the children. Among these, Prince Charles was most interested because of his candidacy for Norway and his wife Maud of England. He is a very good looking slim person. Then Prince Harald, whom the Emperor invited to the maneuvers. The Prince and Princess Waldemar with their five children. All the gentlemen are of exquisite kindness. I do not think one can find a second court in the world of such natural humanity and friendliness, of such a pleasant, distinguished atmosphere. Emperor and King were mutually very pleased with each other. Last night there was a dinner at our envoy Schön. The Emperor was in radiant spirits. We did not return on board until about 12 o'clock. We set sail this morning at 10 a.m. and are now sailing in sunshine and calm weather through the Sound to Saßnitz.

Saßnitz, 3 August 1905.

It is certain that we are living in serious political times. There is no need to fear the worst right away, but you are quite right that there is enough fuel for the fire. The worst thing for us is England's jealousy of our burgeoning trade and industrial development. If you look at the English newspapers, you are shocked by the systematic and spiteful German agitation that runs through the papers of all parties. The press is downright bloodthirsty and would like to exterminate us with stump and handle in order to be able to dominate and exploit the world without restriction. These newspaper writers and screamers cause a lot of mischief and unconscionably play with fire. When it comes to blows, they don't need to wear their skin to the market, of course, they stay at home, dip their feather in poison and bile and let the others beat themselves to death.

Saßnitz, 5 August 1905.

I will probably not return to Berlin until the 8th or the following day, since I have to spend another day on Norderney, where I have an imperial commission to deliver to Bülow.

Berlin, 9 August 1995.

Today I was at the General Staff, but I did not see Count Schlieffen, who this morning, while riding in the Tiergarten, received a blow to the shin from a rider's horse as he rode past, which penetrated the boot and left a wound several centimeters long. It is fortunate that the bone is not shattered, so that the matter will probably be over in not too long. The old gentleman had to be carried up the stairs as he could no longer walk.

Berlin, 10 August 1905.

The political situation seems to have cleared up somewhat recently. The attempt to bring about a meeting between King Edward and the Emperor has proceeded from the English side. After the undoubtedly cherished plan to bring France into conflict with Germany failed because of the French unwillingness to go to war, the peace chimes are now being blown in England. The good English would have liked to fish in the mud as *tertius gaudens*. While Germany and France were butting heads, they would have calmly ruined our dangerous trade, perhaps destroyed our little fleet, and pocketed our African colonies, in order to carry out their plan of a new South African world empire under the British flag. The scheme was not badly conceived, and the complaisant of England, M. Delcasse, was well on the way to carrying it out, until the French, in consequence of the German objection in the Morocco affair, suddenly realized that they were to be used to pull the chestnuts out of the fire for the English, and that if the scheme went wrong they alone would have to pay the piper. With the fall of Delcasse, the beautiful plans began to melt away, for the French do not want a war in which they alone have to deal with Germany. Russian help, which they had counted on for years, fails because of Russian weakness. So England is left to her own devices, and now suddenly finds that there is really no reason to quarrel with her German cousin! This is the way things are, and it is the undeniable merit of Bulow to have recognized the web that tightens around Germany and to have torn it with a strong grip. The Morocco affair, which was perhaps hardly understood by us, was the star operation for France. The German people, however, have no idea how close the doom hovered over their heads.

Berlin, 11 August 1905.

Old Schlieffen is doing relatively well. However, he will have to lie still for some time, as the bone of his leg is slightly cracked. Fortunately, the horse that hit him was not shod in the back, otherwise the bone would undoubtedly have been shattered. I don't think he'll be able to do the maneuver. I have been provided an automobile for the cavalry reconnaissance exercise in Prussia. For the maneuvers we have some forty machines at our disposal, which will be distributed among the corps and divisions, so that we can work with quite modern aids.

Berlin, 12 August 1905.

I received the following telegram from the Emperor today.* You can see from it that I once again had to get something in order, but it is nice of him to inform me.

Berlin, 21 August 1905.

Count Schlieffen has now moved over to the chaise longue, as the adjutant tells me. He does not let anyone pass, so that I have not seen him yet either.

Uncle Helmuth's image column is now erected. He stands there wrapped in a large sheet like in a death sheet. Apparently, all kinds of *allotria* are made to the outer surroundings, without which our modern sculpture can no longer create. The figure itself is kept simple and without *brimorium*, without genius of the art of war and other gods. That is at least something.

Things look bad with the peace negotiations in Portsmouth. The Russians don't want to pay because they can't, and Japan absolutely wants coin, since it is almost bankrupt itself. I almost think it is going on again, the Russians are constantly reinforcing

---

* The Kaiser thanks Moltke for his efforts. (The editor.)

their army in Manchuria and are now sending out three new corps again, bringing their army up to five hundred thousand men. The Tsar's manifesto is too much for the conservatives, too little for the freedom fighters. At least it is a beginning. It is not impossible that the Duma to be convened will molt in the same way as the National Assembly in Paris did at that time. In any case, a firm hand will be needed to guide this huge body of state when it goes off the rails. Nicki will probably not have it!

The friendly visit of the English fleet in the Baltic Sea is upon us. Hopefully we will keep cold blood from top to bottom, though my hope for that is minimal. A government communiqué prescribing rules of conduct for the Germans and recommending decent behavior to them is well-intentioned, but will leave no trace in the political and educational immaturity of our people. Our unfortunately quite uneducated press will probably celebrate orgies.

Berlin, 22 August 1905.

I conscientiously do J. P. Müller's exercises every morning, and they are excellent for me. This Muller would be a blessing for mankind and put an end to countless doctors if he were generally followed. But again, most people are too comfortable for that, they let it go as long as it can, and when the neglected body takes revenge and becomes ill, then medicine and baths have to come in to fight the symptoms, while the basic evil remains unattended.

The Japanese-Russian peace negotiations seem to have finally broken down, and soon the slaughter in Manchuria will probably begin again. In the general political mood, nothing has changed in and around us. All the other nations are pretty much unanimous in railing against Germany and in telling the most stale lies about us. I believe that nothing would be able to arouse such general world joy as if Germany were soundly beaten up. Everything claims that we are the troublemaker, and no one realizes that Germany wants nothing more than to be left alone.

Berlin, August 25, 1905.

I go to Homburg already on September 6, in the morning, where the Emperor arrives early on the 7th. On the 8th, the parade of the XVIII Corps is there. On the 10th I am in Koblenz, where the parade of the VIII Corps is on the 11th. On the 13th, 14th, and 15th are the maneuvers. Probably the second general staff trip will immediately follow the completed maneuvers. That depends on whether Count Schlieffen is fit for field duty again by then, which I would like to believe, since he is already up and sitting in the chair again. I haven't seen him yet, he doesn't let anyone in except his adjutants.

Next Sunday there is a big nailing of the flag here in the armory. We still think that in a fight to the death we will win the victory with a rag of embroidered cloth! We are caught up in a terribly peacenik outlook, I am horrified when I see all this nonsense, over which the main thing, to prepare for war seriously and with bitter energy, is completely forgotten. Colorful strings are attached to people as rifleman's badges, which only hinder them in handling the rifle, ambition is stimulated by all kinds of external awards instead of developing a sense of duty, the uniforms are becoming more and more shiny instead of being designed to be inconspicuous in the field, the exercises become parade-like plays, decorative is the slogan of the day, and behind all this frippery grins the Gorgon head of war, which hangs over us like a weather cloud. And no insight and no turning back on this path, it only gets worse and worse.

I met today ... in the zoo, who is terribly nervous down and almost finished. He complained that it was almost unbearable. Yes, he has many fellow sufferers. How much good will there be in so many, and how hard it is made for everyone who would like to use his best skills and who can never say yes with joy. We all live under a dull pressure that kills the joy of creation, and hardly ever can one start something without hearing the inner voice: What for, it is in vain after all. But now enough with this Jeremiah letter . These are clouds that pass away, but the sun is still in the sky, and it is the faith in the future of our people and fatherland.

What you say about the need for a healthy soul life is certainly true. Unfortunately, we are extremely far from having one. The Latin has the saying: *"Mens sana in corpore sano,"* which means: "A healthy mind in a healthy body". Where the two meet, the highest is achieved. I think we should always start with the body, and it seems to me that Müller is a good guide to this.

Berlin, 31 August 1905.

Count Schlieffen still cannot walk again. He will not take part in the maneuver. It's a good thing I put it on this year. I still haven't seen him. The department heads now come to me with all the lectures and signature matters, so that I am constantly occupied.

Berlin, 1 September 1905.

I went to see Schlieffen for the first time today. He was lying on the sofa and looked miserable. He got a new plaster cast yesterday, which goes from the thigh down the whole leg. He complained about the agony of having his leg nailed down like that. His mood was quite depressed, he talked to me about leaving, he was about to leave, I tried to encourage him and as I left him he seemed somewhat comforted. I was with him for almost two hours, and at the end we were both very nice towards each other. I do feel sorry for the old man; he clings to his position with every fiber of his being, and it must not be easy to give it up. By the way, he told me he couldn't have stayed much longer anyway, because his eyes and ears were getting too bad.

Berlin, 3 September 1905.

You ask whether the peace will last? That is difficult to answer. All the preconditions for a new outbreak of hostilities are in place, but it will probably take several years. The division of Sakhalin Island is quite alarming, as is the division of the Manchurian Railway, of which from now on each state is to guard its part.

There will be many points of contention. The mood in Japan will also urge the resumption of hostilities. The country is not satisfied with the mild terms of peace; there is said to be a very profound ill-feeling. The fact that Japan gave in to all demands is proof that she was close to the end with her achievements, she just could not get any further, probably mainly for lack of money, and I think a tactical success of the Russians in the field would have been enough to overturn the whole situation. That the Russians could not muster a vigorous effort was fortunate for Japan. The haughty conceit of the Russians, who are now already declaring that they have had some misfortune but have not been defeated, showed itself in the most beautiful light during the peace negotiations, but this time it has had a good success; it seems to have been a bluff for the Japanese.

What further consequences the conclusion of peace will have in great international politics can hardly be overlooked even now. England seems to me to derive the greatest benefit from it. As usual when two nations butt heads, it has stood quietly in the background to wait out its advantage. Under the new treaty of alliance with Japan, England has secured the aid of the Japanese in case she should be attacked in India. It has thus obtained a considerable safeguard for this its Achilles' heel, and would take much pleasure in seeing the Japanese shoot themselves to death for it, while England had only to contribute a few ships and some money to the cause. The quid pro quo would supposedly be English aid if Japan's gains from the Russian war were threatened. That Russia is the only country which could undertake this, but that it will not be able to do so for many years to come, the English know only too well. So it will be a good while before their part of the jointly issued bill will be claimed.

For the rest, one can only rejoice that the war is over. I believe, however, that the internal difficulties in Russia are now much greater and will only now unfold. The war that the Tsardom will have to wage against the desire for freedom of its subjects, first of all against the precursors of radical reforms, the bands of robbers and murderers of the subversive parties, will be much more bitter than the war against the Yellows.

CABINET ORDER.

At the end of the maneuvers held by me, which I have entrusted to you for the first time in full confidence in your abilities, I gladly take occasion to express to you my lively appreciation for the warlike arrangement and the instructive course of the exercises. I wish to express my gratitude for this and my gracious benevolence by awarding you the Order of the Red Eagle, first class, with oak leaves and the Royal Crown, the insignia of which I hereby send to you.

Koblenz, 15 September 1905.

Wilhelm R.

To My Adjutant General, Lieutenant General v. Moltke, Quartermaster General.

Berlin, 16 September 1905.

I have been very lucky with the maneuvers. They will probably have a decisive effect on my further fate. The Emperor did everything I thought I had to ask for; he did not lead, although it became bitterly difficult for him, he did not intervene violently in the course of the fighting, and any unnaturalness was avoided. I have fought many a battle with him, but I have always found him to be an equally kind master, and he has never resented it when I have confronted him frankly. After these experiences, I would look forward to the future more calmly if I did not know exactly that the main difficulties for me will only begin when I have definitely assumed the position that the Emperor has intended for me. Up to now I have been an insecure cantonist to him, always on the verge of breaking out of it, but with the office the chain will be put on me, on which my convictions will chafe and tug, and it is difficult to break a fetter which one has voluntarily allowed to be put on. The Emperor has awarded me a very high order, which I would be quite indifferent to, but he has, contrary to all usage, connected the award with a cabinet order.

As the maneuver closed, the Emperor called me over, shook my hand and told me: "I feel the need to thank you. It is not a figure of speech, it is sincerely meant. I have never had such interesting and such truly warlike maneuvers as this time. I would have liked to express this gratitude to you in my meeting, but I feared it would not be pleasant to you."

I then said to the Emperor: "I thank Your Majesty that you have made no mention of me, for there is nothing in the personality. But if Your Majesty says that the maneuvers have proceeded in accordance with the war, this has only been made possible by the fact that Your Majesty has left me full liberty, that you have supported me in all my views, and that Your Majesty has refrained from any interference in the course of them."

Sweden, Tulesbo, 28 September 1905.

Yesterday the local pastor was here to visit M., a very pleasant man, thoroughly liberal, clever and well-read. We had a long religious talk together at M.'s bedside, and I was pleased with the views he developed. With these he would probably have been challenged before the consistory in our country long ago. He is of the opinion that the development of the human soul continues after death, that an intermediate realm exists; he thought that after death the soul is drawn by sympathy into circles that are attuned to it, that higher spirits take care of the souls of the deceased, instruct them and gradually lift them from sphere to sphere. What would Pastor H. say to this brother minister! – He read a lot, including the writings of the German theologians, knew all the ancients, Origines, etc., the Buddhist teachings, was very knowledgeable in all the different religious systems and had a clear view of all of them. I was extremely surprised to find such a man here in the solitude of a small country pastorate.

CABINET ORDER.

It gives me sincere pleasure to appoint you Chief of the General Staff of the Army, leaving you in the position of my Adjutant General. I am entrusting you with this position, which is of such great importance for the Army, because I have absolute confidence in your insight, which is well known to me, in your military qualities and knowledge, as well as in the energy and reliability of your character, that you will succeed in solving

the manifold and difficult tasks of the General Staff, especially those that fall to you as Chief of the General Staff, in a way that is beneficial for the welfare of the Army as well as for the fatherland.
Berlin, 1 January 1906.

Wilhelm R.

To My Adjutant General, Lieutenant General v. Moltke, Quartermaster General.

CABINET ORDER.

I am pleased to take occasion today, at the conclusion of this year's great autumn exercises, which have fully met My expectations in arrangement and course, to give you renewed proof of My satisfaction and My gracious esteem and to award you the following Star of Commanders of the Royal House Order of Hohenzollern.
Liegnitz, 13 September 1906.

Wilhelm R.

To My Adjutant General, Lieutenant General v. Moltke, Chief of the Army General Staff.

CABINET ORDER.

I have today promoted you to the rank of General of the Infantry and it gives me particular pleasure to announce this to you.
Bonn, 16 October 1906.

Wilhelm R.

To My Adjutant General, Lieutenant General v. Moltke, Chief of the Army General Staff.

General Staff Berlin, 19 May 1907.

You understand that the things of this world, for which I am so heavily responsible in my position and possibly will have to come up once again in the most serious way, are still closer to me at the moment than your striving. I always have the consciousness that I must not arrange my life as I would perhaps do if I lived only for myself; I must put aside my own interest in this and live and work as my position requires. Since I am now placed in this position, I have to put its demands above everything, you know that too.

General Staff Berlin, 24 May 1907.

The Emperor has placed me on May 20 on occasion of the Ribs Festival *à la suite* of the Alexander Regiment, which has been a great pleasure for me, since I now belong to the regiment again and can wear its uniform. At the parade on 1 July I will be able to pass the regiment.

Freiburg i.B., 17 June 1907.

My mare has stopped in Müllheim, the vet thinks that she will not be fit for transport before eight to fourteen days. The big chestnut marched here today with the small horses. When he arrived, he was lame as a post, was examined, and it was found that he had kicked a finger-length nail into his hoof. So I have two vets in action and two broken horses. It is my old horse bad luck, which I cannot deny despite my best will, even if you call me a pessimist.

General Staff Berlin, 1 July 1907.

This trip to the North Country is a bit hard on my stomach, I will not easily get used to the local flavor, which has already become unfamiliar to me, and I also have a bad conscience when I think of the precious time I will be forced to waste. But this, too, is service for the fatherland.

Norway, Bergen, 7 July 1907.

The Emperor is very chipper and very amiable. The political prospects also seem better than the weather. Unquestionably, Uncle Edward's very friendly invitation means a turning point in the English direction against us. What has caused this change is not yet quite clear to me, whether it is conditions in France, those in India, or opposition from the government in London, I do not know. But there must be some weighty reason, and in any case this invitation is a symptom. I therefore believe that the next few weeks will be quiet.

It is Sunday today, and we began the service with the obligatory cursing from the Old Testament and then, for comfort, heard a sermon on faith based on the words: "He who believes will be saved, but he who does not believe will be damned." – The author of the sermon demonstrated how one could not give oneself faith, thus basically the most pronounced doctrine of predestination, namely that God only gives faith and thus blessedness to certain people, while the others, may they torment themselves as much as they want, remain lost, one of the most barbaric and bleak doctrines there is. Once again I got a real horror of this kind of religion, and I just want to know what the poor sailors were thinking during the argument – if they were thinking anything at all!

I must first gradually find my way back into this life, which I had already pretty much weaned myself from, but it is quite good that I am going on the trip, for various reasons, I don't see it as a matter of pleasure, it is just a service like any other, and I think the Emperor also likes me to be with him, since he is very open with me about what he needs.

Norway, Bergen, 9 July 1907.

In the morning we were ashore with the Emperor and made the scheduled visit to the widow of the old ship's captain, who lives in a small cottage on the outermost cliff in front of the harbor, and whom we have always visited for ten years now. The old man died three years ago. His widow lives up there with her sister and two already elderly daughters. Her brother is an umbrella manufacturer in Bergen, the one daughter a store maid. The Emperor sits on the same chair every year, I sit on the same pouf, and the same conversation is made every year. There is a glass of homemade currant wine and homemade cake, the old ladies talk like waterfalls and I have to do the interpreting.

Norway, Victoriahavn, 17 July 1907.

I don't remember whether I wrote to you that I would be released from Swinoujscie at noon on August 1, so that I would be back in Berlin on the evening of the 1st.

I long for this day. Under these climatic conditions the journey is simply a penitence, also I do not get used any more to the basic tone of our circle attuned to the calumny and miss my serious work.. So I feel cold inside and outside. However, I am able to cope with the situation from the point of view of fulfilling my duty, and my health has not suffered. Thank God that I do not need Karlsbad* bath or the like.

General Staff Berlin, 4 August 1907.

As I just wrote the date, it occurred to me that there is some similarity with today's August 4, 07 and the same day thirty-seven years ago, August 4, 70, only the last two digits are rearranged. On August 4, 1870, I had my first combat, at Weissenburg. How long ago that was, and yet how clearly it all stands before me.

The *entrevue* between the Emperor and the Tsar seems to be going according to program. Of course, the most adventurous combinations are attached to it in the press. In my opinion, it is of no significant political importance. The interests of countries are not determined by the meetings of monarchs; they take their own course and lead consistently and inexorably to collisions or to understandings. At present, as far as I can judge, the world situation does not look threatening. Our western neighbor has too much to do at home to pursue aggressive policies, and England

---

* A spa city in modern Czechoslovakia known for its hot springs, now known as Karlovy Vary.

seems gradually to be entangling herself in her wide-stretched coalitions. As long as we remain calm and strong, we have nothing to fear, though both are necessary, especially the latter. A weak Germany would be the greatest danger to European peace.

CABINET ORDER.

In grateful recognition of your unceasing and successful efforts to arrange and direct the great maneuvers held by me this year in a manner appropriate to the war and instructive, I award you the Grand Cross of the Order of the Red Eagle with oak leaves and the Royal Crown, the insignia of which are enclosed.
Wilhelmshöhe, 11 September 1907.
Wilhelm R.
To My Adjutant General, General of Infantry v. Moltke, Chief of the General Staff of the Army.

Norway, Odde, 14 July 1908.

That you will have the joy to withdraw into the pure atmosphere of art in Bayreuth, I begrudge you with all my heart. There is so little here that you can really enjoy. The mood on board is a good one, not as stupidly silly as usual. The seriousness of the world situation is also making itself felt unconsciously in our society. I also quite like the supreme mood.

Norway, Bergen, 18 July 1908.

If I do not go along on all your journeys, it is because I have a very real profession and must stand with both feet on this earth as long as I want to do justice to it. You also know that and have understanding for it.

General Staff Berlin, 12 September 1908.

The maneuvers have gone well, we have had four days of good weather, which is almost a necessity for maneuvering in the heavy soil of Lorraine, which becomes unfathomable when wet. Everything has gone as desired, and the maneuvers have, I think, been generally satisfactory. The Emperor was in good spirits and abstained from any intervention. The Archduke Franz Ferdinand, who will ascend the Austrian throne after the death of the old Emperor, pleased me very much. He spoke to me repeatedly and at length, is a clever and sharp-eyed gentleman who obviously knows what he wants. The people of Lorraine were very enthusiastic where they got to see the Emperor.

The troops were outstandingly good. The combat training was impeccable, everything was orderly and of great calm. At the same time, good endurance of the marches, some of which were enormous. The military railroad transports went off without a hitch; the railroad department of the General Staff proved itself excellently. In his final briefing, the Emperor gave both corps the highest praise. Now you know enough about the maneuvers.

Moltke's request to be relieved of his position as Chief of the General Staff.

Berlin, 25 February 1909.

On the 25th, I had a lecture with His Majesty at the New Palace. I asked His Majesty for a discussion in private, which His Majesty granted me immediately. I told His Majesty that the letter contained a reproach for me that could not be more serious, the reproach of indiscretion and disclosure of secret matters, and added that since His Majesty did not agree with the direction of the training and reproached me with this, he could not expect anything else from me than that I ask to be relieved of my position as Chief of the General Staff.*

After His Majesty thereupon declared that nothing was further from his mind than an accusation that I had misunderstood his words and that he was in complete agreement with my leadership, that there could be no question of my leaving, I declared that "in view of the critical political situation after this declaration of His Majesty, I will continue in my office."

Kiel, 8 July 1909.

By the time this letter reaches your hands, everything will probably be settled, and you will then be wiser than I am now, because I do not yet know who is to become Reich Chancellor. I sincerely regret that Bülow is leaving. Despite all his weaknesses and faults, he still has his great merits, and it is very much a question of whether he will be replaced by a better man.

T., our envoy in Christiania, is the only one with whom you can talk about a serious subject. The Emperor is well and in good spirits. One should not think that we are facing a decision which is after all of some importance for the Empire. Probably on Sunday

---

* At the end of February 1909, the Kaiser sent a letter to Moltke in which he strongly opposed the idea that younger officers assigned to the General Staff should have to work on a topic regarding the war on two fronts as a final examination assignment. The Emperor feared that such a task would reveal the most important military secrets. In addition, tasks of this scope were only suitable for army commanders and chiefs of staff to work through, not under any circumstances for junior officers. The Emperor's letter concludes with the request that in the future a selection for the work be made from the proven framework of a limited topic, which would be closer to the gentlemen and would not allow any conclusions to be drawn about intentions in a serious case.

For Moltke, this matter was a question of principle. Moltke had chosen the topic in question in order to familiarize the younger members of the General Staff with such lines of thought at an early stage, which Moltke had to assume would come to the attention of many General Staff officers in the event of war. He considered it necessary that these younger general staff officers should also be given the opportunity, beyond the scope of a limited topic, to form an opinion about such situations that would presumably arise in the event of an emergency.

It was this principled standpoint that led Moltke to ask to be relieved of his position in response to the Kaiser's letter. (The editor.)

or Monday he will go to Berlin to bid farewell to Bülow and appoint his successor, then he is to go to Norway.

Kiel, 16 July 1909.

I met Bülow-Botkamp on the railroad, who had just returned from a petroleum exploration in Hanover. He said he had found large sources of petroleum with the divining rod, and that drilling was now to take place. He can now detect petroleum with the iron rod and water with the wooden rod. It must soon show whether he has guessed correctly.

Karlsruhe, September 1909.*

The days in Austria were very pretty. Wonderful weather, interesting maneuvers. I was received extremely comradely and was shown everything I wanted to see. The old Kaiser was touchingly gracious. I met T., who was commanding a division staff. I was on the road for thirteen hours that day, partly on horseback, partly by car, and arrived late at the court table, where I was placed opposite Emperor Franz Joseph. He was pleased that I showed so much interest in the maneuvers. I am doing excellently.

CABINET ORDER.

The well-prepared arrangement of this year's great autumn exercises and their particularly instructive course have thoroughly met My expectations. I am therefore pleased to be able to assure you today, at the conclusion of the maneuvers, of My highly deserved recognition and My Royal thanks. As a token of this gratitude, I bestow upon you My High Order of the Black Eagle, the insignia of which are enclosed.

Mergentheim, 17 September 1909.

---

* Publisher's note: The original German edition does not contain a day in this date.

Wilhelm R.
To My Adjutant General, General of Infantry v. Moltke, Chief of the
Army General Staff.

Frankfurt a.M., 19 September 1909.

My maneuvers went well, I am generally satisfied. I got along well with His Majesty, got annoyed from time to time, but that also worked. He was very pleased and, as you have probably read, awarded me the Order of the Black Eagle. I was literally ashamed of myself. Uncle Helmuth used a victorious campaign to win this highest Prussian award. We imitators do it with three days of maneuvering!!!

My health is excellent. I have received many compliments about the maneuver, but I do not pay much attention to it. I have not yet received the assessment of the press. My friend G. will probably have detected the peak of idiocy in me again. The Archduke Franz Ferdinand, the heir to the Austrian throne, was quite enthusiastic about what he once told me concerning the other; I was especially pleased that my Austrian colleague, General Conrad von Hötzendorff, was very pleased. About the Emperor I had several occasions to be sincerely pleased. He did what I told him to do, and especially in the final meeting he said exactly what I had put before him, remained thoroughly objective, and delivered the best criticism I have ever heard from him, so that everything was quite delightful.

I put the rich blessing of the order, which poured over me from all sides, with the rest – in the second drawer of my dresser!

Moltke's speech at the unveiling of the Moltke bust in the Valhalla on 10 May 1910.

Full of gratitude that the grace of His Royal Highness the Prince Regent has allowed us to participate in the uplifting celebration of today, and deeply moved in the memory of our great creator and former chief, we, the representatives of the General Staff, have entered this consecrated room, which speaks to us more forcefully than words could of German spiritual power and greatness.

That which the men have created, to whose name this proud building is consecrated, they have bequeathed to us, the now living, as a sacred legacy; it is incumbent upon us to faithfully preserve that which has been hard won. We look up to them in awe and admiration, and the example and the teaching they gave us stand immovably before our minds.

With the General Staff, in which the members of all German contingents are united as in no other military organization, the entire German Army and in it the German people celebrate the memory of their immortal leader and teacher, Field Marshal Count Moltke.

With full justification, the Minister of War has called him a national figure. Untouched by party hatred and favor, his image stands in pure grandeur before the eyes of the nation, the image of a man equally admirable as a commander and as a man, an example to every striving and fighting man, be he soldier or citizen. He himself was a fighter all his life, one of the bravest and noblest who ever fought and fought. At the age of seventy he fought the battle that made the thousand-year-old dream of the Germans a reality; at the age of seventeen he had to take up the battle with life, which confronted him with lack and privation. In hard schooling he steeled his character, he learned renunciation, self-chastisement and contempt for all outward appearances, he learned to conquer and master life, whose changing phenomena his clear and penetrating mind sorted out according to their value and lack thereof, he acquired the ability to classify the many-sided and contradictory under a few, uniform points of view. In this crystal-clear knowledge of things and circumstances lies the greatness of his command, which can only be achieved by genius.

And this man, who quietly and humbly bore the glory that the admiring world paid to his deeds, remained true to himself until his last breath. Duty was the guiding principle of his long life, work his companion, loyalty the core of his being. He never sought his own advantage, always subordinating his person to the cause he served. His king, his people, the army to which he belonged, were the focus of his efforts and worries, his work and labor.

These are the ideal goods he has left us, the path he has marked out for us, illuminated by the rays of his genius. Our serious task remains to preserve these goods, to strive along this path.

To the memory of our great Chief we dedicate this wreath, which I lay at the foot of his bust on behalf of the General Staff, and with it we offer the never-extinguishing feelings of our love and gratitude.

Plön, 19 June 1910.

Since yesterday we are here on this beautiful spot of earth. Of course, I don't get to see much of it, since I couldn't get away from my desk all day yesterday and today. I have already held two reviews of the operations that have taken place so far, which is always a hard job, since I have to have everything in my head, reproduce it and assess it. Yesterday evening, the second meeting was held in the large hall of the local cadet house. Tomorrow morning is the third, the final meeting, which concludes the whole trip.

General Staff Berlin, 26 June 1910.

That you can see all these old places again is a great joy to me. It is the same with these places as it is with us people, who have changed in the course of the long years and yet are still the same as we were thirty years ago.

How wonderfully the childhood home embraces one when one enters it again after long years as an older person, I felt so deeply during my visit to Ranzau last year and also occasionally during my general staff trip to Holstein this year. It is as if the old places stretched out their arms to you, as if the trees greeted you as an old acquaintance, as if the air breathed lighter and more pleasantly, and the smell of the earth was fragrant to you. How beautiful it all is, how dear and familiar, and what a flood of memories flowing from the places of childhood! As we rode through the magnificent beech forests of Holstein, I felt like a child again, listening to the hundred birdcalls and nodding to the sunbeams that flickered golden through the proud dome of green foliage. How familiar it all was and how beautiful!

Norway, Bergen, 14 July 1910.

It is 10:30 in the evening, I sit with the window open and write without light. On the highest mountain peaks the sun is still glowing, our ship is in the shade. Never in my life have I seen a more beautiful panorama than tonight, it cannot be described. The deep violet shadows of the mountains, the red shining peaks, the rosy snow fields – as Goethe says: "Inflames all heights, calms every valley" – I had the impression as if these mountains were overflowing with light, glowing with love towards their creator and as if his eye had to rest on them with silent delight. How magically beautiful is this Norway when it bathes itself in sunlight and God's love.

Norway, Molde, 22 July 1910.

We were all aboard the "Nassau" and viewed this giant ship in all its parts. It is most interesting to admire the sum of intelligence that has become action in the complicated mechanism. Such a ship has its brain and nerve cords, like a living creature. The electric wires control every limb, and with the same ease with which we extend an arm or lift a leg, the ship moves its giant guns right and left, up and down, and sets its machinery in action.

CABINET ORDER.

I hereby grant you a four-week vacation from mid-April to mid-May 1911 to Karlsbad.
    Venice, 27 March 1911.

Wilhelm R.

To My Adjutant General, General of Infantry v. Moltke, Chief of the General Staff of the Army.

Karlsbad, 19 April 1911.

I had to tell the doctor my medical history and he immediately said that the forcible treatment of my tonsils had driven the disease substance into the body and that I was probably still suffering from the consequences. He was quite satisfied by the cardiac activity. He said that after he had tapped me for a long time, there was only a slight indisposition of the stomach and a slight swelling of the liver.

TELEGRAM.

General v. Moltke, Königsplatz 6, Berlin.

Magdeburg, May 23, 1911.

On your birthday I send you, my dear Julius, my warmest congratulations. I am pleased to hear that the stay in Karlsbad has removed the last remnants of your illness and hope that your incomparable working power will remain with me for a long time for the good of the Fatherland. May the clock, which is sent to you today as a token of my remembrance, strike only happy hours for you.

Wilhelm R.

Molsheim, 19 June 1911.

Moving around in the country gets me excellent, I feel completely fresh and well, have no trace of any discomfort, neither while riding nor during the long rides in the car, nor during the occasional climb uphill. This morning I rode first as far as Oberehnheim. The air was so clear that one could clearly see the heights of the Black Forest, while to our right stretched the chain of the Vosges with its beautiful wooded hilltops and numerous castle ruins.

We then drove to the famous monastery of Odilienberg, which is situated on the top of the mountain and offers a wonderful panoramic view over the Rhine plain and the foothills of the Vosges. It is an ancient settlement, mentioned already in the year

800 under Charlemagne. In a wide, ten-kilometer-long arc around the top of the mountain stretches the so-called pagan wall, a cyclopean wall from primitive Celtic times, piled up with huge blocks, one hardly understands how human forces could have moved them, it is one of the strangest structures of its kind, both in terms of extent and thickness, the wall is in places ten meters thick and just as high, it is incomprehensible how people have begun to lift the stones, some of which have a weight of a hundred hundred hundredweights. In the monastery there is now a kind of summer resort with boarding house, which is much visited. It is a convent for lay sisters, who serve the guests in their black religious habit and white stiffened hoods.

In the afternoon we were at the Feste Kaiser Wilhelm, where our lectures are held. Tomorrow we go to Zabern, the day after tomorrow to Dieuze, then to Metz. I am thinking of holding the final meeting on Monday, the 26th, going to Cologne on Tuesday for a tour of the railroad command and returning to Berlin on the 28th.

Kiel, 4 July 1911.

We reported to the Emperor last night, who was very amused and gracious. This morning we all visited the work on the extension of the Kaiser Wilhelm Canal, which is as grand as it is interesting. A whole new lock entrance is being built, in which the lock gates will be laid out from the present thirty to forty-five feet wide, and the stretch of canal behind it straightened out. The entire canal will be widened and deepened accordingly. The enormous walls of the new locks are already partly in place, and one looks with amazement at the tremendous earth-moving that is being carried out here. The most diverse machines are at work everywhere. As if it were a rational being, it bites into the soil with an iron jaw, eats earth, sand, stones, even whole boulders, then raises its soil-filled mouth and, after a slight twist, spits the entire contents into a waiting railroad car, filling it with a morsel. Then it turns back to the ground, opens its mouth and eats again, while the train moves on by one car length. Thus, with such a train, the otherwise hour-long work of a hundred people is accomplished in half a minute. The whole soil-eating monster is operated by two men.

There, on a steel cable, a giant basket filled with cement rolls up. Arriving above the place where the material is needed, it stops, lowers, opens and empties its contents. Immediately it floats back up into the air and hastily runs away on its rope to fetch a new load, while the first one is tamped down and smoothed with mechanical, electrically driven tampers. You see almost no people in the entire work area. Here the human mind works, transposed into machines, and matter willingly follows, albeit puffing and groaning, steaming and sputtering, the laws laid down for it. This is really impressive, and it must be a proud consciousness for the engineer to convert his thoughts into work in this way.

At Sea, 9 July 1911.

The mood on board is good. The Emperor is relatively calm. The political situation is still in limbo. I do not believe that anything serious will result from the appearance of our ships on the Moroccan coast. It will help to create clear conditions.

Baleholm, 16 July 1911.

A few days ago I had a very interesting conversation with His Majesty about religious issues. He was extremely unhappy with the pastors, their narrow-mindedness and orthodoxy. He was of the opinion that death was only the beginning of a further development, thought a lot about these things in general and is much freer in his views than one should believe. He is looking for truth, and everything dull formulaic is an abomination to him. He does not want a standstill in religious development, but progress, and feels the need to bring religion and science into harmony. He told how he had told the pastors that when the children see and hear the development of the world in the "Urania"* and then they are told in religious education that in six days God created the world, doubt must be sown in their hearts. If you pastors do not progress, science will pass over you, and if you do not know anything new to say, the stones will speak.

General Staff Berlin, 19 August 1911.

The unfortunate Morocco story is beginning to grow on me. It is certainly a sign of praiseworthy perseverance to sit steadily on coals, but it is not pleasant. If we creep out of this affair again with our tails between our legs, if we can't summon ourselves to make a vigorous demand that we are prepared to enforce with the sword, then I despair for the future of the German Reich. Then I will leave. But before that, I will propose to abolish the army and place us under the protectorate of Japan, then we can make money and bullshit undisturbed. You will probably have little interest in politics at the moment, your occupation is also more interesting and useful in any case.

Bukovina, Koszczuja, 1 October 1911.

Curious to see how things will develop between Italy and Turkey. When the little Balkan dogs start barking, there's no telling what will come of it.

Karlsbad, 6 April 1912.

Dr. H. examined me very thoroughly today and is very satisfied. The heart is quite all right. There is still a slight irritation noticeable in the kidneys, but, as he says, so little that he would not even notice it if he did not know that there was irritation last year.

---

* A science center in Berlin, founded in 1888.

He thinks that over the course of the present year it will disappear completely. The findings confirmed his assumption that it was an infection in my case. He says that the kidneys always need the longest time to become completely free again, usually about two years, which would also be true for me.
    I don't need to take it easy, I can walk and climb. I am very happy about the favorable result of the examination, even more so because Dr. H. is a very meticulous and precise examiner.

Karlsbad, 24 April 1912.

Politically, everything is apparently pretty quiet. The Italian-Turkish war drags on laboriously, with no end in sight. In the German Reichstag, the draft bill has finally come up for discussion, introduced extremely weakly by a speech by Bethmann. This man will never get up the nerve to speak clearly and energetically. Here again the old milk sauce. No one thinks of war, Germany is quite peaceable, and so are the other powers, yet one cannot know what might happen one day, and therefore a reinforcement of the Wehrmacht is necessary. It would be a laughing matter if it were not a crying matter! – Nevertheless, the bill will apparently be accepted smoothly. The people have a healthier sense of the world situation than their appointed leaders.

Telegram from Moltke to the Emperor.

Berlin, 23 May 1912.

Your Majesty would please accept my heartfelt thanks for the inkwell graciously sent to me for my birthday and the gracious words accompanying it. The root of my strength lies in the trust that Your Majesty has placed in me so often and has expressed again today; everything I have been able to achieve is due to this trust. I ask God to give me the strength to continue to show myself worthy of this highest good.
    Your Majesty's most faithfully obedient

General v. Moltke.

Norway, Baleholm, 8 July 1912.

In the newspapers that came with the courier it said that I would be dismissed in the fall and replaced by General v. W. I don't know who concocted this nonsense. I do not know who concocted this nonsense. The Kaiser had written next to the news: "Impudent!" For the rest, I am not upset about it. If it is to be, I will know best. It is not that far yet.

Norway, Baleholm, 20 July 1912.

Yesterday afternoon the Emperor was with four gentlemen, including myself, on an English yacht which had arrived here, belonging to a Sir Watchman, an old gentleman who propagates the crazy idea of universal world peace!

General Staff Berlin, 18 August 1912.

Although the weather was not very favorable, we nevertheless undertook the flight with the "Hansa";[*] unfortunately, it could not take place in the originally planned route. On Saturday morning we drove out to the hall in which the mighty ship is housed. At one hundred and ten meters long, it took up almost the entire length of the hall. The weather was dull and cloudy, the wind quite fresh, but at least it was not raining. The leader of the ship told me that it had been established by trial balloons that at the height of eight hundred meters a strong wind was blowing of fifteen to sixteen second gusts, and that he assumed that strong gusts would come down around noon, so we could only make a trip of a few hours and would have to be back in the hall around noon. At 8 o'clock we boarded, and the ship was pulled out of the hall. It has a very spacious cabin that can seat sixteen people comfortably, we were only eight.

---

[*] A Zeppelin first flown in 1912 by DELAG, the first commercial airline.

One has a comfortable wicker chair to use, sitting by the large open window looking down on the world. You don't notice a draft and absolutely no vibration. There is a steward on board who has a small galley with cold kitchen and a small ice cellar where the wine is on ice. On small tables you can spread the cards in front of you or hold your meal. The cabin is very nicely done in light lacquer, and so high that I could stand comfortably in it.

Wonderful was the ascent. After the ship had turned with its tip against the wind, the mooring ropes were released by the crews at a command, the propellers began to turn, and slowly the giant craft rose into the air. It was noticeable only by the fact that the people, houses, trees, etc. became smaller and smaller, the panoramic view larger and larger. In a few minutes we had reached the altitude of three hundred meters, which we now maintained continuously, with slight deviations. The ride went away across Hamburg, which was shrouded in a murky haze of smoke and fog, the Alster flashing brightly through the smoky air. The wind was strong, about ten meters a second, nevertheless, as the ship has an inherent speed of twenty-one meters, we made rapid progress. The "Hansa" has four propellers on its two gondolas, and in the middle between the two gondolas is the cabin, connected to the front and rear gondolas by a narrow passage, but not to be entered by passengers. One sits in the cabin just like in a saloon car, the noise of the propellers does not disturb at all, one can talk in peace. Now we are above the harbor with its countless ships and small steamboats, shooting back and forth, churning the water incessantly. All the ships greet the "Hansa" with their steam whistles, we wave from the windows with handkerchiefs, down below people stand with their white faces turned upwards and wave back. Then we sail down the Elbe. The view of the leafy heights of Blankenese, the numerous, brightly gleaming villas, the ships passing below us on the tide is charming. Everywhere gathered people greeting up; from the windows, from the roofs they are waving white cloths. With one glance we overlook the many inlets of the harbor, the docks, the quays, everywhere the meals are steaming, and the screeching of the cranes sounds up. Incessantly drones the sound of work, weaving and swirling trade, industry. Ships are unloaded and loaded, bales of goods are shipped, the railroad lines gleam and trains crawl along them like black caterpillars.

Gradually the city fades behind us, we follow the course of the mighty river, see its two banks, the dredging operations, the islands and river signs. On the great world trade route the ships pull, the fast steamer rushes through the water, using the expiring low tide, we overtake it playfully, the trains on the shore cannot keep the same speed with us. So it goes down the stream to Kuxhaven, and in front of us lies the sea in lead-gray color. We have covered one hundred and thirty kilometers in two hours. But towards us comes a blue-black wall over the sea, the clouds chase past us, often enveloping us so that the view disappears, the wind gradually gets stronger, and we have to turn around if we don't want to be caught by the approaching squall. Too bad, too bad, but it doesn't help, because we're not going on a war cruise, but a pleasure cruise, and we mustn't endanger the ship. So back we go.

Now we are drifting before the wind. The engines are running at half power, yet the landscape is passing below us like a panorama of change. We have a speed of one hundred and twenty kilometers per hour. Admiringly, the ship obeys the helm. We descend to a few meters above the water level, then we rise again into the air. It is a wonderful feeling to float in the air, like a bird, rising and falling as it pleases, and always in steady flight, without any vibration.

Now we fly in a northeasterly direction over the land, leaving the stream behind us. Below us, in regular squares, lie the fields, stand the houses and farms, graze the cattle. The effect of the ship on the animals is interesting. The horses grazing in the paddocks raise their heads, and with waving tails and manes they run away at a stretched gallop, as do the cows and sheep, all running away as if to save their lives. The chickens in the chicken yards behave like mad. They flutter and fly in confusion, duck flat to the ground, run into the coops to hide. From above we look into the woods, see the racks like straight lines, here and there a few roe deer seeking a thicket in the fastest flight, some storks fearfully fluttering away over the meadows. Everywhere fear and fright with the animals, only humans stand and greet and wave up! – We fly over the Holstein Geest, heath, fields, woods, villages and individual farms alternate with each other.

Now we are over Elmshorn, then we take the direction to Barmstedt, whose flat church tower I recognize from far away. There's Voßloeh, where we ate warm beer and buttered bread as children, then the beech forest, in which we wandered around, in the vague sense of its immense size! Now we survey it with a glance, a green island in the landscape. Now we see the much-curved Pinau, and now comes Ranzau. There lies the old house of our beautiful youth on its little island, surrounded by green and by water. Every spot I can recognize, every spot where we played, the trees where I cut my name. The windows behind which I lived, the bridges over which we walked. How unchanged everything is, and how deeply etched in memory. There is the garden where I sat many a winter night in the snow to shoot the hare that came to the cabbage at night, the pond where the many crucians were, the old firs in whose tops W. and I used to hide in when we skipped our drawing lessons, the Bornholt mill, the court house, the district court judge's apartment, everything is there, everything seen from above, everything built up like a toy, and here again children as in those days, staring up, interrupted in their playing, happy as we were, and thinking that this wonderful existence will never end, as – we thought it would!

The propellers of the "Hansa" rattle over the old dear spot of earth and water, we make a loop and go over the whole piece of the past once again. The propellers rattle, and in their sounds I hear the children's cheers of the old days, the voice of the parents, the rustling of the leaves, the murmur of the days gone by. How far away, how remote that time lies behind him who now floats up there in the air and feels how past, present and future mix. If it didn't sound so trivial, I would like to say: Who would have told us that back then!

But we have to tear ourselves away, because the weather is riding behind us on the wings of the storm. We turn off, and in ten minutes we are over Altona, then over Hamburg, now already over, the hall. On the square in front of it lies a white sheet with a red arrow mark indicating the direction of the wind, for we must land against the wind so that it does not catch the giant body of the ship from the side. The crews stand ready to catch the descending bird.

Now we turn against the wind. The top of the ship lowers, and in an oblique glide we descend to just above the green lawn. The mooring ropes are thrown out, grabbed by the people, the engines stand still. The soldiers pull the ship to the front of the hangar, straighten it, and then the propellers turn once more, and the "Hansa" plunges through the mighty gate into the interior of the hangar, stops and is moored. We disembark, all aware that it has been a wonderful trip.

Two minutes later, the weather we escaped so quickly approaches, and the rain pelts the tin roof of the hall. Just in time under roof! Masterfully timed.

General Staff Berlin, 14 September 1912.

The maneuver went well and smoothly. The Emperor was very pleased and expressed his appreciation to me in a particularly warm manner; I also heard that the maneuver was generally satisfactory. It did not come to the complication I had feared; I had already spoken to His Majesty on the Nordland voyage, and he kept himself in check with great self-sacrifice. His Majesty the Emperor held a very nice meeting. Tomorrow morning I will now leave for Wilhelmshaven to attend the fleet exercises on the "Hohenzollern" on Monday.

General Staff Berlin, 17 September 1912.

The day at the fleet was very beautiful. A proud sight, 66 torpedo boats, 14 submarines and 46 large ships. The passing lasted almost an hour. I was with the Kaiser on the liner "Deutschland." – I am fine. I am told that the maneuver has received much acclaim in the press. From the military side I have heard a lot of appreciation.

Bankau, 21 September 1912.

As far as the maneuvers are concerned, I have had – as they say –

a "good press." The newspapers seem to have gotten out of the habit of calling me a jerk now!

General Staff Berlin, 16 May 1913.

It seems that the dance in the Balkans will start again. Serbia and Bulgaria cannot agree on the distribution of the bearskin and are facing each other with weapons in hand. Greece is also in conflict with Bulgaria, which has a huge appetite for land. If war breaks out among the existing allies, Serbia and Greece will be against Bulgaria. To what extent this war will affect the behavior of the major states, no one can predict. So we are still quite far from definite peaceful conditions.

CABINET ORDER.

It gives me particular pleasure, on today's day of My twenty-fifth anniversary in government, to again express My gracious benevolence to you by appointing you Chief of the Fusilier Regiment Field Marshal General Count Moltke (Silesian) No. 38. The regiment preserves with its name a deep reverential gratitude for the immortalized Field Marshal, and thus in memory and in the present there are relations to the name "Moltke" which make me assume that you will recognize in the appointment as Chief of this regiment a proof of my special recognition of your always proven, faithful and good services rendered to me in all official positions, especially as Chief of the General Staff of the Army. I have instructed the regiment to submit the report and the officer's rank list to you in accordance with the regulations.
Berlin, 16 June 1913.

Wilhelm R.

To My Adjutant General, General of Infantry v. Moltke, Chief of the General Staff of the Army, *à la suite des* Kaiser-Alexander-Gardegrenadier-Regiments No. 1.

General Staff Berlin, 16 June 1913.

Today the Emperor appointed me Chief of the Fusilier Regiment

Field Marshal General Count Moltke No. 38. The regiment was formerly in Schweidnitz, now in Glatz.

General Staff Berlin, 17 June 1913.

Berlin is still celebrating and jubilating; from early morning, clubs, guilds, students, etc. parade through the streets with music corps and flags, perform a mad spectacle and block all traffic. The Emperor was very fresh and in good spirits yesterday. There is something great in this huge participation in his jubilee, and he may well feel that.

Kuxhaven, 9 July 1913.

The new Minister of War, General von Falkenhayn, is reporting today. I don't know if you remember him; he was on the General Staff for a long time.

Norway, Bergen, 11 July 1913.

Events in the Balkans are not going as I would have liked. The Bulgarians seem to be at a disadvantage everywhere. Their behavior is incomprehensible to me. The king seems to have been eliminated altogether; nothing is heard of him. His much-vaunted diplomatic skill seems to have failed completely. I have the impression that he is at the mercy of the military party without a will. Bulgaria is playing *la banque*; it cannot possibly carry out the war against Serbia, Greece and Romania. Turkey also seems to be stirring again; it would also be foolish if it did not take advantage of the situation. Incidentally, the reports from the theater of war are so contradictory that it is almost impossible to get a clear picture of the situation.

Norway, Baleholm, 19 July 1913.

We are all somewhat numb to the events in the Balkans. No one knows anymore what is to become of it. Now the Turks are also starting again, taking advantage of Bulgaria's defenselessness and marching on Adrianople. Bulgaria has staked everything too senselessly to lose again, as it seems, everything gained. *Qui trop embrasse, mal étreint!**

I think to myself that the next event, when Bulgaria is finished, will be the war between Serbia and Greece, the two now allies. It would be best to surround the whole Balkans with a fence and not to open it again until everything there has been beaten to death. As long as Austria and Russia do not interfere in the turmoil, I see no danger of a European conflict. One can feel sorry for the unhappy country in which the belligerents take turns slaughtering the inhabitants as they get somewhere. What terrible atrocities are committed there, for one is worthy of the other; the Serbs slaughter the inhabitants just as regularly as the Bulgarians, and the Greeks seem to do no better.

Norway, Baleholm, 22 July 1913.

As far as the development of the warlike events in the Balkans and their political repercussions are concerned, I think we can be quite satisfied with the way things have gone. Russia, which so much wanted to play the role of protector of the Balkan states and to exercise a decisive mediation, has been badly caught in the nettle. The belligerents simply turned it down and declared that they would settle their matter among themselves without mediation. Greece, through its successes, is coming more and more to the fore in its dealings with the Bulgarians, and if an understanding is reached between it and Romania, as seems to be the case, it will provide a counterweight to the Pan-Slavist aspirations in the Balkans and establish a group of powers that will not march to

---

* "He who embraces too much, embraces poorly!"

Russian command.

Austria, too, finally seems to realize that it must reckon with the conditions as they are and not with those it would like to have. The unpleasant tension between Austria and Romania seems to have been resolved, which is of great importance for us in view of a possible clash between Germanic and Slavic peoples.

Bulgaria is in a hopeless fix. The Romanian cavalry is already roaming in the area of Sofia and King Ferdinand's heart may well have fallen quite deeply into his pants! There is nothing left for him but to make peace and to grant everything that his opponents demand. Such a turnaround from the greatest success to complete impotence is without precedent in world history. By the way, the Bulgarians are to be congratulated. After the atrocities they have committed, they are no longer to be considered a belligerent state, but a horde of criminals. In the town of Serres, when they retreated out of 2700 inhabitants, they left only a few hundred alive and burned everything, the pure Huns. I believe that peace will soon be established, because they are at the end.

In China, too, all hell is breaking loose again. The South is outraged against Beijing and Yuan Shi Kai. The war is on, and already Russia is stretching out its greedy hand to Mongolia and northern Manchuria. How many people are killed every day!

Poznan, 27 August 1913.

General Pollio, who is here, has pleased me well, he speaks only French, seems to have a sincere admiration for our army.

General Staff Berlin, 22 December 1913.

The command of the Crown Prince charges me with a not easy and responsible task. Not personally, because he is a very charming and kind gentleman, but factually. He must be educated to work, at least to the appreciation of work, he must learn to understand that the fulfillment of duty is more important than sports.

Moltke's speech on the birthday of His Majesty the Emperor January 27, 1914.

Gentlemen!

On behalf of the General Staff, I would like to express our pleasure at being able to celebrate today the Army's most beautiful holiday, the birthday of our Most High Warlord, in the company of a large number of former members of the General Staff, and I would like to thank these gentlemen for expressing the feeling of comradely togetherness by their numerous attendance.

The General Staff is the most succinct expression of this comradely togetherness, which encompasses all parts of the entire army, for it unites in itself the members of all German federal contingents for joint work for the Kaiser and the Reich.

But it is not only comradeship that has brought us together today, it is the faithful devotion to our Imperial Lord that is common to us all.

Gentlemen, as a birthday gift to our Emperor, let us renew our vow to stand firmly by him in good days and bad. The more a unpatriotic demagogy is at work to sow discord and strife among the German tribes and estates, the more it works to undermine the last and firmest support of state and monarchy, the army, the more it becomes our duty to unite firmly to preserve the sacred goods handed down to us by a great past.

Knowing that the entire Army, borne by the spirit of loyalty and duty, stands united behind our Most High Warlord, let us raise our glasses to the future of Germany and to the welfare of our Emperor and Lord.

General Staff Berlin, 22 February 1914.

With the coming spring, as every year, there is again a political crisis. Austria is facing a political action by Russia and Austria has put itself in a difficult position militarily by its incomprehensible policy against Romania. Now Berlin is supposed to make up for it. But it is not so easy!

General Staff Berlin, 7 March 1914.

This morning I gave a lecture on photostereoscopy to a number of members of the Reichstag in the library room of the General Staff, with photographs. It is a matter of the fact that I have requested one more department head and that there was no understanding for this matter in the Reichstag. In order to teach them this, this event took place. They all showed a lot of interest and expressed their amazement at the technical possibilities of exploiting photography.

General Staff Berlin, 9 March 1914.

Tomorrow I have a dinner for twelve people on the occasion of the presence of an Italian military mission.

General Staff Berlin, 11 March 1914.

I drank to the Italian General Zuccari at the table without making a speech, whereupon he got up and made a speech at me, saying that I had earned the greatest merit, that people in Italy and Austria looked to me with the greatest confidence, etc., etc. I was quite embarrassed, as you can imagine.

General Staff Berlin, 22 March 1914.

I was at the opening ceremony of the New Library this morning. The building is very beautiful, with mighty domed hall, whose dome is supposed to be somewhat larger than that of St. Peter's Church. Built entirely of reinforced concrete, which looks exactly like gray sandstone. Quite a number of speeches were made, among which the Emperor's was the best.

Karlsbad, 27 April 1914.

The Mexican story, as far as I can tell, is going to be a washout for the Union, because the whole country is uniting against the Americans, and it will not be easy for them to deal with the country, which is about four times the size of Germany. I think President Wilson will be glad to come out of this affair with a black eye. The matter will not lead to international entanglements.

Baden-Baden, 30 May 1914.

Today we were on the battlefields of Weißenburg and Wörth, where I received my baptism of fire forty-four years ago. You can imagine that on these blood-soaked terrains the memories of the great time are vividly reawakened. I was handed the battle report which I had written as an ensign in the bivouac on the evening of the Battle of Weissenburg and which, strangely enough, had been found in the war files. I had to write it at that time, since all the officers of the company had fallen and I was leading the company. Had completely forgotten about it. The report, written on a sheet of rough paper, I liked quite a lot, it is simple, factual and quite reasonable, without boasting, I spoke of myself modestly only in the third person as: the ensign. I enjoyed the paper. It is interesting to find again the lines in the terrain, which I walked in the fire at that time.

Metz, 5 June 1914.

It is a pleasure for me to introduce the Crown Prince to the circumstances of our borderlands. He is full of interest in the matter. He has a lot of good qualities; the young grape may make a good wine one day.

Kyllburg, 7 June 1914.

You are certainly right with your explanations about the development of the freedom of the soul, I have read them with great interest. You know that today (Sunday) is my working day, I have a lot to do, have already written for hours and have to be brief, therefore I cannot go into more detail on your topic today. I am thinking of holding the final meeting in Cologne on the 11th. In the afternoon I want to go to Homburg and from there to the maneuver area for one day on the 12th. On the 13th, in the morning, I think I will arrive in Berlin.

General Staff Berlin, 16 June 1914.

We have been separated for a long time, let us hope that we will be granted a longer time together again. On Thursday, I hope to have a lecture with His Majesty, then I will ask him to release me from the North Country trip. It will have to go without me for a while.

General Staff Berlin, 18 June 1914.

If I am released from the North Country trip, I think to come to Karlsbad on July 2. I can't get away well before then because I still have too many official things to do. If you stay there for five weeks, we would still be together for about three weeks.

General Staff Berlin, 19 June 1914.

Yesterday evening, I asked His Majesty to excuse me from the North Country trip. The matter did not cause any difficulties, although he was very sorry that I would not be going.

Karlsbad, 17 July 1914.

As far as your trip to Bayreuth is concerned, according to the latest news I have received, you will be able to make it quietly. Nothing decisive will happen before the 25th.

Karlsbad, July 18, 1914.

I very much hope that you will not change anything about your Bayreuth trip. Even if I am alone in Berlin for two days, it really does no harm at all. I am very much looking forward to our being together in August when you return from Bayreuth.

Karlsbad, 19 July 1914.

I don't really believe that we will be able to live together in August. Either you will go to Olga or, if things go badly with your mother, to Gvesarum, or something else will happen.

Karlsbad, 21 July 1914.

I am glad that you saw and talked to Dr. Steiner, it is always such an inner refreshment and strengthening for you to talk to him. I would also be happy to see him in August, when he should come to Berlin.

So now Thursday is supposed to bring the decision! I'm starting to get a little skeptical about this!

General Staff Berlin, 26 July 1914.

Here at the General Staff, W. was waiting for me and we had a longer meeting. Later – it is now 10 o'clock – I want to go to the Foreign Office in order to discuss things with J. The situation is still quite unsettled. The further course of events depends only on

Russia's attitude; if it does not undertake a hostile act against Austria, the war will remain localized. Last night thousands of people passed in front of the Austrian Embassy and gave ovations, until late at night the cheers lasted, people sang patriotic songs, it was almost as if we had mobilized ourselves. The mood in the press is good, even the "Berlin Daily Journal" writes energetically in the Austrian spirit. But you will probably return on Tuesday. By then, hardly any major decision will have been made. Enjoy the beauty that is still offered to you.

General Staff Berlin, 27 July 1914.

This morning I was at Bethmann's for a long time, I have just returned from there and have to go to the New Palace in an hour, where the Emperor will arrive at 3 o'clock. The situation is always rather unclear. It will not clear up very quickly; about fourteen days will pass before anything definite can be known or said. You can stay in Bayreuth for the rest of this time, you don't have to worry about me. I endured yesterday, which was somewhat different from the spa day in Karlsbad, excellently, I feel well and fresh.

Luxembourg, 29 August 1914.

I'm sitting here in the school where we also built our bureaus here. Everything is still unfinished and nowhere near as comfortable as in Koblenz. We have neither gas nor electric light, only dim kerosene lamps. All the brighter light shines for me from the reports that have come in from our armies today. In the East a full victory has been won, so many prisoners that the army does not know how to take them away. In the West, the 2nd Army under Bulow reports a full victory, fought today against five and a half French corps.

We are all staying together, that is, my staff and I, in the Hotel de Cologne, which has a German landlord. It is not very nice, but one has to make do in the field. It doesn't matter whether you have it a little better or a little worse.

I am glad to be by myself and not at the court. I get quite sick when I hear the talk there; it is heartbreaking how clueless the High Command is about the seriousness of the situation. Already a certain hurricane mood arises, which I hate to death. Well, I continue to work calmly with my good people. With us, there is only the seriousness of duty and no one is unaware of how much and how difficult still has to be done.

Luxembourg, 31 August 1914.

The success in the East is great and will hopefully cleanse our unfortunate province of the Russians. The devastation they have wrought must be healed by a later time, when we are at peace again. Also in the west again a success with the 2nd Army under Bülow, to which the Guards Corps belongs. It is said to have suffered heavy losses. Today and tomorrow the armies of the center fight, it will be a decisive battle, on the outcome of which depends infinitely much.

Luxembourg, 1 September 1914.

Today, on the day of the battle of Sedan, we won another great victory over the French. At my request, the Emperor was outside today with the High Command of the 5th Army, with the Crown Prince, and will stay outside for the night. It is good for him that he comes to the troops once and that they see him, also that he is on French soil.

Luxembourg, 2 September 1914.

I just got back from France. I was at Fort Longwy, which was bombarded right after the invasion. The effect of our heavy artillery is devastating. The whole fort, which enclosed a small town, is a heap of ruins. The Emperor returned from the troops today, in a jubilant mood. Things are going badly in Austria. The army is not advancing. I see it coming that it will be kicked out.

Luxembourg, 3 September 1914.

Nothing new has happened today. Things are going badly with the Austrians and we cannot help them at the moment, we must thank God if we can cope with our enemies. God grant that soon some event will occur in Russia that will relieve us of the Muscovite masses.

Luxembourg, 7 September 1914.

Today a great decision is made, our entire army from Paris to Upper Alsace has been in battle since yesterday. If I had to lay down my life today to fight for victory, I would do it with a thousand joys, as thousands of our brothers have done again and thousands more have done. What rivers of blood have already flowed, what nameless sorrow has come over the countless innocents whose homes and farms have been burned and devastated. I am often overcome with horror when I think of it, and I feel as if I must take responsibility for this terrible thing, and yet I could not do otherwise than what has happened.

Luxembourg, 8 September 1914.

It is difficult for me to say with what nameless heaviness the burden of responsibility has weighed on me during the last days and still weighs on me. For the great struggle in front of the entire front of our army has still not been decided. It is a question of preserving or losing what has hitherto been gained with infinite sacrifice; it would be terrible if all this blood should be shed without a resounding success. The terrible tension of these days, the absence of news from the distant armies, the consciousness of what is at stake, is almost beyond human strength. The terrible difficulty of our situation often stands before me like a black wall that seems impenetrable. Tonight somewhat more favorable news has arrived from the front. God grant that we may once more have a success with our melted-down troops. The Guards Corps has been heavily engaged in battle again, and is said to be down to almost half its strength.

It is a difficult time, and countless victims have already been claimed by this war that will continue to claim them. The whole world has conspired against us; it looks as if it is the task of all the remaining nations to destroy Germany once and for all. The few neutral states are not friendly toward us. Germany has no friend in the world, she stands all alone on her own.

It depends on today's decision whether we will stay here. Not for a long time, in any case. The Emperor must enter France, get closer to the army, he must be in enemy territory like his troops.

Luxembourg, 9 September 1914.

Things are going badly. The fighting to the east of Paris will be to our disadvantage. One of our armies will have to retreat, the others will have to follow. The beginning of the war, so full of hope, will turn into the opposite. I must bear what happens, and I will stand or fall with my country. We must suffocate in the struggle against East and West. How different it was when we opened the campaign so gloriously a few weeks ago – the bitter disappointment now follows. And how we will have to pay for everything that is destroyed.

The campaign is not lost, just as it was not lost for the French, but the French enthusiasm, which was on the point of being extinguished, will flare up powerfully, and I am afraid that our people, in their enthusiasm for victory, will hardly be able to bear the misfortune. How difficult this will be for me, no one can better judge – than You, who live entirely in my soul.

TELEGRAM OF HIS MAJESTY THE EMPEROR AND KING.

With best wishes
Luxembourg, 14 September 1914.   Wilhelm.

Chief of General Staff.

The Vilna Army, II, III, IV, XX Army Corps, three to four reserve divisions, five cavalry divisions, has been completely defeated by the battle of the Masurian Lakes and the ensuing pursuit. The Grodno Reserve Army, XXII A.-K., remnant of VI A.-K, parts of III Siberian Corps, has suffered heavily in the particular engagement at Lyk. The enemy has heavy losses of killed and wounded. The number of prisoners is increasing. The spoils of war are extraordinary. With the width of the army's front of over one hundred kilometers, the tremendous marches of one hundred and fifty kilometers in four days in some cases, with the fighting going on all along this front and depth, I cannot yet report the full extent. Some of our units have come sharply into the fray. However, the losses are still only minor. The army was victorious all along the line against a stubbornly fighting but finally fleeing enemy. The army is proud that an Imperial Prince fought and bled in its ranks.

Signed Hindenburg.

(Written in the Emperor's own hand and sent to Moltke on 14 September 1914.)

Mézières, 27 September 1914.

I'm leaving here again at noon today for Brussels to get things going there. Our situation in France is still unchanged. We need a success at some point, it comes and does not come.

Mézières, 3 October 1914.

Our situation is still critical, but here in France, too, a turn can occur any day, as we had a fine success yesterday outside Antwerp. One such success in the West, and everything is saved. You know that I was reluctant to call in sick and leave, you know that I told you my place is here, I stand and fall with the army. I may return to Brussels tomorrow, where the decision is ripening, and it is good for me to be there, so that unity is maintained. The Guard Corps has moved to another place and will probably have to fight new battles again.

TELEGRAM FROM THE EMPEROR.

Colonel General v. Moltke, *Gouvernement* Brussels.

10 October 1914.

I express My Royal Thanks for your successful participation in the capture of Antwerp, which will forever be one of the most glorious feats of arms, and I award you the Iron Cross, First Class, in high recognition of your excellent services rendered to Me so far. I am full of thanks to God for this glorious success.

Wilhelm LR.

Mézières, 11 October 1914.

I try as much as possible to orient myself about everything that is being done and to maintain the relationship between Falkenhayn and me, it is not easy, but I do what I can. I think a harder test can hardly be imposed on a person. Yesterday I returned from Antwerp. I was at least able to help a little there, while here I am only a spectator. The case of Antwerp was at least a success for a long time.

Mézières, 22 October 1914.

I have now collapsed after all, after my body had held up so well so far. It is an inflammation of the gall bladder and congestion in the right lobe of the liver. In and of itself the thing is not bad, but I have to lie down. Dr. N. from Kaiser treats me in a nice and pleasant way, he expects that the matter will be completely overcome in another eight days. For me this illness was a hard blow, just the day before I had spoken with His Majesty. It was as

I had thought. The Emperor had the idea that I was actually in charge of the matter and that Falkenhayn was only an assistant to some extent. I now made the matter clear to him and said that I was completely switched off. He said that he wanted "remedy" to occur.

Mézières, 24 October 1914.

The Emperor was with me for an hour yesterday, very graciously, personally he apparently remained the old man toward me. I don't think he has a clear insight into the situation he has put me in. I could not talk about it yesterday either, but must do so when I am well, in three or four days I think. P. told me that the Emperor wanted to offer me one of his hunting lodges if I wanted to recuperate for some time. Maybe this is the only way to come to a decision, I do not know yet, would like it very much.

The success we hoped for has not come, disappointment again and again. It is as if nothing more should succeed for us, and yet success must finally come if we are not to suffocate in the mass of our opponents.

Mézières, 26 October 1914.

There is no progress in our operations. All the hopes we have placed in the new corps have been deceptive. We can't come to a decision, the campaign is dragging on like a stagnant swamp. Physically, things are getting better every day.

Mézières, 28 October 1914.

I am very worried about the situation in Russia. I see it coming that after the Austrians have been defeated again, our army will have to go back. This Austrian defeat is the heaviest blow we could have suffered.

CABINET ORDER OF HIS MAJESTY THE EMPEROR.

As a result of your illness I have, to My greatest regret, found it necessary to place the post of Chief of the General Staff of the Field Army in other hands, and I have appointed Lieutenant General von Falkenhayn, Minister of War, as your successor. It touches Me painfully in the highest degree that you will now no longer be able to translate your many years of untiring and beneficial peace work into further deeds yourself and to participate in the success of your work at close quarters. However, your merit for the General Staff remains undiminished and your personality and your activity at the head of the German General Staff, which is gloriously known throughout the world, will remain unforgotten by Me and My Army. With all my heart I wish you a speedy recovery and hope that you will fully regain your former sprightliness.

I have gladly complied with your request to be accompanied by an officer of the General Staff, and have instructed the Minister of War to continue to provide you with your previous salary.

Grand Headquarters, 3 November 1914.

Wilhelm R.

To My Adjutant General and Chief of the General Staff of the Field Army Colonel General v. Moltke.

Moltke's preface for "The German Soldier's Book."*

Written November 1914.

This book is dedicated to you, German warriors, who have left your parents, brothers and sisters, wife and child, house and farm, to go out to war: It shall bring you a greeting from the homeland, which you protect with your blood and life. It is a sacred cause for which you are in the field. Germany did not undertake this war out of selfish interest. We wanted to keep peace with all the world, and we did not seek foreign property or land. The war was forced upon us by the envy and hatred of our numerous enemies, who wanted to destroy the Reich, German life, German culture and peace work. They wanted to eradicate Germany from the ranks of culture and spoil what we have created in long, quiet peace work. In defense

---

* Publisher: Deutsche Bibliothek, Berlin W.

of our national life, for the existence of our country, we are waging this war, and we will not lay down our arms until we have won a peace that will enable our children and grandchildren, safe from new attacks, to rebuild and carry on what the war has destroyed. But it is not only a matter of material goods, let us not forget that; it is a matter of something higher, of preserving for the whole world the leading German spiritual life. That is why it is a holy war that we are waging; the whole German people knows and feels that, and they stand unanimously in loyal brotherhood behind their army. It will endure with you and make every sacrifice until victory is won. And when you then return home, you will bring back with you from the field as your most precious possession the certainty that Germany was invincible, that she stood together with all her tribes and parties like brothers, and you will carry in your heart the consciousness that the German national soul harbors infinite powers when it allows ideal goals to revive within itself. It is the fervent wish of all those who remember you today and every day that this good will be preserved for the German people in the future, even after the war. Hold out, you German warriors, no matter how hard the battle may be. Remain faithful and firm, as you have been up to now, and you will be victorious.

EXCERPT FROM A LETTER FROM CROWN PRINCE WILHELM TO MOLTKE.
Stenay, 15 December 1914.

Your Excellency

I have wanted to write for a long time how much I feel for you in this difficult time for you. It cut into my heart how I had to see you so lonely and ill in Mézières. From old times I have always thought so much of Your Excellency and especially as a really loyal, sincere friend of my father, who unfortunately has little of this kind. During my time in the General Staff, I found only kindness and forbearance and understanding from Your Excellency regarding the loss of my regiment. Finally, I owe my present command to you alone, and should God let me return home in good health after the war, the battles of Longwy, the Lotaine, the Meuse crossing, and the battles at Varennes and in the Argonne will always remain glorious, uplifting memories for me until my last moment. All this gives me the right now, in the days that are gloomy for you, to come to your side and to squeeze your hand tightly in the feeling of respect and loyal attachment, I am sure that I am understood, even if I express myself clumsily, I have never been able to make many words, but the feeling is warm and real.

Now goodbye, Your Excellency, and a warm greeting to your dear wife, who can be the only real comforter at this time.

In old loyalty

Wilhelm.

CABINET ORDER OF HIS MAJESTY THE EMPEROR.

I hereby appoint you Chief of the Deputy General Staff of the Army for the duration of the mobile relationship.

Grand Headquarters, 30 December 1914.

Wilhelm R.

To My Adjutant General, Colonel General von Moltke, Chief of the Fusilier Regiment Field Marshal Count Moltke (Silesian) No. 38, *à la suite* of the Kaiser Alexander Guard Grenadier Regiment No. 1.

Part IV – Moltke After the Battle of the Marne

Moltke to Reich Chancellor v. Bethmann Hollweg

Berlin, 8 January 1915.

Your Excellency

I apologize if my handwritten reply to your letter of the 5th of this month makes it difficult to read, but I do not wish to entrust this letter to a copyist.

Trusting in the path of purely personal communication chosen by Your Excellency, I speak as openly as the difficulty of the matter allows me.

There is no question, and I have been opposed here from various quarters, that the union in one hand of the office of Chief of the General Staff and that of Secretary of War is viewed unfavorably in wide circles of the country. Personally, I do not consider this union favorable. The General Staff and the War Ministry are two authorities which must counterbalance each other if work is to be done in an expedient manner. Moreover, the Minister of War belongs to Berlin, to the central office of his effectiveness. Personally, the unification of the two offices is certainly very convenient for the holder; where opposing views confront each other, he can decide dictatorially. This has recently been shown in the question of the reorganization of the corps, where the War Ministry and, I am told, General v. Falkenhayn, as Minister of War, were against the reorganization and in favor of strengthening our Western Army, while General v. Falkenhayn, shortly afterwards, as Chief of the General Staff, ordered the reorganization. In this case I would have gone along with the view of the War Ministry.

But it is very difficult for me to give a well-founded judgment on these matters, since I lack any orientation as to the actual situation of the army. From the moment when His Majesty had the Chief of the Military Cabinet tell me to report sick and go to Berlin, since General v. Falkenhayn was to be put in charge of operations, I no longer had any influence on the conduct of the war. Since General v. Falkenhayn told me at the same time that he could only assume responsibility if I did not interfere in any way, I held back and since then have neither been asked for my opinion nor informed in advance of the intended measures of the army command. Since I was called up on 1 November, I went to Homburg at the request of His Majesty and there, after two days, received the order for my dismissal from my previous position, I have no longer been able to inform myself about the situation by means of a survey of the General Staff, since I was now completely switched off. I do not say this to complain, but only to show how difficult it is for me to make a well-founded judgment about the operational events and an evaluation of them.

The only thing that I can see, and that all the world can see as well as I can, is the result of the last months of war. I see that our entire Western Army is in the trenches and that operational warfare has ceased. The difference between warfare in the East and in the West must be clear even to the military layman. It is obvious that the restoration of the possibility of operations in the West can be effected only by disengaging from the enemy and concentrating the army groups further back. To this measure, which would seek a decision in open field battle against the enemy, which must necessarily follow, one has not yet decided. I am as little informed about the reasons as I am about the objectives now being pursued in the West. Nor do I know the views of the army leaders on this, and I do not know whether they have been consulted about it.

I would understand the conduct of the war in the West if it were based on the idea: first stall in the West, then bring about a decision in the East. It is incomprehensible to me that the importance of the latter was not recognized long ago. If we had come to peace with Russia, I believe that everything would have been won. Whether it will now be possible to bring about this decision, I cannot judge from here. In any case, with the failure of Austrian warfare, it has become much more difficult than it would have been two months ago.

Your Excellency says that Your Majesty and General v. Lyncker wish to retain General v. Falkenhayn as Chief of the General Staff under all circumstances, even if the two functions now united should be separated. The question is thus decided from the outset. General Ludendorff is probably too young to be Chief of the General Staff. He would be excellently suited as Chief of the Operations Department or as Chief Quartermaster, but he is a headstrong personality who goes through walls with his head, and he would never be able to work together with the present Chief of the General Staff. He is very capable and ambitious, has a justification for that too, but he would only subordinate himself to a personality he respects.

In my opinion, Colonel General v. Bülow is the most capable of our army leaders.

I do not know whether General v. Falkenhayn is trusted in the circles of the latter. It would be very desirable that it should happen, because trust is an important thing.

Your Excellency will hardly be satisfied with my remarks, I feel that myself. However, it is impossible for me to express myself with certainty. Your Excellency will understand. If you want a competent judgment, get in touch with General v. Bülow. Whether this is possible without you appearing to interfere in military matters, I do not know.

In recent days, I have been visited several times by gentlemen who have raised grave concerns about the food issue. I will soon report to Your Excellency on this matter, which is of vital importance. There have been representatives of agriculture, industry and the grain buying society, all of whom have expressed the same concerns.

314 *Moltke to Reich Chancellor v. Bethmann Hollweg*

It is with the greatest respect that I thank Your Excellency
very devoted

v. Moltke.

Moltke to Reich Chancellor v. Bethmann Hollweg

Berlin, 10 January 1915.

Driven by deep concern for the fatherland, I beg to submit the following lines to Your Excellency.

I have been in contact with various authorities concerning the food supply of our people: Privy Councillor Sering, Professor Eltzbacher, Professor Ballod, and others; moreover, I have been approached without being called: Mr. v. Wangenheim, Klein-Spiegel, representatives of major industry, Mr. Stinnes, Müllheim, Privy Councillor Hugenberg, Essen, as well as many private individuals, all driven by the same concern for the country.

Unless immediate action is taken, and that with ruthless energy, we will, in the opinion of all, be heading for a catastrophe. The guidelines enclosed are the result of the joint judgment of all the gentlemen with whom I have spoken. Your Excellency will perhaps be of the opinion that I am concerned here with matters that do not concern me. But the question of feeding the people is of such drastic importance to the conduct of the war that I feel obliged to raise it. Our armies are of no use to us in the last analysis if we are compelled to ask for peace for want of food, especially bread grain, before a decision has been brought about by arms, and no one can know how long the war will last. I have heard that so far radical measures have been refrained from by the Federal Council, so as not to excite discontent among the parties on the left. Our people will now calmly accept vigorous measures, they are still ready to make sacrifices and even demand in wide circles that the government intervene with a strong hand, but the same people will demand accountability from the government when emergencies occur that could have been avoided at the last hour. On the government will fall all responsibility with full gravity if nothing is done. I therefore implore Your Excellency to intervene immediately. If commissions are convened again and endless consultations are held, all of which, according to experience, will be inconclusive, precious time will be lost, and, as Your Excellency can see from the annex, we have no more time to lose. It is not a matter of doing the absolute best, it is not possible to take into account all special interests, which will constantly contradict each other. This is not about individual interests, but about the entirety of the people and the existence of the state and the monarchy.

The awareness that it is a matter of safeguarding our highest goods has prompted me to write this letter.

A second important question, about the decision of which I am not informed, is whether the military means that will become available in the near future should be used in the East or in the West. Your Excellency must be informed about this in order to be able to guide the policy of the empire. I believe to be of the same opinion with Your Excellency that the only great aim which we must still pursue now, in spite of the fact that the opportunity has already been missed once, is to bring about a decision against Russia which will open to us the possibility of peace with her. I told Your Excellency weeks ago that if this succeeds, I believe the war is as good as won. I consider the decision to be taken here to be the most important, both militarily and politically, of all the warfare to date.

With the greatest reverence
Your Excellency very humble
v. Moltke.

ENCLOSURE.
Sent to the Reich Chancellor on January 10, 1915.

Detailed reports and consultations with prominent figures in finance, industry and economics have shown that we have only small stocks of bread grain left in Germany, namely wheat for only one or two months, and rye in such limited quantities that it will probably be completely lacking for the last two months of the harvest year.

The regulations of the Federal Council on the increased milling of bread grain have already been taken into account here.

The extended provision of baking potato flour into bread is by no means able to remedy the deficiency.

The task now is to eliminate all waste and luxury consumption by all means, even the sharpest.

Furthermore, the supply of human food must be increased by preventing the use of rye and potatoes for animal feed with all possible energy. Every use of human foodstuffs means a waste of valuable national assets. The huge pig stocks can therefore not be sustained.

The only encouraging thing is that our large roughage harvest allows us to keep the dairy cows reasonably full, so that milk, cheese and butter consumption will probably not be restricted beyond tolerable levels.

The only surplus we have is sugar. This must be used to make up for the shortfall in fats imported from overseas and to fill gaps in the grain supply. It is quite inadmissible that the quantities of sugar exported so far should remain locked up in order to enable the owners to engage in large-scale speculation after peace has been concluded. It must not be a question of benefits to individuals, but to the people as a whole. In detail, the following measures are considered absolutely necessary by all authorities in the field of national economy:

1. Immediate lifting of the maximum prices for wheat.

2. Authorization to wartime grain companies to pay higher prices than maximum prices for rye, wheat, and barley, without any

commitment.

Instruction to wartime grain companies to bring in all grain stocks, especially all wheat stocks, as far as it is at all possible.

3. Maximum prices for rye are to be raised provisionally by thirty marks, those for table potatoes by thirty to forty percent.

4. Pigs are to be slaughtered and preserved by up to fifty percent of the herd through large purchases by the municipalities with the support of the Reich. Quota according to the population figure. The army administration shall participate in the purchase.

5. Complete prevention of any export of foodstuffs to foreign countries. Austria-Hungary must replace the quantities of grain received so far with other food or fodder, e.g. pulses, as beans, etc.

The Army Administration cannot continue to supply the Austro-Hungarian troops in Poland with rations, which have so far been provided by Germany.

6. Utilization of sugar reserves:
   a) by increasing the non-blocking quotas in such a manner that a quantity of sugar is made available for consumption by at least one-half each month as compared with the preceding year,
   b) by reducing the sugar tax from fourteen to seven marks for the quintal,
   c) by the purchase of one million quintals of sugar by the Army Administration for the troops,
   d) by the addition of sugar to the oat feed on the part of the army administration, for every ten pounds of oats, two pounds of raw sugar.

7. The railroad administration shall use coke for consumption instead of coal, if it has not already done so; this shall apply in particular to military transports.

8. Use prisoners to a much greater extent than hitherto for the reclamation of wastelands and moorland crops, in order to be able

to develop them in the spring.

9. Securing legumes (including summer cereals) for sowing by granting the right of eminent domain to the Chamber of Agriculture.

10. The prisoners are to be fed to a much wider extent with fish (stockfish), which can be obtained in large quantities from Norway.

v. Moltke.[*]

---

[*] A judgment on Moltke's economic activity is cited here:

Berlin, August 6, 1918.

Dear Excellency!
    The "History of the German National Economy during the War" is now being written. Your late husband played a major role in the development of our food economy. The man, whom I highly admire, called upon me several times for consultations on this subject, and it seems to me to be an imperative of justice and historical truth to withdraw his merit from oblivion. I am convinced that it is only thanks to his determined and, as always, selfless efforts that famine did not break out in the very first year of the war——

M. Sering
Privy Councillor of the Government, University Professor.
Currently Chairman of the Scientific Commission of the Royal Prefecture. War Ministry.

Moltke to His Majesty the Emperor

General Staff Berlin, 10 January 1915.

Your Majesty
I humbly inform you that I have today submitted a report to the Imperial Chancellor on the food issue. I humbly request Your Majesty to hear the questions and proposals raised in this report. The securing of supplies for the army and the people is so serious that I have felt obliged to raise it.

I have contacted many leading personalities in the field of food supply, and everywhere I have encountered the view that we are facing a serious crisis if the most energetic measures are not taken immediately.

I have submitted to the Imperial Chancellor the guidelines within which they would have to operate, and which all gentlemen, some of whom have come to me with the request to explain the situation to Your Majesty, and some of whom have been asked by me to bring their views to my attention, have agreed are necessary. I have been told unanimously from all sides that it is the twelfth hour when help is still needed. I need not explain to Your Majesty that this matter is of the most vital importance for the conduct of the war. The strongest army will not be able to assure Your Majesty the happy outcome of the war if Your Majesty is forced to make peace for lack of food before a final decision on arms has been reached. The people will now be ready to recognize even the most severe intervention of the government as justified; it is even demanded in wide circles. If the emergency feared by the authoritative authorities in the field of food supply occurs, which could have been prevented by timely intervention, the worst consequences are to be expected.

The concern for the future of the monarchy and the fatherland presses the pen into my hand. I implore Your Majesty to order that an iron hand intervene here; only in this way can help be provided.

In former times I have been able to enjoy the confidence of Your Majesty and in the certainty that Your Majesty still believes me that I know no other motives than Emperor and Fatherland, I ask to be allowed to add the following about the great aims of the war as they present themselves to me.

According to my innermost conviction, the decision of the war lies in the East. If it is possible, even now, to defeat the Russians in such a way that a peace agreement can be reached with them, France will very soon give up its resistance. Your Majesty will then have as good as won the war. As long as Russia is in the field, France will not make peace. It will not make peace even if it should succeed in breaking through its lines or inflicting a partial defeat on it; it will not and cannot give up the war as long as Russia is not finished and as long as an English soldier stands on French soil. England will see to that. But if the hope of Russian help is destroyed, England's power over France will also be broken. I therefore consider it absolutely necessary to use all available forces to defeat Russia, and all the more so since Austria is apparently failing more and more militarily. Not for Austria's sake, but to counter the danger that after a separate peace of Austria we will be confronted with the entire army power of Russia.

I am not informed about how Your Majesty will decide, and I ask Your Majesty to forgive me if I express my view to the Highest of All without being asked. However, I have always considered it my duty to serve Your Majesty openly and without regard to my

person, and I will adhere to this view until my death.
In deep reverence, I remain as Your Majesty's most humble
v. Moltke , Colonel General.

Moltke to General ——

General Staff Berlin, 12 January 1915.

Your Excellency,
The letter of the 3rd was only delivered to me by Major —— on the 10th. I see from it that the Imperial Chancellor and Your Excellency have attempted to inform the Emperor of the generally prevailing mood against General v. Falkenhayn.

That this mood is the same not only in the army but also among the people is becoming more and more apparent to me every day. I have remained silent until now, since His Majesty has never asked me for my opinion, and since I must assume from the orders I have received from him that I am dismissed for him, but the concern for the Emperor and the empire almost squeezes my heart. I fear that if no change is implemented, we are heading for the most serious catastrophe.

Even though I have been completely eliminated, I can see the results of the warfare of the last few months. They are downright frightening. We have given our enemies three months of time and lost any initiative of our own. General v. Falkenhayn has great personal ambition, but the ability to judge correctly the great circumstances of this tremendous war, to take powerful decisions, to recognize the moment and the place where a success of importance is to be won, to set himself great goals and to pursue them vigorously, is evidently lacking in him. It has been muddling along for three months. Forty-some army corps have been lying in the trenches for months. There is no longer any talk of an operation. General v. Falkenhayn has not been able to decide to make the army mobile again.

This could have been accomplished in two ways. Either by concentrating the armies backward in groups, in order to seek the decision against the enemy, who had to follow, in the field battle, or by shortening the line now held by withdrawing the arc projecting to the west, thus creating the possibility of freeing strong forces. Had it then been recognized that the decision of the whole campaign lay first in the east, for a crushing defeat of the Russians would probably have brought us peace with them, had the forces thus made available been employed there in time, infinitely great things could have been accomplished. General v. Falkenhayn did not realize this. He may have shied away from giving up some of the ground he had gained. But the important thing is not to assert a few kilometers of ground, but to bring about a decision.

Standing still in the west only makes sense if one wanted to wait for the decision in the east here first. For months we have heard nothing more than that a trench has been taken here, one lost there, that's all. In November, great things could be achieved in the East. The pleas and ideas of Field Marshal Hindenburg have gone unheard. Whether it will now still be possible to achieve there what has been missed, I cannot judge from here. Our military strength has been terribly dispersed. We are heading for a catastrophe if change is not implemented.

Your Excellency knows that I am not passing this judgment in order to bring myself into commendable memory by criticizing my successor. I have finished with my life and work and would never be able to return to my old position. But I see things as they are, and I believe that the whole army judges as I do. Just ask the honest and judgmental people in the General Staff, Colonel H. and Colonel B., you will be horrified when they openly tell you their view. Trust has gone to the devil, and trust is a giant force.

May His Majesty take General Ludendorff, perhaps he can still save what can be saved. He is not a comfortable personality, but God knows that is not what matters. What is at stake here is throne and country and the future of a people that has already made endless sacrifices and shed rivers of blood. God help us on.
Faithfully yours
v. Moltke.

Moltke to Field Marshal General v. Hindenburg

Berlin, 14 January 1915.

Your Excellency,
Please accept my best thanks for your last letter and the affirmation of your comradely feelings, which was a heart-satisfying pleasure for me. You may rest assured that I will cherish and preserve the same feelings towards you, whatever may be the fate of my life in the future.

I know how difficult it has become for your royal heart to translate the thought you have about General v. Falkenhayn and your judgment of him into the deed of your letter to His Majesty the Emperor. God grant that your action may be successful. This man is plunging us all, throne and fatherland, into ruin. If your step achieves its goal, you will not only be the savior of Prussia and Silesia, but the savior of our entire country.

I do not know the contents of your letter, but I know and share the thoughts you have expressed. Only you could and had to write like this. What can be higher than to give one's whole self for the fatherland. I squeeze your hand, your Excellency. I stand and fall with you. Hold out unswervingly and uninfluenced. The weal and woe of the country is at stake.

Yours faithfully

v. Moltke.

Moltke to His Majesty the Emperor

Berlin, 15 January 1915.

I humbly ask Your Majesty to allow me to present the following thoughts on the further conduct of this world war, which will decide the fate of Germany.

As I dared to point out to Your Majesty in my letter of the 10th of this month, since warfare in the West has come to a complete standstill for months, the next objective of operations must be the defeat of Russia and Serbia, in order thereby to obtain the possibility of a special peace with Russia. Should it prove possible to bring the war with Russia to a successful conclusion, I believe that the neutral Balkan states and Italy could also join our cause. It seems to me very probable that France will then no long be willing to continue the war in the allegiance of England. The possibility, granted by a peace with Russia, of employing in the West all the forces hitherto standing in the East will certainly make France inclined to peace.

On the other hand, I consider it quite unlikely that England will join in a peaceful settlement between Germany and France. It is my firm conviction that she will continue the war against us alone, even then, in order to prevent a rapid revival of our economic life and our foreign trade.

The likelihood of continuing the war against England would have to be considered already now. In my opinion, a crushing blow against England cannot be struck with our fleet.

If a blockade is not feasible according to Your Majesty's authoritative judgment, then – provided that we have come to an agreement with our other adversaries – the old Napoleonic idea of an attack against England's most vulnerable point, Egypt, would have to be taken up again. Napoleon's plan failed because it had no railroads at the time. Today we possess this formidable means of war. The extension of the gaps in the Baghdad Railway still existing in the Taurus and Amanos, and the construction of a branch line of the Hedzhaz Railway as far as the Suez Canal, would establish a direct rail route from Germany to Egypt, and give us the opportunity of bringing about a great decision against England on the land, which cannot be expected from the Turkish enterprise at present carried out with insufficient means. At least it may be hoped that the Turkish expeditionary corps can hold on in the Sinai to cover a railroad construction.

The completion of the Baghdad railroad lines in the Taurus and Amanos will take about a year with the utmost effort of all forces. Their cost is about fifty million marks. A temporary construction would take about half the time and cost. If this, too, is not feasible at the present time, the upgrading of the existing roads for large-scale truck operations would have to be considered.

The fruits of the enormous sacrifices which Germany has had to make in this war, besides economic advantages on the continent, can only be claimed by England through the expansion of a German-Central African colonial empire. France and Russia have great gains – especially territorial ones – not to offer Germany.

The commencement of the construction of the railroad under discussion would also, in the event that England should be inclined to peace with Germany sooner, provide a valuable instrument for possible peace negotiations, in which we would be able to exert tremendous pressure on England by means of this railroad.

I consider it so important to clarify the thoughts about the possible continuation of the war in time and to initiate their implementation in time that I have dared to submit the foregoing to Your Majesty.

I humbly request Your Majesty to consider the proposals and, if Your Majesty agrees with them, to order their immediate implementation.

In deep reverence, I remain as Your Majesty's most humble
v. Moltke, Colonel General.

Moltke to His Majesty the Emperor

Berlin, 17 January 1915.

Your Majesty!
   Through Field Marshal v. Hindenburg I learn of the grave crisis in which the Monarchy and the Fatherland currently find themselves. As the oldest and most loyal servant of Your Majesty, I must, even at the risk that my step might be misinterpreted, if not by Your Majesty, then at least by others, dare to express my opinion to Your Majesty openly and without reservation in all reverence.

   I am firmly convinced that General v. Falkenhayn is not suited, either by character or by ability, to be Your Majesty's first advisor in the military field in these difficult times. His person constitutes a serious danger for the fatherland. In spite of an outwardly strong will and skilful external appearance, he does not possess the inner strength of mind and spirit to devise and carry through generous operations. The operations proposed by him in the West of His Majesty and carried out have not led to any result, they are a strategy of missed opportunities.

   Through his short-sightedness – I deliberately do not say his ambition – we have suffered a grave failure at the Yser, and in so doing have missed the opportunity which presented itself at the time to end the campaign against Russia by a swift, decisive blow. There is a serious danger that the same mistake will be made at the present moment. Our whole war situation is now so critical that only a whole and complete success in the East can save it. There is no time to lose if the danger is to be invoked that Rumania and Italy will side with our adversaries. It will be averted if we succeed in decisively defeating the Russians and coming to a peace with them. I believe that this can be achieved if we make minor demands. But it is only possible if we use all the forces at our disposal in the East, including the rifles that may still be expendable in the West, even at the risk of getting into a difficult situation there and being forced to shorten our lines.

As I have already explained to Your Majesty, we can now achieve only partial successes in the West, which will have no influence on ending the war. If we now also deploy insufficient forces in the East, only partial successes can be achieved there as well, and Your Majesty will soon be forced, in view of the unreliable attitude of the neutrals, to draw even stronger forces than are now necessary from the West to the East. This will lead, as it has done before, to a drip-by-drip deployment without any decisive success. If there is no such success now, Rumania and Italy will move against Austria and force it to make a shameful peace, which must also deprive us of the fruits of the heavy and bloody sacrifices of this war.

By chance it has come to my knowledge that Field Marshal v. Hindenburg has suggested to Your Majesty that I be recalled to my former position. I implore Your Majesty to refrain from this under all circumstances. Not because of my health, which has been completely restored, but because I have the feeling that Your Majesty no longer has the old confidence in me. From the day when Your Majesty took over the management of the operations from me, I have no longer been asked to express an opinion, and it would be impossible for me to write this letter if it were based on a selfish intention. My person is not important at all now. What matters is to save the fatherland from its grave crisis. At the present moment, any person capable of recognizing the demands of the strategic situation and having the character to carry them out with determination is suitable for the post of Chief of the General Staff, a man whom Your Majesty is entitled to trust.

From the above statements, Your Majesty will recognize that there are only objective reasons which make the removal of General v. Falkenhayn from his position as Chief of the General Staff appear to me to be in the best interests of Your Majesty and the Fatherland.

General v. Falkenhayn has so little confidence in the army that new operations must not be begun under his leadership. Even if he should now, under the pressure of circumstances, be inclined to meet all the demands of the High Command East, tomorrow he will not keep his promises, and there is a danger that he will create new difficulties for the conduct of the war in the East instead of supporting it with all his strength.

If Your Majesty does not take these frank remarks as the expression of my unconditional devotion to Your Majesty's person and to my fatherland, but as an unauthorized interference in the conduct of the war and Your Majesty's resolutions, I beg to be dismissed with grace. My words will then have been the last warning advice of a faithful servant who, with a heavy heart but driven by a sense of duty, has decided to take this step.

In deep reverence I remain as Your Majesty's most submissive
v. Moltke.

Moltke's additional remark.

His Majesty has replied to the above letter in the enclosed unopened letter. Before the letter came into my hands, I received a telegram from Colonel General v. Plessen, telling me, by order of His Majesty, not to open the letter until Colonel General v. Plessen had been with me to give me verbal explanations. Colonel General v. Plessen arrived with me on January 24, at 10 o'clock in the morning. One hour after his arrival the enclosed letter was delivered to me. I explained to Colonel General v. Plessen that, after having received his explanations, I would not open His Majesty's letter, since after learning of its contents – as had become clear to me after the oral communications of Colonel General v. Plessen – I would be forced to draw the consequences. I will place the letter on file unopened and request that this be reported to Your Majesty. With this, I would have gone as far as I could in order to be able to serve the country even further.

Berlin, 24 January 1915.

v. Moltke.

Urgent!
TELEGRAM.

Colonel General v. Moltke, Berlin, Königsplatz, General Staff Building.
Grand Headquarters, 23 January 1915.

I will be with you in Berlin tomorrow, January 24, at 10 o'clock in the morning. Please do not open His Majesty's letter before my arrival.

By order of the Most High

v. Plessen,
Adjutant General.

Moltke to Field Marshal General v. Hindenburg

Strictly confidential.   Berlin, 23 January 1915.

Dear Field Marshal!
    Major v.—— returned from the Grand Headquarters yesterday evening. Before he arrived here, a telegram was already here with his transfer to the General Staff of the Governorate...and the order to leave there immediately. He left today, so was unable to carry out his intention of reporting to you personally. With him, I have lost my best assistant; he was my Ludendorff in the local circumstances.
    His mission has failed, completely. It is received very ungraciously, without understanding. The good man, who gave his existence for his fatherland, without any consideration for his person, who was ready to take all consequences upon himself, is now separated from me. The step which he, you, Field Marshal, I and the Empress had taken, all guided by the same concern for the country and the outcome of the war, has at least had the effect that four corps are now placed at your disposal. My request to withdraw everything that is expendable from the West and send it to the East remains unfulfilled. Whether it will be possible for you

to achieve as great a success with these four corps as we need if we are to end this war at all, I am not in a position to judge. God grant you know my views, which coincide with yours. The second success is the return of General Ludendorff to you. I am very glad about that. It seems to me that we must now refrain from further steps which can only worsen the mood. After all, it all comes down to the matter at hand.

H. said that the full independence of your operations would be preserved. In response to your suggestion that I be recalled to my old position, His Majesty summarily declared that I was too ill, as reported to him by Colonel v. M., who had inquired of my physician. The latter is a lie, he has neither been to see him nor has he inquired in writing. For the rest, I am doing well, I am completely back on my feet.

I have not yet received an answer to my letter to Your Majesty. Tomorrow comes P., who will probably bring it to me. I look forward to it with calmness and, like H., I am prepared to bear all the consequences.

I beg your pardon if I advise you to be quite cautious with regard to any envoys from afar. Your remarks about the mood in the General Staff have been reported to His Majesty and have led to sharp reprimands.

Field Marshal, I have done everything in my power to help you and the fatherland. The fate of the latter is now in your hands. May our God in heaven not abandon his German people and may he be with you in the hours of decision.

Faithfully yours
v. Moltke.

Moltke's Speech on the Birthday of His Majesty the Emperor, 27 January 1915

We have gathered here today on the birthday of the German Emperor under very different circumstances than we were used to under earlier circumstances. We are in the midst of a war, a war that will decide the fate of our fatherland like no previous one. There our souls are not in the peacetime mood of jubilation which tends to prevail on the Emperor's birthday, a mood which hardly rises above the thought of a love feast or other festivities to be held, – today we are deeply serious, for today we face the fate which will decide the death and life of an entire people. I think this serious mood is particularly appropriate today. We place the fate of our people before our souls when we have gathered here today in a simple manner. Millions of German hearts are united today in a common thought. It is directed towards the Emperor, and by understanding in him, as it were, the totality of the German people, he forms the central point in which everything flows together that lives in the totality of the German people's soul in terms of wishes for our country. So today we also want to direct our wishes to our people and our country. We want to hope that it will emerge strengthened inwardly and purified from many ugly sides of the long life of peace from the difficult test which God's counsel has imposed upon it.

Today we do not want to join in a hurrah, we want to go apart seriously and quietly, and on this Emperor's birthday we want to vow to serve the Fatherland with all our strength, and we all want to say: God bless, God protect, God keep our German Fatherland.

Moltke to General Ludendorff

Berlin, 29 January 1915.

Dear Ludendorff!
I am sincerely grateful for your letter and for the fact that, in spite of your work overload, you wrested the time to write to me in such detail. You hardly know what a boon you have done me with this sign of trust. Anyone who, like me, is eliminated, trampled on, slandered, feels doubly grateful.

My heart is torn when I think of the months of warfare that have passed, that have been lost, since I was deposed. I don't want to say that I would have done better, but differently anyway. But no one, not the Emperor or anyone else, has asked about me since. The Emperor did not even bother to inquire whether I was healthy or ill, whether I wished to return to my old position or not.

My successor and the military cabinet have thrown me to the dead. I have heard nothing from the Emperor since General P. returned to the Grand Headquarters with my answer.

I am now trying to control the misery of the country here as much as I can. I know that I will make many new enemies with it, I don't care at all.

Moltke to General Ludendorff

My dear Ludendorff, the future of Germany now rests on you and the Field Marshal. If we don't have peace with Russia in two months, I don't know what will become of us. Not militarily, but economically. In a sacrilegious manner, the country's sources of aid have been squandered. Month after month has gone by without anything significant happening, the people have always been under the illusion that we have an abundance of food. Now the sad truth is revealed. I have written to the Emperor, to the Chancellor of the Reich, yesterday for the second time, and ruthlessly exposed the imminent danger. But what value has the voice of a deportee! I now expect to be removed as a troublemaker – in God's name!

At least I have the consciousness of having done my duty, without any consideration for my person. You see, dear Ludendorff, that is why it is of such infinite importance that you act quickly and with ruthless energy. We must reach an agreement with Russia, we must at least succeed in getting Rumania to permit us to import bread grain. An infinite amount depends on the shaping of the military situation in the East. The fact that this has not been recognized for months by leading authorities is a mistake which can take its most serious revenge on the country and the people, on the throne and the monarchy. About fifty army corps lie in the trenches in the West; any thought of making this giant army operational again has been abandoned. One cannot decide to give up one meter of land and seek the decision in open field battle. This is no longer warfare, it is a complete fiasco.

I can only follow your operations in thought and with hot wishes. I think what you intend is absolutely right. Moving the operation to the right bank of the Vistula is, in my opinion, the only right thing to do. If it succeeds, the Russians will have to get out of their mouse hole. They will use all means to cut their lifeline, the railroad to Warsaw. God be with you.

I know that if there is anyone who can still save the Fatherland, it is you and your Field Marshal.

Faithfully as in old time yours

v. Moltke.

Chief of the General Staff of Field Army No. 227

Grand Headquarters, the ... February 1915.

On the occasion of a conference, I happened to learn of a memorandum on the food question of Germany in its relation to the war, which the Deputy General Staff had addressed to the Reich Chancellor. I do not know from which office in particular the document was edited, nor did I wish to inquire about its contents in detail. However, I would like to ask Your Excellency to take measures to prevent any statements by the Deputy General Staff that could influence the decisions of the Supreme Army or State Administration from reaching the outside world before I have received them.

To the Chief of the Deputy General Staff, Colonel General v. Moltke, Excellency	Received without date and signature on Friday, February 5, 1915. v. Moltke.

Moltke to General ——

Berlin, May 4, 1915.

Your Excellency
      I would like to thank you for your letter of the 30th of March.
   The frankness with which you wrote to me is the best proof of your sincere friendship. Nothing is worse than being confronted with unclear circumstances. Now I know where I stand and I know the reason for my constant exclusion, which was inexplicable to me until now.
   I cannot deny that your message that my activity in the matter of people's nutrition is interpreted as a sign of nervousness has surprised me and I must frankly admit that I would never have come to this thought without your clarification. It gives me about the impression as if one would say of a person who sees the house burning and who alarms the fire department that he does this out of nervousness! I think that at the Grand Headquarters they are not very well informed about the conditions in the homeland. This is understandable, since warfare is naturally in the foreground of interests and since the newspapers are completely tied down by

censorship. This may explain why the necessity of what I have done has not been recognized. But I can assure that it was very necessary to open the eyes of the responsible authorities if mischief was to be prevented. Since there was no one else who wanted to do this, I did it. I have also received thanks for this from an extraordinarily large number of people.

If my intervention was used against me in the surroundings of His Majesty, I regret this, but I cannot change it and would act in exactly the same way in a second case. However, it has already come to my attention that the retreat from the Marne in September of last year has recently been attributed to nervousness on my part. This insinuation is just as false as the one above. The retreat was an unavoidable necessity in the current situation, which I had to order with full deliberation, even if with a heavy heart, and I am sure that the history of the war will prove me right one day. But I only mention this in passing.

As I came here at the end of September, numerous gentlemen from the circles of industry, agriculture and science came to see me. They all came independently of one another, but all with the same request for help, and all with the same conviction that if business continued as before, an economic catastrophe would be inevitable. This was not a pessimistic view on my part, but the view of the most competent assessors of our national economy. In the five months of war that had just passed, virtually nothing had happened, everything had continued as in peace, and all admonishing voices had gone unheard. I was urged to report to His Majesty and ask for his intervention, in which many saw the only salvation.

I did not easily decide to intervene in these matters, which, after all, I faced as a layman, and I did so only after I had come to the conclusion that a radical change in the previous procedure was necessary in the interest of the country. It was necessary that a unified and generous economic plan and an organization of the national economy adapted to the war *coute que coute*[*] be brought about.

---

[*] "At all costs."

I knew that I was stirring up a hornet's nest, but that did not matter to me; what mattered was the matter at hand. I also believe that I took the right path by sending a memorandum to the Imperial Chancellor in which I described the situation and at the same time asked His Majesty to be lectured on it. At that time, His Majesty expressed his thanks to me. That seems to have been forgotten. Not everything, but nevertheless the main part of what I proposed in this memorandum after detailed consultation with our most eminent national economists has been introduced today – though unfortunately only after months. Some difficulties, for example the oat calamity, could have been avoided if the cumbersome apparatus of our civil administration could have been set in motion more quickly. Nevertheless, what I wanted to bring about has essentially been achieved, and I am satisfied in the knowledge that I have done my duty and rendered good service to the Emperor and the country.

I do not think it was a mistake that I acted very energetically in view of the importance of the matter. I think that here at home, except perhaps among those who saw in my action a violation of their privileges, it would be difficult to find the opinion that I acted out of nervousness.

If this is now presented to the Emperor in this way, I can well assume from which side this is coming, and I will also resign myself equanimously to this. I can assure Your Excellency that after the experiences I had to make from the first day of mobilization, my calm and my inner balance can no longer be shaken by anything.

Forgive this long letter. I am grateful that you have always kept good comradeship with me and it was only important to me that you do not get the wrong idea about me. But this shall be the last time that I bother you with my person.

Faithfully yours
v. Moltke.

Telegrams from the Emperor to Moltke

New Palace, May 23, 1915.
Colonel General v. Moltke, Königsplatz, Berlin.

My dear Moltke! Receive my warmest congratulations on your birthday. The past year brought us the most difficult war in the history of the world! The fact that my army was perfectly prepared for it and achieved brilliant successes in the first part of the campaign was largely due to you, for which I and the Fatherland remain deeply grateful to you for all time. Since then, Providence has always increased our tasks, God's grace helped us to accomplish them happily. Our firm trust in God will continue to help us. With this confidence, I wish you God's blessing for the coming year of your life.

It is a special pleasure for me to give you the letters of Frederick the Great, who, like me, also had to fight against a world of enemies and had to struggle through the most difficult times.

Wilhelm I. R.

Pleß, Schloß, August 7, 1915.
Colonel General v. Moltke, Königsplatz, Berlin.

On the return of the day on which, a year ago, the fortress of Liege was taken in the onslaught of heroically advancing troops and the deployment on the Western Front was secured, I gratefully commemorate your services. It was your work that the army entered in an exemplary manner into this greatest of all wars forced upon us, that mobilization and deployment of immense masses took place in an impeccable manner, and that in a rapid run-up the greater part of Belgium and northern France fell into our hands with great fortresses which were thought to be impregnable. In the long years of peace you have been able, in the spirit of your predecessors, whose work I commemorate with high esteem, to further educate the General Staff and to train it for the great tasks now incumbent upon it, so that the General Staff performs its duty admirably wherever our arms are fighting. I and the Fatherland are always grateful to you for this. On today's commemorative day I award you the Order *Pour le merite*.

William I. R.

Moltke on the Retreat on the Marne

Berlin, Summer 1915.

I have never been mistaken about the severity of the struggle which Germany would have to fight through if the conflagration should once break out in Europe. My annual memoranda to the Reich Chancellor on the military-political situation, not least the one in which I called for the last army reinforcement three years ago, which unfortunately did not come to fruition to the extent I wanted, could provide information on this.

The most serious decision I faced as Chief of the General Staff was whether Germany should conduct the expected two-front war defensively or at least offensively on one side. After thorough examination and study, I decided in favor of the latter and arranged the deployment in such a way that the offensive in the west could be conducted with the strongest possible forces and the simultaneous defensive in the east with a minimum of forces.

It was hoped that a quick decision would be brought about in the west. Such a decision was necessary to gain freedom of further action, but it could only be expected if the French army could be met in the open field. An attack against France's fortified eastern frontier would in all probability have to lead to a protracted war of position and postpone a decision. The events of the war in the 6th and 7th Armies speak for the correctness of this view. The result was the necessity of bypassing the French fortified belt, which could only be done by using Belgian territory because of space and army strength ratios.

As far as that was concerned, my opinion agreed with that of Count Schlieffen. It differed substantially in the execution. The deployment worked out by my predecessor was designed in such a way that the German right wing of the army would have to advance via Roermond, thus crossing not only Belgian but also Dutch territory. Count Schlieffen was of the opinion that Holland would confine itself to a protest and would otherwise allow the violation of its territory to take place unhindered. I had the gravest reservations about this view; I did not believe that Holland would calmly accept a violation, but I foresaw that the German army wing would be deprived of such strong forces by a hostile Holland that it would have to forfeit the necessary striking power against the West. In my opinion, the advance through Belgium could only be carried out under the condition of a strictly neutral Holland.

Although I did not know what attitude England would take in the event of a German war against Russia and France, I considered it more than likely that this state would join our enemies as soon as we violated Belgian neutrality, all the more so since England had already declared this to be a casus belli in 1870. It was clear to me that for this reason alone the preservation of Holland's neutrality was an absolute necessity, and I accepted all the difficulties that would have to arise for our deployment and advance if we did not want to set foot on Dutch soil. Immediately after the announcement of mobilization I declared to the Dutch envoy in Berlin that I solemnly vouched for strict respect for Dutch neutrality on the part of Germany. I believe that the circumstances have proved me right. One need only imagine how they would have turned out if we had had to deal with a hostile Holland whose coasts were open to an English landing, what would have become of the enterprise against Antwerp on the assumption of a non-neutral border, how many troops would have been necessary for our rear guard in the advance to the west.

I was and still am convinced that the campaign in the West would have had to fail if we had not spared Holland. Moreover, I was clear about the fact that this country had to be preserved at all costs as a kind of windpipe for our economic life. If, on the other hand, we spared Holland, England, having declared war on us ostensibly to protect the small neutrals, could not possibly violate Dutch neutrality for her part.

However, the planned advance through Belgium was complicated to a great extent by the elimination of Holland: our deployment, conditioned by the railroad lines, had to be extended with the right wing to the area of Krefeld. It became necessary to advance the strong 1st Army, which was to form the encircling wing in the further advance, southward over Aachen. Between Liege and the Dutch border there was only one crossing at Vise, which lay outside the fire of the fortress.

In order to be able to meet the immense technical difficulties which were to be expected in this approach, I had theoretical work carried out for years on the advance of our army corps along a road and the regulation of rearward communications, and I believe that in this respect the administrative general staff tours which I instituted have been rewarding.

Of the utmost importance for the execution of the planned operation was the early seizure of Liege. The fortress had to be in our hands if the advance of the 1st Army was to be made possible at all. This consideration made me decide to take Liege by *coup de main*.

In all earlier drafts of operations, an orderly siege of Liege was expected, first the deployment was to take place according to plan, then the advance was to be launched along the entire line, Liege was to be surrounded and attacked artillery-wise. But even for this, the earlier planned advance of the right wing of the army through Holland was a prerequisite. Certainly, the siege would have cost a lot of time and troops, the Belgian army would have completed mobilization and deployment in the meantime, we would have found Liege built up for war, and it would have been absolutely necessary to reckon with the destruction of the Verviers-Liege railroad, the preservation of which would have been of the utmost importance for our advance through Belgium.

In my intended *coup de main*, everything depended on speed of action. I had reconnoitered the situation at Liege in great detail and had established all the routes along which columns could advance against the inner city without coming into the field of vision of the outer forts. Five such roads had been established, officers to lead the columns even at night had been trained by local reconnaissance and were constantly replenished. Despite the generally prevailing prejudice against undertakings with immobile troops, I designated five peace brigades for the enterprise. It was important to carry out the *coup de main* before the intermediate works in the forward line could be developed.

I was fully aware that if the enterprise failed, I would be reproached by the entire military world for having wanted something impossible and for having proved my total incompetence by daring an infantry attack on a modern fortress. But the very fact that Liege was a modern fortress, i.e. one without inner ramparts, made me plan to advance through the interstices of the outer forts directly into the interior of the fortress.

I put all my eggs in one basket with this venture and won the game thanks to the bravery of our troops.

No such modern fortresses will be built in the future.

Only with the fall of Liege was the way clear for the action of the 1st Army; moreover, the Belgians had no time left to destroy the Meuse railroad. Thus a great deal was gained, as became apparent in the later course of events, where the railroad over Liege formed the only available line for our troop movements.

The idea underlying the operations that now followed was to push the Belgian army, if at all possible, away from Antwerp, as well as the French army, which I expected to find on the Meuse and Sambre, by surrounding its left wing, away from Paris and to the southeast. While the 1st-5th Armies, with Metz-Diedenhofen as their pivot, made a swing to the south, the 6th and 7th Armies were to cross the Meuse between Nancy and Epinal in order to regain contact with the 5th Army south of Verdun.

Nothing had become known to us about the intentions of the French before the opening of the war, nor did we have any certain news about their planned deployment. The strong emphasis on the offensive idea, which had become prominent in French military literature in recent years, had not gone unnoticed by us. We had no indications that this idea would be realized by the attempt of an advance to be undertaken with strong forces on both sides of Metz.

The strong 6th Army, however, was so provided in Lorraine by the deployment instructions that it could be used both north and south of Metz. Only the action of strong French masses between Metz and the Vosges after the French deployment was completed brought clarity.

I had instructed the 6th Army, to which the 7th was subordinated, to initially evade the French advance; it was my intention to let the enemy advance as far south of Metz as possible, in order to then possibly attack his two wings from the north and south with all the greater prospect of a decisive success. The declaration of the 6th Army commander that he could not let his troops retreat further without endangering their internal support, that he would have to attack, did not allow this intention to be carried out.

The battle of Lorraine was fought before the 7th Army and the replacement divisions provided to the 6th Army had arrived in full force. It brought full tactical success, but the pursuit came to a halt at the Meuse River and the planned thrust between Nancy and Epinal did not succeed. Here, for the first time, the strength of the defensive in field-prepared positions, which imprinted its character on the whole course of the war after the Battle of the Marne, became apparent. It soon became clear that the defensive line established by the French between Nancy and Epinal would be opened only by the advance of the 5th Army.

While the 1st-5th Armies were in victorious action over the Meuse and Sambre, conditions in the east, where the Russians had rapidly penetrated East Prussia against expectations, made it necessary to send reinforcements there before a final decision against the French-English army could be reached. I intended to take these reinforcements from the 7th Army, which, like the 6th, had been unable to advance despite a long and difficult struggle on the Meuse. The definite reports from both armies that the enemy was constantly facing them with superior forces and that their own losses were so great that another use of parts of the 7th Army would only be possible after replenishment, were the reason for taking two corps from the German right wing after the fall of Maubeuge and leading them to the east. I recognize that this was a mistake that paid off on the Marne.

The news received about the grouping of the French forces during the advance toward northern France had always been that Paris was as good as denuded of troops. In the army reports, there had been constant talk of a "hasty retreat" and of the "incipient disintegration" of the enemy, and the army high command had repeatedly emphasized that "ruthless pursuit" would complete the destruction of the enemy. Only in the last days of August did reports come of transports of French troops from the east toward Paris; the enemy seemed to be pulling them out in front of the 6th and 7th Army fronts. The removal of the 7th Army to St. Quentin was now ordered; the intention was to use it on the right wing of the army.

A French advance from Paris against the right wing of the 1st Army now became probable. The news of this was communicated to the armies of the right wing, they were instructed – if I am not mistaken – on August 28 or 29 (I do not have the file material): the 1st Army between Oise and Marne, the 2nd Army between Marne and Seine to stop. At the same time, the 1st Army was advised not to approach Paris any closer than the preservation of operational freedom permitted. By the time the above directive reached the 1st Army, it had already crossed the Marne with parts of it. It requested to be allowed to continue the pursuit for one more day in order to reap the fruits of its victories. This was granted, but at the same time the necessity of staggering and securing against Paris was again emphasized.

The French counterattack now took place against the right wing of the 1st and the front of the 2nd, 4th, and 5th Armies. The 1st Army, in order to repel the threat to its right wing, moved its two left wing corps around to the right wing behind its front. This created a 25 kilometer-wide gap between the 1st and 2nd Armies, into which three British divisions penetrated, whereupon the 2nd Army withdrew its right wing.

On September 7, news arrived that indicated that the 1st Army was in a very difficult position. It seemed necessary to give an order for the possible case that it should be thrown. I therefore sent

Lieutenant Colonel Hentsch to the 2nd and 1st Armies. He was to get an idea of the situation, but was not ordered to lead back the I. Army, but only to instruct it, in case it could not hold, to move out into the line Soissons – Fismes, in order to regain the connection with the right wing of the 2nd Army – and thus to close the gap that had been created. How little I thought of giving Lieutenant Colonel Hentsch the order for the I. Army to simply retreat behind the Aisne can be seen from my radio message of September 10, 10 o'clock in the evening, to A.O.K. 1 and 2: "1st Army stands ready as rear echelon. Surrounding the right wing of the 2nd Army is to be prevented by attack." The 1st Army claims that Lieutenant Colonel Hentsch delivered to it the order to retreat; Lieutenant Colonel Hentsch denies this, he reported to me on his return that the orders for the army's retreat had already been worked out when he arrived there. That the 1st Army was no longer in a position to act freely is evident from the fact that it did not succeed in joining the 2nd Army at Fismes. It had to fall back on Soissons with its left wing instead of its right, so that the gap between it and the 2nd Army was not closed and later the 7th Army, which had arrived in the meantime, had to be deployed here.

I went to the army high commands on September 11. I had ordered the 3rd, 4th, and 5th Armies to stand. I believe that the order I dictated to the 4th Army must be in the files of the 4th Army. However, I did not pass it on then for the following reasons: As I came to the high command of the 3rd Army, the commander-in-chief told me that his army was no longer able to hold the cross-country line located between the 2nd and 4th Armies if the French should attack him. The army had suffered such heavy losses, he said, and was so fatigued by its intervention partly on the left wing of the 2nd Army and partly on the right wing of the 4th Army that it no longer had any combat power.

I now drove back to the 4th Army to discuss the situation again. Here I received a report from the 2nd Army to the following effect: "Enemy seems to be directing main pressure against right wing and center of 3rd Army in order to break through here. This is questionable in view of the width of the army fronts and reduced combat strengths. This can be countered by withdrawal of the German center under firm annexation to the left wing 2nd Army at

Thuizy up to the height of Suippes - St. Menehould and to the east. Later new offensive from the right wing then promising."

If the view of the 2nd Army was correct, and I had no reason to doubt it, I had to fear, from the impressions received by the 3rd Army, that it would no longer be able to repel the imminent enemy attempt to break through. If it succeeded, the 4th and 5th Armies would be in such a difficult position that a catastrophe was to be feared. At a meeting I had with the commander-in-chief of the 2nd Army in Rheims on the evening of September 11, he confirmed to me his view, on which the telegram of the 11th had been based, that he certainly expected the French to attack the 3rd Army as early as the 13th.

I therefore had to decide to assign the 3rd Army a shortened line in which, in my opinion, it could hold with certainty. This was possible only by withdrawing the army. This also necessitated the withdrawal of the 4th and 5th Armies. The assembly of the 3rd, 4th, and 5th Armies in the Rheims-Dverdun line meant a considerable shortening of the front line and must make it possible, after it was achieved, to draw troops out of the front to reinforce the threatened right wing of the army. I therefore, since swift action was required here, issued an order on September 11, 4 o'clock in the afternoon, according to which the 3rd Army was to reach the Thuizy (excl.) – Suippes (excl.) line, the 4th Army the Suippes (incl.) – St. Menehould (excl.) line, the 5th Army the St. Menehould (incl.) – and east line. The lines reached were to be expanded and held. The line thus assigned to the weak 3rd Army had a frontal width of only 20 kilometers; the total extension for the 1st through 5th Armies, when combined, was about 150 kilometers.

Since the French attacks of the last few days had been repulsed in front of the left wing of the army, it could be expected that the armies would be able to reach the designated positions without difficulty. Unfortunately, as mentioned, the 1st Army did not succeed in gaining the link with the right wing of the 2nd. Similarly, the 5th Army declared that it could not halt at St. Menehould but had to fall back as far north as the Argonne Forest. (See 5th Army operations files of 11 September.)

Thus the merging of the army in the line I had intended did not come to fruition.

On 13 September I ordered the withdrawal of one corps each of the 3rd, 4th, and 5th Armies and the departure of these corps to the west in order to reinforce the right wing of the army and to close the gap between the 3rd and 2nd Armies. This became necessary because the 7th Army had only reached St. Quentin with the beginnings.

On September 14, the further direction of operations was transferred to General v. Falkenhayn, and at the same time my Chief Quartermaster, General v. Stein, was appointed Commanding General of the XIV Reserve Corps.

Thus ended my military activity.

Part V – Moltke's Final Years

Moltke and the Founding of the "German Society 1914"

Moltke's speech at the opening of the "Deutsche Gesellschaft 1914" on 28 November 1915.

As an elder of the committee for the foundation of the "German Society 1914," the honorable task of opening the meeting falls to me, and I initially take the chair.

Gentlemen, while we can assemble here in secure peace, outside the war rages, our brothers and sons stand in battle against a world of enemies, ready to lay down their lives daily and hourly, in order to preserve, by the sacrifice of their individual lives, the life of the whole, of the nation, from the ruin which our adversaries have intended for us, in order to win for the German Reich a victorious and lasting peace in a hot, bloody struggle. Shoulder to shoulder they stand and fight, without distinction of class, profession, birth, political orientation – a great, unified mass, the collected strength of the people, held together and glowing with the one great thought of the Fatherland. Our people, which seemed to be torn by factions, which had so often wasted its best strength in petty quarrels, was united by this war. The sacred flame of patriotism melted the barriers that the egoism of the well-being had erected among us, we came to know each other as brothers, we experienced the words of Lagarde: "To be one people is to feel a common need," and it is this unity that makes us insurmountable.

It is true that war tears down many things, destroys many valuable things, lives and goods, but it also generates and reveals forces and abilities with the help of which not only the tried and tested can be re-established, but new paths promising greater things are pointed out to the work of mankind. Who should not feel that this war is one of the great turning points in world history, that its outcome will be decisive for the direction that will be given to human development, to human culture for centuries to come. This war must bring us a new time, new possibilities of development, a new consolidated community life, new forms of activity of the spiritual life. We will have to leave behind us many things which before seemed to us worth the greatest effort and which nevertheless proved to be worthless in this great, iron age. But we have the conviction that in our people lives the magic power to erase the terrible traces of the struggle, and to awaken new, creative life on the sites of death and desolation.

This creative power, which has already manifested itself so gloriously in so many ways, this unity of spirit, which has taught us to subordinate special desires and special interests to a great common goal, we must cultivate and preserve as our greatest asset, as the surest guarantee of an upwardly striving future. In 1871 we became one empire; now we must become one people.

These are the thoughts on which the foundation of the "German Society 1914" was based. That they have found a well-prepared field is proven by the number of our members and the stately count in which you have appeared this evening for our inaugural meeting. I thank you and welcome you warmly.

Letter from Moltke to the editor of the "Tat" of 1 January 1916.*

With great attention I have read your essay on the foundation of the German Society. I have also read the other articles of the number of the "Tat", and I will gladly declare that the spirit and the attitude which prevail in them have found in me joyful approval. The program of your magazine: To embrace everything that seriously strives for the renewal of life, the renewal of Germany out of the irrational dispositions of its people – encompasses the thoughts that also moved me to participate in the founding of the German Society. That we are in dire need of a renewal of spiritual life was a certainty to me long before this war put our nation on the gold scale of world development, and with all my soul I hoped that it might prove worthy of the high task which world guidance has set it.

Here we are dealing with spiritual weapons, only with them the future can be conquered. There is so much that is ideal and striving upward in the soul of our people. For a long time it was suppressed by the thick script of material life; it broke through it when the war made the externals of existence disappear before the ideal storm of love for the fatherland that swept through all hearts. If God loves our people, he will preserve this spiritual elevation for them. But everyone must cooperate in this.

That is what you want with your magazine, and that is what I wanted with the call to life of a society which is not to be, as you

---

* This letter was published in the July 1916 issue of the "Tat" with the following introduction:

The sympathetic personality of the initial leader of our war operations was generally remembered in the obituaries on his sudden death, for Moltke was not only a professional soldier, but a warm-hearted, cultivated person with idealistic tendencies. Thus, he was particularly preoccupied with the emergence of the new Germany after the war, and, as is well known, the founding of the "German Society 1914" in Berlin can be traced back to him. The January issue of the "Tat" dealt in detail with this foundation, and it may be of interest to the readers of the "Tat" how Moltke felt about the "Tat" on the occasion of this essay.

He later wrote again to the editor on the occasion of the March issue: "If one is of the opinion that the way of thinking of your monthly expresses that of the coming youth of Germany, I am convinced that one may look forward to the future with joyful confidence."

say, a "political club," but a meeting place for all those spirits who have the strength to put aside individual desires and aspirations in the service of the German idea of unity. Divided into classes, separated into parties, we hardly knew each other before the war. We wanted to break down the barriers that the egoism of individual existence had erected between us and bring man closer to man. Certainly, you are right, it will be important to help the nobility of the soul to triumph over the business spirit, to nurture the little plants that have been growing in many people for years, and of whose quiet development everyone could convince himself who looked into our national life with open eyes. We have all been aware from the beginning of the difficulties in overcoming the mechanical view of life that we have been taught for years. But one must not shy away from the difficulties where great things are concerned. After all, an ideal thought will once have been born into reality. It is known that if one wants to reforest a forest on a ground which was not a forest ground before, the first planting often perishes after a number of years, but the second one then thrives. One must only not despair. If this time the throw does not succeed, then a later generation will take up the once born thought again. We must work for the future. We are going there soon, but our people should live into the coming centuries, they should live upward, and every seed that is planted now will one day sprout. This is my hope and confidence and faith in the world mission of our people.

Excerpt from a Letter by Moltke

Berlin, 20 March 1916.

The present time offers many unpleasant phenomena, among which, first and foremost, the dispute between the government and the parties of the Reichstag. Where is the famous truce and where is the unity between the people and the government? It seems to me that the latter is not at all aware of the deep-rooted dissatisfaction of wide circles, and, worst of all, it is making attempts, on the one hand, to gag the newspapers by tightening censorship and, on the other hand, to influence them by means of official announcements that do not always fully correspond to the facts. I see in this a regrettable lack of trust in the people. God grant that a decision in the military field will soon fall to us; it is time; the war must be brought to an end if we do not all want to sink and rot with it.

Being a spectator, as I have been, is difficult. I have often been on the verge of despair, especially when I saw how some things were done differently than I thought they should have been. Only after long and difficult struggles have I been able to conquer myself, and have learned to bear the weight of the pressure. I do not think of myself, but only of our fatherland. Not being able to serve it is the sacrifice I have to make again every day.

Yesterday I was with Tirpitz, also a comrade in fate. He feels it like a salvation to be out of official circumstances that had become unbearable for him. May the Emperor never regret having pushed aside men who might have been of use to him.

Bethmann will have a hard time in the Reichstag. How nonsensically this man is acting by failing to make contact with the people and their representatives.

Excerpt from a Letter by Moltke

Berlin, 21 April 1916.

It was a great and heartfelt pleasure for me to receive a message from you again after a long time and to hear from your words the old tone of heartfelt affection that outlasts all vicissitudes of life. Thank you for this loyal friendship, which, as you well know, I return with all my heart.

I also thank you for what you write to me about your conversation with His Majesty. If the high lord has such friendly feelings towards me as you think, he has in any case only expressed them in a purely platonic way. At Christmas 1914, I reported to him personally in good health and also telegraphed that I was ready for any assignment where and when His Majesty ordered it. Since then nothing has happened, I have been cared for as little as if I had been buried long ago. I have never in my life asked for anything for myself and never will.

If His Majesty really wanted to use me, he could have asked me himself whether I thought I was capable of taking over this or that position, and he could have had the confidence in me that I would have answered purely factually. But I never heard a word from him. If he now says that he was always told, when he wanted to use me, that my health forbade my use, I do not know who was so oriented about me as to be able to know this. My doctor was never asked about me.

I wrote to His Majesty a few times during the first months of my imprisonment. After General —— informed me that I did not wish to comment on the war situation to the Emperor, as this might make him uneasy, I refrained from correspondence. Writing about the weather had no appeal for me.

Last spring, I did my utmost to write to the Chancellor of the Reich in order to get the people's food question, which was developing in a very bad way. Even then it was obvious to those with foresight that the sad circumstances which have now really come about and which could have been avoided by a generous, uniform organization and precautionary measures encompassing the whole of economic life, were bound to occur. I have received thanks from many quarters in the circles of agriculture, industry, national economy, for having intervened where our administrative authorities failed; from the General —— on the other hand, I have heard that at the highest level my efforts have been judged as nervousness, pessimism, and undue interference. The Emperor could not entrust the responsibility of commanding an army to such a sick man. That settled the matter for me, and I did not press further.

By the way, I congratulated His Majesty on the successes in Russian Poland by telegraph. You see, dear ——, that I have no reason to approach His Majesty again.

I have never learned to beg in my life.

I know very well that the Emperor personally does not have the will to leave me on the left, but he is just as powerless against the influences that are directed against me as I am.

Couldn't he, for example, now have offered me the supreme command in Schleswig-Holstein? Again, not a word to me. My past has been erased; for me it has only the value of the awareness of having done my duty.

God help our country and our incomparable people, we will still have to go through much hardship. May the Emperor then not lack men who have only the thought of serving him and the country and who subordinate their person to the cause.

Farewell, dear ——, you will do my hard-pressed heart good if you let me hear from you now and then. I will always remain your old friend

                                                Moltke.

Moltke's Speech at the Funeral Service for Field Marshal General Freiherr von der Goltz*

18 June 1916.

Esteemed attendees!

The picture of the man for whose commemoration we have gathered here has been portrayed in such a detailed, brilliant and truthful manner that you will not want to consider it presumption on my part if I ask you to lend me an inclined ear for a very brief word. There are two reasons that move me to speak to you: First, my long-standing personal, comradely, I may well say friendly relations, which have connected me with the deceased. And secondly, the feeling that at the grave of a soldier, a word must also ring out for him from a soldier's mouth; for he was a soldier first and foremost.

I was a young officer, as I was commanded from the War Academy to the General Staff and came into relations with the then Major v. d. Goltz. He had already used the rich experience he had

---

* Almost immediately after finishing this speech, Helmuth v. Moltke died of a heart attack on June 18, 1916, during the memorial service for Field Marshal Frhrn. v. d. Goltz in the Reichstag building.

gained in the course of the campaign of 1870/71 with the army of Prince Friedrich Karl in writing for the benefit of the army, and we already looked up to him with a certain shy reverence. This reverence, however, soon gave way to a sincere veneration and devotion. How quickly we got to know the man who approached us not as a superior, but as a comrade, in the endeavor, we all want the same thing, we all want to work for the army and for our country. I believe that if the Latin saying "*Homo sum, nihil humani mihi alienum esse puto*"* applies to anyone, it was the deceased. His outstanding human qualities, his kindness of heart won him the hearts of all who came in contact with him. These feelings of companionship have remained with all those who had the good fortune to enter into personal relations with him. In my case, they lasted until the end of his life, and they ended in an exchange of letters that was concluded only a short time before the death of the Field Marshal.

Ladies and gentlemen, I must not repeat what has been said here. You know the course of life of the deceased, you know that he went to Turkey as a young officer, that he served the Sultan there for twelve years, and that he then laid the foundation for the friendly relations which today unite the Ottoman Empire and the German Empire in joint war undertakings. You know that he, having returned from there, took over the business as Inspector General of the Pioneers, and all those who worked with him at that time still cherish his memory today, for even this matter, which was foreign to him, he knew how to master accordingly after a short time.

Then came his most beautiful time, when he was appointed by His Majesty as Commanding General of the 1st Army Corps. How his heart rejoiced, there he was in his element, tireless in living together with the troops, making the highest demands on himself. Sparing no effort, he lived with his soldiers as father, friend and comrade. He then had to take on the position of Inspector General, which put the troops at a distance from him, and it was only after the opening of the present campaign, when the General

---

* "I am human, I consider nothing of human affairs to be foreign soil to me."

Governorate of Belgium was transferred to him, that he returned to active duty. At that time I had the opportunity to meet with him several times. When I came to Brussels – during the siege of Antwerp – he was seldom met at home; it was always, "The Field Marshal is out at the front." – It did not keep him at the desk, he had to go out, and those who were with him told with what indescribable bravery and contempt for death he stood in the middle of the battle in the ranks of his soldiers, as if he were standing on the parade ground. And when he returned in the evening, he would discuss the day's events as one discusses a maneuver with complete calm and objectivity. And some of those who were with him in the trenches did not return; the field marshal himself was also wounded.

But even if, with untiring loyalty and sacrifice, his keen intellect enabled him at first to bring the shattered parts of the occupied country back into orderly conditions, his heart was not in the matter; he was a soldier, and I believe he did not resign unwillingly from his difficult and thankless post when he was then summoned from there, at the Sultan's request, to Turkey as the chief link between the Ottoman and German armies. He experienced the tremendous struggle of our allies on Gallipoli, he saw the fruits of his years of activity tangibly before him, and then came the moment when he himself had to take command and went out to Baghdad to take up the fight against the English. When he arrived in Baghdad, he found the English in a strong position at Kut el Amara. His task was to repel them. How difficult the conditions were, how bad the access roads were, how far away he had to travel before reinforcements could be brought in at all.

Ladies and gentlemen! It is often repeated in history that heroism and tragedy stand side by side. It was the same here. Just as Moses was once granted a glimpse of the Promised Land, but not to enter it, so too the Field Marshal General was not granted the chance to witness the final battle of his army, but his keen eye must have done the looking into the Promised Land, for surely he foresaw the victory of Kut el Amara.

Ladies and Gentlemen! I have only been able to add a personal note to the picture of the Field Marshal. I did it because I believe that in this case I may well speak on behalf of the Army and on behalf of the General Staff, to which we both belonged for many years.

I do not want to speak of the deep pain that also seized me when the news of the Field Marshal's tragic end arrived, and I do not want this day to pass without our having placed a laurel leaf on the bier that day.

Telegram from His Majesty the Emperor

18 June 1916.
Excellency Mrs. von Moltke,
Berlin, General Staff Building.

I have just received the shocking news of the sudden death of your husband. I am at a loss for words to give full expression to my feelings on this occasion. Deeply moved, I remember his illness at the beginning of this war, the brilliant preparation of which was the content of his restless activity as Chief of the General Staff of the Army. The Fatherland will not forget his high merits, and I will keep in grateful memory, as long as I live, what this upright, clever man with the golden character and the warm loyal heart was for Me and the Army.

In sincere sorrow I express my heartfelt sympathy to you and your children. I know that I have lost a true friend in him.

Wilhelm I.R.

The letter received in my presence on January 24, 1915, from His Majesty the Emperor and King to Colonel General v. Moltke was returned to me today unopened by Her Excellency Mrs. v. Moltke after the death of her husband, for return to the hands of His Majesty.

Berlin, 23 June 23, 1916.

v. Plessen,
Adjutant General.

Letter from Crown Prince Wilhelm

8 July 1916.

Dear Madam!

On purpose, I am writing only now, after some time has passed. I do not need to say much. You know how much I loved and adored your husband. I would like to squeeze your hand to express my heartfelt sympathy. I will never forget that it was the old chief, who passed away too soon, who got me the command of the magnificent 5th Army, saying to His Majesty: "Just like the others, the crown prince will do the job for a long time to come." And then, as my father had told me I had to do what Knobelsdorff advised me, your husband warmly pressed my hand and said: "Just don't let your own sound judgment be eliminated, you are and remain the army commander who alone is responsible to His Majesty!" – I took these words to heart throughout the campaign and did well.

His memory remains great and pure in my heart. It kisses your hand, dear madam, your faithful

Wilhelm,
Army Group Crown Prince.

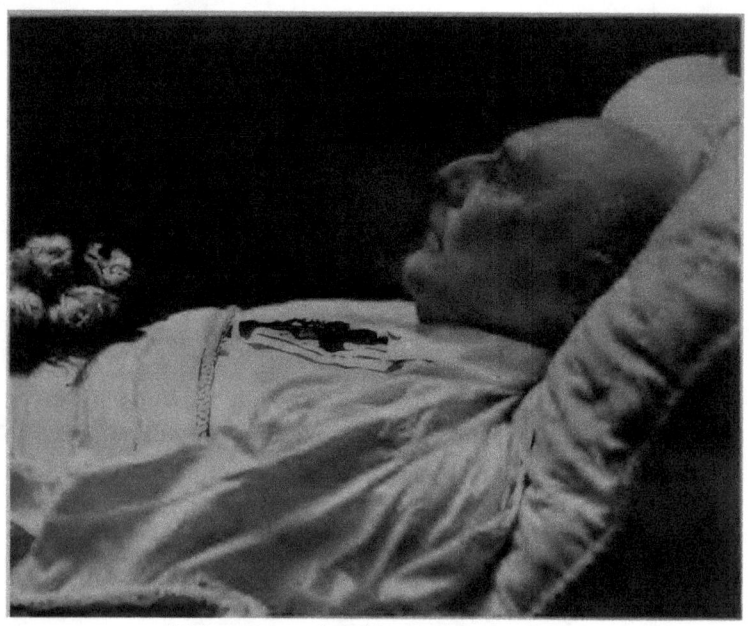
Helmuth von Moltke on his deathbed

About the Author

Helmuth Johannes Ludwig Graf von Moltke, a.k.a. Moltke the Younger (1848-1916) was a Prussian army officer and the nephew of Count Helmuth von Moltke the Elder. After serving several years in multiple positions in the German army, he became the Chief of the General Staff in 1906 and led the initial campaign in France in 1914.

After his death his wife Eliza (1859-1932), edited and published his letters and papers in an attempt to rehabilitate his reputation.

www.ingramcontent.com/pod-product-compliance
Lightning Source LLC
Chambersburg PA
CBHW050512170426
43201CB00013B/1930